TOM HART DYKE
AND PAUL WINDER

THE
CLOUD
GARDEN

Complete and Unabridged

CHARNWOOD
Leicester

First published in Great Britain in 2003 by
Bantam Press, London

First Charnwood Edition
published 2004
by arrangement with
Transworld Publishers, a division of
The Random House Group, London

Lines from 'Always Look on the Bright Side of Life',
copyright © Python (Monty) Pictures, are reproduced
by kind permission of Eric Idle.

British Library CIP Data

Dyke, Tom Hart
    The cloud garden.—Large print ed.—
    Charnwood library series
    1. Dyke, Tom Hart—Travel—Darién (Panama and
    Colombia) 2. Winder, Paul—Travel—Darién (Panama
    and Colombia) 3. Orchids—Darién (Panama and
    Colombia) 4. Hostages—Darién (Panama and
    Colombia) 5. Large type books 6. Darién (Panama
    and Colombia)—Description and travel
    I. Title II. Winder, Paul
    917.2′874′0453

    ISBN 1–84395–136–3

Published by
F. A. Thorpe (Publishing)
Anstey, Leicestershire
Set by Words & Graphics Ltd.
Anstey, Leicestershire
Printed and bound in Great Britain by
T. J. International Ltd., Padstow, Cornwall

This book is printed on acid-free paper

To Mum, Dad, Anya (Bristles) and
my grandmother, Crac
(Tom)

To Mum, Dad, Bill and Kevin
(Paul)

CONTENTS

ACKNOWLEDGEMENTS

From Tom: Lots of love to my dearest Mum for her determination in trying to find me in Colombia. To Dad and Anya for their constant comforting and support for Mum in what must have been times of severe hardship. And for their understanding on my return home.

Hugs and kisses must shower down on relatives and friends who helped — in particular my ever-supportive college friend Tom, alias 'The Hipster'. To persons not mentioned, many thanks and love to you all.

Lastly and most importantly a huge flurry of hugs and kisses to 'Crac', my influential grandmother, for her endless encouragement throughout my life.

From Paul: Much love to Mum, Dad, Bill and Kevin for their constant support. To family in Ireland, all of my friends and other kind strangers who tried to find me, I am forever indebted. To James Spring and Matthew Shultz, my thanks for their advice and commitment in the search.

Thanks to the staff at the British Embassy for welcoming us back into the real world with luxuries and friendly faces; and to the International Red Cross and the Colombian Red Cross for extracting us from the Darién quickly and with expertise.

Special thanks to Dan Waddell for pointing us in the right direction and showing us how to choreograph our story; his patience and humour were vital. Thanks to Mark Lucas, our agent, and his assistant Alice Saunders for smoothing our way through the world of publishing. Thanks also to Peta Nightingale for all her valuable input. Thanks to Doug Young and Prue Jeffreys from Transworld. It goes without saying that Transworld is made up of dozens of fun and friendly people who all worked diligently and enthusiastically on publishing our little adventure.

To the guerrillas of the Darién, we hope we can meet again one day, under more peaceful circumstances.

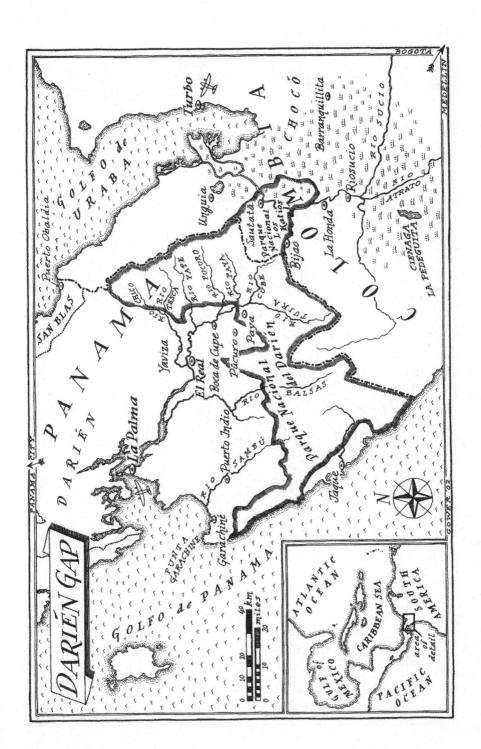

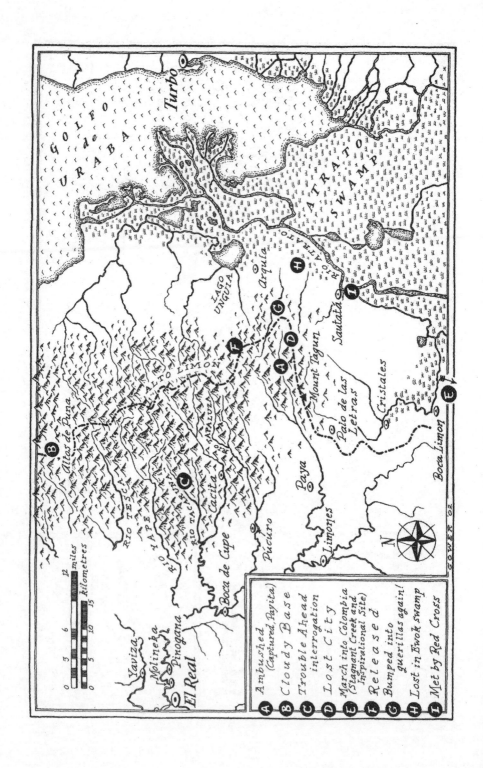

1

CAPTURE

PAUL: I hit the ground face down. Three men in combat fatigues were yelling in Spanish. One was pointing his automatic rifle directly at me. My mind struggled to absorb what was happening. We'd been ambushed. Just a few minutes earlier we'd been laughing about what a picnic the Darién Gap was, despite its reputation as the world's most dangerous stretch of jungle. We'd even been passing round lollipops, for God's sake. Now my face was in the dirt while a group of armed and angry men bellowed orders I couldn't understand. Was this really happening?

One of the men ripped off my rucksack, pulled my hands tightly behind me and bound them together. Tom and I were ordered to our feet. The whole thing couldn't have lasted more than a few seconds. We were marched back in the direction we'd come. My glasses were snatched from my face by a branch that hung across the path. I stopped, and the men cursed us, but Tom was able to pick them up and put them back on me because his hands were tied in front of him. They pushed us aggressively on our way. Tall razor grass crossing the path cut into my bare neck and face. Down the track we marched, my heart thumping hard.

Shit, I thought, we're in deep trouble now. They might drag us off into the jungle and shoot us in the back of the head. I had never felt so close to death.

We arrived at the stream in which our guides, Carlos and Francisco, had bathed just minutes earlier and waded across it to a small clearing. Were they going to kill us there? I looked around and saw that Carlos and Francisco were gone. Ordered to our knees, I gave Tom a quick glance as I went down. He looked absolutely terrified. I felt the same. Any sense of calm had long since disappeared. This was serious. This was really happening.

Over Tom's shoulder I could see heavily armed and camouflaged men coming and going across the river. The group must be larger than the six I had seen so far. We waited, Tom and I kneeling opposite each other, guarded by two taciturn and menacing men, AK-47s at the ready. Occasionally my eyes met Tom's, but neither of us knew what to say or even think.

After what felt like an eternity a man they referred to as El Jefe, the boss, came to talk to us. He looked down at us, emotionless, his dark eyes fixing me intensely. The only sound was the gentle gurgling of a stream. I braced myself for what was to follow.

'Do you have fear?' His eyes were narrow, severe.

'A little,' Tom replied nervously.

'Would you like water?'

'Yes.'

Some was quickly brought to us from the

river. My throat was tight and dry and I gulped it down.

Thankfully, El Jefe ordered his guards to loosen the cord around our hands, and my hands were then retied in front of me. I felt a little less vulnerable. I wasn't sure why but with my hands in front of me I felt I could protect myself a little bit.

'*¿Donde está la brújula?*'

I didn't understand. I looked at Tom.

'The compass,' he said.

Our guides must have told them we had it. I took it out of my pocket with some difficulty and gave it to El Jefe with shaking hands.

'He wants everything else you have in your pocket,' Tom added.

I handed over my money belt, which I had stuck in my pocket that morning to pay the guides later in the day when we crossed the Darién. We had come *that* close to traversing the most dangerous strip of jungle in the world. A few more hours of walking and that would have been it: Colombia, our destination.

El Jefe disappeared towards the other clearing. There was very little we could say to each other.

I looked at Tom. For some reason, he was sniffing a rotten guava.

★   ★   ★

TOM: Marching back down the overgrown trail, I braced myself for a swift execution and burial. All I'd heard about paramilitaries, or seen in films and on TV, made me think they would steal

3

our stuff then shoot us. They had what they wanted, now they would get rid of us. As we walked, I felt all energy drain from me. It was 16 March 2000, my sister's birthday, and at that moment I desperately wanted to see her. Then I got angry. 'What the hell did you think you were doing?' I asked myself. 'How did you get yourself into this?' I said a few silent prayers.

We crossed the river and were ordered to kneel on the floor opposite each other. Paul's face was sheet white. Then I saw a series of rectangular beds of overgrown plants and vegetation. They looked like graves. In all, there were about a dozen. That confirmed it: we were going to be shot. The rest of the group disappeared, leaving just two guards with AK-47s levelled straight at our heads. I fully expected to hear the sound of a gunshot.

In front of me, I saw a guava fruit lying on the jungle floor, rotten and teeming with maggots. God knows why, given the circumstances, but I was feeling quite peckish, so I picked it up with my bound hands. I could see the maggots crawling around in its putrid flesh. I sniffed it, and that got a reaction from our captors: their stone faces morphed into a look that said 'We can't let the gringo eat *that*!' But that was what I was after, a human reaction. I believed these men were going to execute us and I wanted to live.

Slowly and deliberately, I began to peel back the skin of the guava, as best I could with my hands tied. I offered the fruit to Paul. His eyebrows almost leapt from his forehead. The look said, 'What the hell are you doing?'

'¿Qué?' one of the men asked.

'Tengo hambre,' I replied.

I offered them the guava and was met with a look somewhere between bewilderment and disgust.

The strangest thing happened. They collected some sticks off the ground and began throwing them at the guava tree, trying to dislodge fresh fruit for me to eat. Despite my hands being tied, I stood up and joined in, throwing a stick or two pathetically in the air. For a second, we were like schoolchildren trying to get conkers out of a horse chestnut tree and the reality of our circumstances receded for a few moments. It ended abruptly — fruitlessly, I suppose you could say — when the boss, El Jefe, returned to question us.

He pointed at Paul. 'I want your passport and your traveller's cheques.'

It was clear this sort of situation was not unfamiliar to him. I translated for Paul. He knew what Paul was carrying: his men had already rifled through my rucksack, seen my possessions, and it was likely Paul would have something similar in his. Paul handed over the traveller's cheques. He asked me if I had anything else. I thought of the dollars in my shoe and shook my head. Then all of a sudden I remembered.

'Oh yes, señor, I have something.'

'OK, let's see it.'

I put my hand into the left pocket of my baggy shorts and pulled out some seeds that had been in there for more than three days.

'These are seeds from a poisonous tropical shrub, *señor*. Would you like some?'

I caught Paul's eye as I spoke. His look, not for the first time since our capture, said, 'What the hell are you doing?' I wanted to make us appear as harmless tourists who had stumbled unwittingly into the jungle. To some extent, that was the truth.

El Jefe was not amused, however, and walked away. He would have been even less amused had he known about the $120 concealed in my shoe.

★ ★ ★

PAUL: When El Jefe returned, so did the sombre, menacing atmosphere.

'*No tiene miedo, no morira en la Selva.*'

'He said, 'Have no fear, you will not die in the forest,' ' said Tom.

I wasn't convinced.

'*¿Si nosotros desatamos ustedes, ustedes correran?*'

'He wants to know if we'll run away if they untie us.'

Strange question. Where the bloody hell could we run? We were miles from safety and surrounded by gun-toting paramilitaries, or guerrillas or whatever the hell they were.

'No,' we said in unison.

We were untied and taken back to the other clearing and our rucksacks. They were much lighter now, our captors having taken all they wanted. A couple of women dressed in combat fatigues joined us. One of them wore a cheap-looking golden plastic tiara on her head. It looked incongruous next to all the combat clothing and automatic rifles.

Tom tried a weak joke. '*La reina*,' he said.

No-one laughed.

We were marched off into the jungle, away from the path and the river, following a small stream up into dense forest, deeper into the jungle. Who were these people, and what did they want? They were clearly well armed and equipped. Could they be FARC guerrillas, or a paramilitary unit, even rogue bandits or one of the many other groups operating in Colombia's civil war? Most importantly, what was going to happen to us? Would they still shoot us?

A guard led the way, splashing in and out of the small stream. I lost track of time, switching to automatic pilot, but it didn't seem long before we arrived at a small jungle bivouac. Here, on a steep slope, was a dilapidated open-sided reed hut. The men quickly built a raised bed with tree branches. A fire was lit. They gave us pasta and tinned meat from my supplies, which I had bought for emergencies. This wasn't what I had in mind. Tom and I ate in silence. They posted a guard and told us to sleep.

I couldn't. I was terrified. I thought of other times I'd been shit-scared. I remembered a close encounter with a falling boulder on an alpine climb; being caught up in the middle of a riot in Lagos, Nigeria; a scuffle in a bar in Central Africa. But each time the feeling of fear had left as swiftly as it had come, tossed to one side and forgotten. Not this time.

2

SERENDIPITY

TOM: It's a long way from the greenhouses of Kent to the steaming rainforest of Central America, but they have one important thing in common: plants and flowers. To study and observe in the wild specimens I cultivated so carefully at my parents' house, Lullingstone Castle in Kent, was the motivation for my trip. But then, plants and flowers have been the motivation for my whole life.

It all began with Gran. Ever since germination she has nurtured a now flowering genus called Tom, species name Hart Dyke. She bought me some vegetable seeds and a trowel when I was tiny, barely old enough to walk, and I started to grow a small garden, just carrots and a few other vegetables. Then I started to put flowers in with the vegetables, the garden grew in size and its cultivation became a hobby. After school, I would go straight down there to do some weeding. Gran taught me everything she knew; the rest I picked up from Geoff Hamilton, the presenter of *Gardener's World*. Every Friday night Gran and I watched it religiously. Geoff was my teenage hero. I could think of nothing better than being him and my dream was to own a greenhouse exactly like the one in which he potted his plants. The man was a trailblazer. Alan Titchmarsh has a lot going for him, but comparing him to Geoff is like comparing Tony Hart to Michelangelo. I can't remember ever missing a programme.

I can clearly recall one of the darkest moments of my life. It was early August 1996, a bright sunny day cooled by a gentle breeze that set the sycamore leaves trembling gently. I'd cycled back to the castle from a gardening job in my local village, Eynsford, and was putting the bike away when Gran came out of the gatehouse to meet me. Tears were welling in her eyes.

'He's dead,' she said.

'Who?'

'Geoff Hamilton.'

I was speechless. I thought him invincible. This didn't happen. Heroes didn't die. Friday nights were never the same again.

When I was nine I discovered orchids, and that was it, game over. A hobby became an obsession. Out of school bounds, on the chalk downs, were masses of orchids: wasp orchids, other bee orchids, man orchids, white helleborines, common twayblades and common-spotted orchids. Just seeing them growing there fascinated me, together with the thrill of sneaking off to stare at them because they were out of bounds. Would the headmaster find out? Would he give me a rollicking? And, of course, the plant is very attractive, mysterious and beguiling. The bee orchid takes the form of a female bee so that when a male comes along, he thinks 'Wahey, I'm in here' and tries to mate with it before realizing

'Oh crumbs, it's a flower'. But he stays there just long enough for the pollen to stick to him. Ingenious. I would just stare at them whenever I had the chance, entranced. One summer, at the age of fifteen, I came home from school and, along with my sister Anya, tried to count every single orchid on the golf course near my parents' house. She got bored by lunch when we reached a hundred. Four days later, I finished. I had counted 63,424.

After secondary school came agricultural college. Dad asked what I wanted to do with my life but I had no idea, other than the vague thought that I might open a nursery. I began to plan a trip with my college friend Tom. Our first plan was to go away for three months, which turned into a year. I worked as a tree surgeon and landscape gardener to save some money between 1995 and 1997. At first, the purpose of the trip was simply to travel, but that all changed in those two years as I became fixated on my greenhouse at home. While my friends went to pubs and clubs and picked up girls, I was at garden centres and nurseries picking up seeds. I even cycled to Lisbon in order to see the horticultural delights of Portugal. A few friends were meant to accompany me but as the day of departure drew nearer they kept dropping out until it became patently clear no-one wanted to come with me, so I set off on my own. It took two and a half weeks to cycle more than a thousand miles. The fact that I couldn't sit down for a week after getting there was academic. It was worth the pain.

With my trip abroad in mind, I managed to obtain a grant of £500 from the Royal Horticultural Society to research potentially hardy, woody plants in Tasmania; another £500 from the Kent Gardens Trust for the same purpose — and a further £100 was made available while I was travelling — and £500 from the Merlin Trust to study orchids in the Malaysian state of Sabah in Borneo. Including the grants, I had a total of some £9,000. I couldn't wait to get started.

Once the trip got under way, in November 1997, my orchid fever became more intense. In Thailand I visited a few nurseries, and after a detour that took us through Laos and China, we went back to Chiang Mai, Tom for western luxuries, me to visit a slipper orchid nursery in Mae Wang, an hour's drive from Chiang Mai. That visit was a powerful lesson for me both in orchid culture and the orchid profession. The owner spoke superb English and was as crazy as I was about orchids. Orchids were strewn everywhere; trophies lined the shelves where others might put family photographs. His wife marched in every now and then, but he paid her no attention. I left thinking, 'I want more. I want more of a rush. I want to see them in the wild.' I was blown away, and once the feeling waned I wanted to experience it again, but with greater intensity. It's like drugs or bungee jumping: you want more, always more. That's how I felt leaving that nursery. I craved another orchid rush.

Tom and I parted company for two weeks in

Bangkok and agreed to meet up in Penang, Malaysia. It was liberating to follow my obsession without feeling I was hindering someone else. We did indeed meet up again briefly before going our separate ways finally and amicably. He'd grown weary of travelling with a plant fanatic.

I went to Sabah where I was informed that a combination of drought and forest fires meant I could not carry out my project for the Merlin Trust, so I went to the Philippines and Brunei before heading to north-western Borneo and the Malaysian reserve of Sarawak. There, in the wild, I saw the Holy Grail of orchids: *Paphiopedilum sanderianum*, a rare, aesthetically wondrous orchid, one of the most desired flowers on the planet. It had three-foot-long pendant petals that were like twisted pieces of ribbon, and five delicately beautiful flowers, fully open. The plant thrust its long spike upward and outward from its limestone home. The yellow and dark red striped dorsal sepal sparkled in the sunlight. The deep labellum, or pouch, was five centimetres long and turned me to jelly. As if that wasn't enough adrenalin to cope with, I realized it was late July — a time of year when this treasure was believed not to flower. What a rush. In the mid-1980s a single specimen's value on the black market was $25,000, yet here was one in front of me. I had to scrabble up a cliff for three hours and perch on a rock to get a look at it but it was worth the effort. I spent two days staring at it, transfixed by its three-foot petals, taking pictures all the time. Eventually I managed to tear myself away, yet still the voice in my head cried, 'More, more!'

Singapore was next, before a five-week expedition to find orchids on the Mentawain Islands off the west coast of Sumatra for the Merlin Trust. After that expedition I simply couldn't get enough of them, and Central America began to feature heavily in my thoughts and plans.

First, there was my research in Australia to complete. After a year, including a paid stint as a landscape gardener, and with my work done, I was at a loose end. I flew to the US to have a look at the redwood trees of California. It didn't last long. I became fidgety. I needed a floral fix, so I made my way down to South America, thoughts of finding new species uppermost in my mind. It was in Creel, in northern Mexico in November 1999, that I first met Paul Winder.

★   ★   ★

PAUL: Every morning, sat bleary-eyed on the 6.43 from Chelmsford to London, I watched people trudge into work, coming alive only to fight for a seat, often the same one in the same carriage every day. After an hour or so they would reach their offices and go through the same old routines: working for the future, building a pension, worrying constantly about what might happen, never concentrating on the present, paying the mortgage. It was not how I wanted to spend the rest of my life. Instead, I was determined to make one last trip before I settled down and fulfilled my mother's greatest wish.

I would arrive at my desk at an investment bank in the City at 7.30 a.m., the phone would blare out and I would know exactly who it was and why they were calling. Staring at the reports and my computer screen, I wanted to care but I couldn't. Every day I was 100, 200, 300, 500 million or a yard short on the euro or the dollar. The trading desk always left the trades short of collateral and we'd have to scramble desperately to fill the void. Somehow the position would be cleared, but I was tired of it. My eyes might have been gazing at the computer screen in front of me but my mind was elsewhere, far away from the City, London, England, focused on distant horizons.

The managers would call us together for meetings, away from the figures on our screen, the trilling phones and the shouting. 'One team, one dream!' they would repeat. My dream was to get the hell out of there. It was all about pulling together, working as a team, all that stuff. But come bonus time, funnily enough, it would resort to every man and woman for themselves. The tension was unbelievable, people fretting about the size of their particular sugar lump. People wanted the cash for their designer labels, the car with the badge or the house with the right London postcode. I only ever thought about travel.

The urge to go had always been there. I could never get rid of it. Yes, I was well paid and that meant I could go climbing whenever I wanted or go to the pub with my friends whenever I liked. I could have settled down, worked hard, and it would have been a comfortable life, if safe and predictable. But always there was the urge, the feeling that I had to get away from all this in order to feel alive. My only motivation for working in the City was earning enough money to escape.

It all started when I was a kid. Maps have always intrigued me. I have a world map that I've always hung somewhere in the houses I shared in London or in my bedroom at my parents' house in Chelmsford. I pored over it for hours, like other people read a book, drawing imaginary journeys across the world: the fabled Silk Route; the Trans Siberian Express; Paris to Dakar; Istanbul to Kathmandu; and Stanley's traverse of Africa. I always felt jealous of the early pioneers and explorers: they had an uncharted world to investigate. I wanted to get off the beaten track, too. Nowadays it is far more difficult. Trails of backpackers have blazed paths in virtually every direction.

No matter how lucrative the contracts in the City became, the urge always resurfaced. I have never been comfortable in one place for too long. Perhaps it's because of my upbringing. I was born in Kitwe, Zambia, in 1971, and I spent most of my early childhood there before returning to England and then to Ireland, my father's birthplace. Then it was back to England for my secondary school education and the usual path to university. When I finished, the only thing I knew was that I wanted to see the world

15

first hand. I needed to get away, so I hitched to Scotland and walked in the hills for three months. I met a Slovenian man who'd done the same. I said that I'd hitch to his country one day. Next year, I did. By chance I found myself a job travelling around the country changing the coin units on vending machines. It earned me the cash to travel. I first thought about travelling overland to Australia, then set off for two months' climbing in the Alps, then decided on crossing Africa via the Sahara and the jungles of Zaire. But the many adventures I experienced in Africa failed to satisfy the urge. On the contrary, they deepened it.

The urge takes me to places others might shy away from. But I love extremes. There is no better feeling than to meet people and see how they live in the most difficult of circumstances, or to go somewhere few others have ventured. It makes me feel alive. On the one hand, there is the bank: people talking of bonuses, bragging down the phone to friends about their new house, car, wife, whatever; there are ringing phones, numbers flashing across a computer screen, meetings about targets and the daily grind. On the other is travelling: freedom, meeting new people, seeing how they live, living each day as it comes, not knowing what it may bring. No competition, really.

I knew from early on in my life that I needed to move. It was natural; it was what a human being was designed to do. For me it is the process of getting there, the scenery and the people you meet on the way rather than the destination that's important.

During one of my many map-scouring sessions I spotted a gap in the mighty Pan-American highway, the mysterious Darién Gap on the Panama — Colombia border, the only missing link in a road that runs from the bitter northern extremes of Alaska through the sprawl of the United States and the tropical heat of the Equator eventually to terminate in the barren wilderness of Tierra del Fuego. This golden isthmus has lured explorers such as Balboa, Columbus and Drake over the centuries. It intrigued me. What other places on the planet have such an aura? And what other places are so untouched by tourists?

To save money for the trip, I moved back to my parents' detached house on a quiet street on the outskirts of Chelmsford. I'd have a few pints after work, board the train, then get the bus back to their house. I'd go straight to my room to go on the Internet to search out as much information as possible, or to scour the map for the best route. Each time I bounded upstairs I would try to ignore the pained expression on Mum's face, the one that said 'Settle down, love. Buy a house, put down some roots.' I promised her this would be the last trip. I wasn't sure I meant it, but I prepared as if it was. I wanted it to be the best yet.

The Darién fitted the bill. It had all the ingredients for adventure: a labyrinth of rivers, tangled thickets, interminable swamps, dense forests and high mountain ranges. It was also dangerous. The Panamanian and Colombian armies are themselves afraid to enter the region, preferring to abandon it to lawlessness and self-destruction. It is one of the last bastions of true adventure left on the planet. Just thinking about that made the urge more powerful. I love adventure, and adventure is nothing without danger.

I couldn't afford to carry on like this, taking off at a moment's notice, so I wanted this trip to be as challenging as possible. Perhaps after doing something like crossing the Darién the urge would disappear and I would be ready to live a 'normal' life.

★   ★   ★

TOM: That morning I had been collecting in the copper canyon and was drying out the seeds of the Mexican strawberry tree (*Arbutus* sp.) and a suspected deep-pink *Salvia* × *jamensis* between the ruts on the corrugated roof of the Casa Margarita, my guesthouse in Creel. The Casa Margarita was a homely hostel on the back-packer trail, very roomy with wooden bunk beds clustered together in dormitory fashion. It resembled a rustic Swiss lodge rather than the usual seedy hovel.

It was early November and the day was bright and cloudless, perfect for drying seeds, even though the Central American winter was looming. Other guests had had the same idea; however, rather than taking the opportunity to dry seeds they had strung their washed clothes across the yard. It gave the air a fresh, invigorating smell.

I was pausing in Creel for a few days before catching a bus to Chihuahua and then on to San Pedro in Guatemala where I planned to take a short course in Spanish. As the seeds dried, I sat on the lip of a cement washbasin cleaning my camera. A pencil-thin man wearing a collar and jeans, rather than the usual scruffy backpacker's garb, walked into the courtyard from one of the dark dormitories, his hands stuffed deep into his pockets. He was blinking in the bright sun behind a pair of wire-framed glasses, like an owl forced to face the sunlight for the first time. His hair was bleached blond and the first signs of a beard grew on his chin. He looked studious, yet friendly enough. Being the sort of person who will speak to anyone I said hello and he returned my greeting. It turned out he was English. We fell into an easy conversation, like many travellers do, about the places we had been to and seen. He appeared laid back, affable. I reeled off a list of places I'd visited, one of which was Cambodia. This immediately pricked his interest.

'Really? When?'

'February 1998,' I replied.

I had been away from home for almost two years.

It turned out we had just missed each other in Cambodia and had even stayed in the same hotel barely a week apart. Then we started talking about places we planned to visit next. As it turned out, we were both aiming to make our way down towards South America.

'Are you going to go by land?' Paul asked.

This seemed an odd question, but then I didn't have a guidebook or, for that matter, much of an idea about South America. My trip was coming to an end, my money was close to running out and I was merely eking out another few weeks before I returned to home and reality. The chance of finding or encountering any new species was fading. I was toying with the idea of getting a plane home from Guatemala.

'I haven't a clue,' I said.

'Have you heard of the Darién Gap?'

I hadn't.

'The Pan-American highway,' Paul explained, 'runs from Alaska to the bottom of South America without stopping, except for a bit of jungle called the Darién Gap, on the border of Panama and Colombia. You can't make a land crossing unless you walk through it. I'm thinking of going.'

'Oh,' I said, 'sounds great.'

To be honest, I wasn't interested. My mind was fixed on going to Guatemala to learn Spanish. The conversation ended, we exchanged email addresses, as backpackers do, and he was on his way. We never sent each other a message and the Darién Gap disappeared from my thoughts. It was the sort of exchange you have on countless occasions while travelling: you speak to someone, ask where they are headed, where they have been, swap emails, wish each other luck and say goodbye.

The next day I left for Guatemala. As planned,

I spent seven weeks in San Pedro learning Spanish. The town is a favourite stop-off point on the 'Gringo Trail', a chilled-out place where many people pause to decide on their next move. Or simply to smoke dope and drink beer. I enrolled on a course and stayed at a hostel, the Valle Azul, the whole time, socializing only in the evening when I would go to a ramshackle Italian restaurant called Nick's Place — for some reason nearly all the restaurants in Central America are Italian — before turning in for the night. At weekends I went out on trips, to places surrounding Lake Atitlan, hunting plants and seed collecting. I met a few people — it was impossible not to — but mine was a solitary existence and those people I did befriend had moved on by Christmas.

My course had finished by then but I decided to spend the festive season in San Pedro because there was a party to celebrate the Millennium. Then I planned to take in Costa Rica, perhaps Panama City, before flying home. It was hardly a merry Christmas: I knew few people and I did not feel like making new friends. In fact, I was bored. My trip was almost done and there was little else to get excited about. On Boxing Day I did what I had done on Christmas Day and most other days before that: I ate a bowl of tasteless spaghetti bolognese at Nick's Place then went back to the hostel.

I stepped into the shower and got an electric shock as soon as I pressed the button to turn it on. Even more fed up as a result, I went straight to bed. It was only 7.30. I turned on the radio.

Voice of America rang out. That wasn't going to relax me. I felt restless. Sleep wasn't going to happen so — and this was something I had never done before — I got dressed and went back to the restaurant, a single-storey house in a row of tumbledown buildings.

The place was packed with backpackers from across the world. Some sat in small groups, chatting quietly about their travel experiences and where they would go next, tips and hints changing hands like currency, while others in larger groups drank beer and told jokes in broken English or halting French to try to impress new friends. Every now and then the noise would be laced with heavy laughter or loud American voices. The chatter mingled with bad pop music that blared out into the street, where more tables were set out down to the water's edge.

Ignoring the stained tablecloth, I picked one of the few vacant tables inside and sat on my own. A surly waiter bored by drunken young Westerners weaved his way through the crowd to me. In my best Spanish, which lifted the frown from his face for all of two seconds, I ordered a pizza, for the sake of variety, and a glass of my usual: Coke. As I ate I was diverted by a rowdy group of Canadians who were loud even by backpacker standards. Next to their table, trying to ignore them, sat three people in conversation: a thin Japanese woman and two men, one of whom sported a thick beard. I looked closer at the bearded man, knowing I had seen him somewhere before. It's a common feeling when

22

you're travelling, seeing a face in the crowd that's somehow familiar without your knowing why. Then I heard the bearded face speaking English in a soft, amiable voice, and that did it. I finished eating and strolled across.

'It's Paul, isn't it?' I asked the bearded man.

He looked at me blankly.

'I'm Tom. We met in Creel a few months ago.'

There was a flicker of recognition.

'Yeah, Tom, I remember.' He stood up and shook my hand. 'Join us.'

I sat down, ordered a Coke and we started making small talk. To break the ice, I told a story I'd heard earlier that day.

'Did you hear about those guys who went up the volcano yesterday?'

Paul and his friend, another Englishman named Simon, hadn't. I described how they had been held up and robbed at gunpoint by bandits just before they reached the summit. Everything was stolen from them: packs, shoes, clothes, underpants, the whole lot. They were forced to walk back down stark naked.

'So don't go up there unless you're stupid,' I finished.

'We've just been up the volcano today,' Paul said.

'Yeah right,' I said, laughing.

'I'm not joking,' he said, deadpan, and then laughed at my embarrassment. 'We never reached the top,' he added. 'I forgot to pack the machete and the jungle got too thick to walk through.'

Discussion turned to travel plans. He asked if

I'd thought any more about the Darién Gap. I'd forgotten all about it, and told him so. He repeated what he had said in Creel, though this time he told me more. Tourists used to go through it, he said, but for ten years it had been considered a no-go area and no-one had crossed it for at least three years. It sounded intriguing. The idea of going somewhere so remote was enormously appealing, especially since my trip was drifting aimlessly towards its close and I had no idea what I would do when I arrived back in England. He explained the dangers of the area, the nature of the civil war in Colombia and that guidebooks warned travellers against going anywhere near the Darién.

Warnings didn't bother me much. I'd visited parts of the Philippines and Cambodia people had warned me to stay away from, yet I'd been there and got away with it. Paul knew what he was talking about, it seemed. And after surviving a dangerous trip up a volcano fully clothed, he seemed the fortunate sort.

Ever since the subject of the Darién Gap had cropped up, Simon had remained silent.

'Do you fancy doing it, Simon?' I asked.

'No chance.'

It was an understandable reaction, but for me Paul's enthusiasm for the place was infectious and once an idea is sown I find it impossible to resist. There was another clincher, of course: orchids. The rainforest of Central and South America is a honeypot of native plants and flowers. On my trip so far I had been to some wonderful places and seen a number of beautiful species: *Eucalyptus deglupta* in the Philippines, saguaro cacti groves in the Arizona desert and camellias and magnolias in the temple gardens of China to name a few. I'd not seen many new species though.

'Is the whole area jungle?'

'There's a few small villages, but that's about it. It's a World Heritage Site. There are national parks on both sides of the border. We'll need a map and maybe a guide, if anyone will take us.'

The bit about the map was academic; the news that it was a World Heritage Site sealed it completely. I knew from what I had read and been told that these sites were dripping with flowers. I had never been to tropical rainforest in a World Heritage Site. There would be orchids there no-one else had seen. No botanist had been near this place for at least a decade. I would be the first! The idea of hunting plants and collecting seeds in near virgin territory made my legs weaken with anticipation. It was the sort of opportunity I had dreamed of ever since spending the best part of a week counting orchids on the local golf course as a teenager. Nature provides the best 'tips' on orchid husbandry and there was every chance I could learn more about light intensity, anchor points, aspect, humidity and so on.

Even if I failed to find any new species, I might encounter the wonderful Dracula orchid, an amazing flower so named because it resembles the face of a vampire. Or I might come across one of the twenty-five species of *Stanhopea*; they grow only in the American

25

tropics. Their huge, deep-veined leaves and long, pendulous spikes that in cultivation grow downwards through the basket have long fascinated me. Each large glossy flower is a decorative 'clamp' shape with a devilishly overpowering scent. Flowers bloom for only a few days a year. I had never seen this plant flower in the wild. There was also the chance I might find an *Encyclia cochleata*, the cockleshell orchid, growing wild. I had desperately wanted to grow it during the summer of 1997 after seeing a splendid specimen in full flower at an orchid show, but I couldn't buy it. *Encyclia cochleata* is a medium-sized epiphytic herb with deep-green, strap-like, lanceolate leaves. The lip, shaped like a cockleshell, is a real treat with creamy white and light green sepals and petals twisting downwards from the decorative, concave labellum, which partly conceals the conspicuous column, the sexual organs, which in some specimens have almost black markings. The flowers are large and are produced from an inflorescence that continues to produce flowers for many months.

These thoughts and images ran through my head like streakers. A trip to the Darién Gap was an opportunity too thrilling and too scintillating to pass up, regardless of the risk. Here was a chance to top the orchid rush in Mae Wang and Sarawak. My mind was made up: I was going.

'When are you setting off?' I said.

'I was thinking about March. I was going to go to Panama City and take it from there. I want to learn to dive in Honduras first. Why, are you interested?'

'Count me in, Paul.'

He seemed delighted. Tentatively, we started to formulate a plan to rendezvous in Panama City on 1 March. Then we went back to our hotels. It was a casual agreement but we were serious about keeping in touch this time, and we vowed to try to recruit others for the mission before meeting up in Panama City.

The next morning Paul left San Pedro. He spent only one night there. Had I fallen asleep after my first meal, had that dodgy shower been wired correctly and not sent God knows how many volts of electricity coursing through my veins, I would have missed him and never seen him again.

★ ★ ★

PAUL: Tom was the first person to react spontaneously and enthusiastically to my idea. I'd asked a few people on my travels down from New York and all of them had thought me mad. Fortunately, Tom was clearly barking.

He was hooked, bouncing around, a whirl of nervous energy and enthusiasm, telling all and sundry about the Darién and the idea of crossing it. God, I thought to myself, there's no stopping this bloke. Did he really know what it entailed? I attempted to pin him down to a few dates, but as I leaned forward he was distracted by something behind me and before I knew it he was racing off down to the dock, his straggly hair flowing wildly

27

behind him, his ragged bamboo-patterned T-shirt billowing in the wind, shouting out Latin names and something about a tree, an incomprehensible tumble of words and yelps. Apparently, the tree in question had been obstructing the workings of the boats' owners so one of them had decided to chop most of it down.

A minute or so later, he returned panting and distraught.

'Paul, I can't believe it! *Eucalyptus camaldulensis* — they've destroyed it!'

I tried to look as if I cared, furrowed my brow to express concern. Was this bad? It seemed as if it was.

'I think they've tried to pollard it but they've made such a mess. They used an axe!'

'Is it dead?'

'No, it will re-sprout from epicormic growths.'

'Oh, right . . . '

A few bewildered glances were exchanged around the table. Who was this guy? I liked him, though. He was like a mad scientist. You don't meet many people with this sort of enthusiasm, I thought. As he sat down I began to quiz him quickly, worried that any minute he would bounce up and go running off in search of another tree.

'What's your travelling timetable? I want to get down there in early March before the rains come and make a crossing impossible.'

He agreed excitedly, his attention back on the Darién. We decided to meet up in Panama City on 1 March 2000. We also agreed to find out as much as possible about the place en route to Panama City. I had researched the Darién from books and maps but this information was probably outdated; on the ground, up-to-date knowledge was what was really needed.

We went our separate ways. I wondered seriously whether Tom would turn up in Panama City, feeling sure that the more he learned about the Darién and made his way down the Gringo Trail to Panama through Central America the more likely he would be to pull out. Yet it was good to find someone who expressed an interest.

3

MIND THE GAP

PAUL: As I moved through Central America rumours about the Darién were legion. Fellow backpackers knew of it, and some wanted to cross it, but not in its present state. Internet sites and discussion boards either drew a blank or said it was impossible. People who had tried had simply vanished: a Canadian had disappeared; a Russian cyclist had been shot and killed; there were tales of kidnappings, and drug smugglers who thought nothing of getting rid of someone they thought might be a witness. In 1984 a cocaine laboratory was discovered deep in the Darién. This became a key part in the case the United States built against Panama's military leader Manuel Noriega and his connections with the Medellín cartel. In 1993 three missionaries were kidnapped from the remote Kuna village of Púcuro; to date, no-one knows what happened to them. In 1997 four tourists were kidnapped on the Colombian side in Los Katios National Park; two died in the resulting shootout with government troops. Shortly afterwards right-wing death squads hunting for rebel sympathizers swept the Darién. Then nothing, the crossings ceased. The grapevine told of nothing but destruction.

I was unable to find anyone with first-hand experience of the Darién. In the year 2000 more people had probably climbed Everest, more had probably trekked to the South Pole than had crossed the Darién Gap. Information was scant, and it soon became clear I could find out about the place only by entering the Darién itself. The adventure of travelling in this forbidden area closed off to Westerners for several years became more compelling the more I looked into it. The risk, the uncertainty, was part of the attraction.

The Darién has evoked such feelings ever since, from one of its peaks in 1513, the Spanish explorer Vasco Núñez de Balboa became the first European to sight the vast expanse of the Pacific Ocean. He and his men hacked and fought their way there for twenty-five days, suffering badly from sickness and continual attacks by local Indian tribes. The Darién, given its position, opened the way to untapped riches, or so explorers thought. Yet Balboa's zeal earned him little renown — even Keats in a poem gave the credit for the Pacific sighting to 'stout Cortez' — and a few years later he was unjustly beheaded at the insistence of a jealous governor.

The area has intrigued people over the centuries; it possesses a mysterious and fatal fascination for travellers and explorers. This could be due to its unique position as a narrow link between two great land masses, Central and South America. In the seventeenth century the Scottish Parliament even set out to establish a colony in the area, Caledonia. The project ended in ignominious failure, malaria claiming the lives of most colonists and Spanish marauders taking care of the rest. The venture virtually bankrupted the country and left a scar on the nation's psyche matched only by a few of the national team's football results.

I made my way down to Nicaragua, then to Costa Rica where I received an email from Tom. He was still keen, though he explained he was having little luck in finding recruits for our trip. I replied:

> *Good to hear from you. I liked Nicaragua alot especially the island on the lago. Yes it is difficult to find others to have a look at it. I know one other English guy who wants to have a look but is undecided at the mo. We can look at it in a rational way, keep going into it, speak to the locals alot and if it gets too dicey turn back and take the boat. There's a couple of different routes as well, some safer than others. This is a method I've used in other so-called dangerous areas and it's worked.*
>
> *Enjoy the travels amigo and I look forward to having a bash at the gap with you.*
>
> *laters*
>
> *Paul*

TOM: After I left San Pedro in the New Year it seemed as if almost everyone I encountered had heard of the Darién — or, more precisely, heard of Paul. He'd been everywhere! I went to Belize, then to Honduras, and whenever I asked people if they fancied walking through the Darién they'd mention that another Englishman had asked them a few days before. In Nicaragua, one hotel owner I asked gave me a strange look.

'Some nutty gringo who was here to climb a volcano a week ago asked me the same question,' he said.

'Was he called Paul Winder?'

'I can't remember his name, but he was skinny, with a quiet voice and a beard.'

It was Paul.

Paul was methodical about who he asked. On the other hand, I accosted everyone I met. 'Hello,' I'd say, 'I'm Tom. Have you heard of the Darién Gap?' If they'd heard of it, I asked them to come; if they hadn't, I asked them to come. Unsurprisingly, given my approach, I encountered few takers. In fact, I think only one person, a Swedish guy, expressed any interest at all, but he changed his mind soon afterwards. 'Tom, do you have a specialist head doctor?' I remember him asking. My interest in the Darién idea waned from time to time but I kept getting emails from Paul that revitalized me.

In Granada, Nicaragua, I picked up an email from Paul filled with facts about the Darién: what to expect, what equipment we should take, the best route, all that stuff. Any worries I had were erased by the realization that Paul knew what he was talking about. Straight away I emailed back, telling him of my failure to find other people to join our expedition. At the end I wrote, with absolute conviction, 'I'm with you. Let's just do it.'

Before arriving in Panama City, I spent three days at a resort, El Valle, a half-hour drive from the capital, from where I could visit forests, waterfalls and, more importantly, hunt orchids. During dinner one night I befriended an American family from Chicago, Steve and Lara and their five children. When I said I was going to the capital it turned out they were going there too and they offered to drive me. In Panama City they booked into a wonderful $100-a-night hotel, while I took the grotty hostel around the corner, five bucks for a bed. We arranged to meet for dinner at a restaurant nearby. Before meeting them outside, I nipped into an Internet café next door to email Paul and let him know I was in town.

'Who's Paul?' Steve asked when we met up.

'He's a guy I'm hooking up with here. We're going through the Darién Gap together.'

'Cool!'

Carl, the couple's twelve-year-old son, was impressed. Steve shot him a stern look.

'Getting killed is not cool, Carl. For Christ's sake, Tom, why would you want to go there? That place is screwed up.'

Just then, as were about to enter the restaurant, there was a screech of brakes right behind us. A drunk had wandered out into the road, forcing a car to swerve to avoid hitting him. The driver jumped out of his car, screaming obscenities. In response, the drunk lifted a shaky middle finger.

'See, Tom,' Lara said, 'it's easy enough getting yourself killed in the city, never mind the Darién Gap.'

'Fair point,' I said, and smiled.

In the restaurant we lined up and chose our food cafeteria style. I plumped for something that at some stage in its life might have been lasagne, but in Central America I had learned not to be fussy. We sat down and Steve started to work on me again, nagging away about the Darién.

'Just what is the attraction of the Darién, Tom? You have a death wish?'

'Orchids,' I replied. 'There'll be orchids everywhere.'

'There must be safer places to collect orchids. Like Iraq.'

I laughed.

'Well, I hope you know what you're doing, but I think you're making a big mistake. There's a reason people don't go to the Darién Gap.'

'Who's going to the Darién Gap?'

The accent was a thick American drawl. The whole table fell silent, even the kids, who'd been chatting merrily. At my shoulder, from nowhere it seemed, appeared an imposing figure, well over six feet in height and as big as a bear. He was chewing gum, his eyes and face hidden behind aviator shades and the peak of a black baseball cap emblazoned with the name of some warship or other. His hands were planted on his hips. Everything — his bearing, his speech, his clothes — screamed ex-military.

'Me,' I mumbled through a mouthful of mince and soggy pasta.

He pulled down his shades and looked at me over their rim, his eyes narrowing as he sized me up. He didn't like what he saw, and he swiftly pulled his shades back up. He let out a derisive snort and shook his head.

'Hell, son, I wouldn't go there even if I was tooled up,' he said emphatically. 'You could give me a Hechler & Koch MP5 sub-machine gun, a Magnum and a whole heap of grenades and I still wouldn't go near that place.'

Well, I thought, this guy knows his guns. Either that or he's overdosed on Schwarzenegger films.

As he spoke, the TV mounted on the wall, which his burly frame was partially obscuring, started to show pictures of an erupting volcano. From the dateline and caption I could make out it was one in the Philippines I'd climbed the year before last.

'Bloody hell!' I said.

'You got it, son. It's no sort of place for a young fellow like you. It's not even a — '

'No, no,' I interrupted, 'I mean the news. I climbed that volcano the year before last.' I looked apologetically at Mr Hechler & Koch. 'Sorry, you wouldn't mind moving aside, would you? I'd like to watch this report.'

'Suit yourself, kid. It's your funeral,' he said, and swaggered off, muttering to himself about 'punks'.

'That guy seemed to know what he was talking about, Tom,' Steve warned, nonetheless looking relieved that he'd gone.

I'd gone through a lot to get to Panama City and I wasn't in the mood for changing my mind now. Travelling through Costa Rica I had thought my travelling days were over when my rucksack went missing on a bus ride from San José to San Vito on the Panamanian border. I got off the bus on the border of Panama and waited for my pack to be unloaded from the hold, it having been too bulky to take on the bus with me. Off came a stream of bags, but not mine. I asked the driver where it was. He said that was all there was. I looked through the luggage; my bag wasn't there. This was bad. Everything was in there: my seeds, my camera films, my credit card, everything. When you travel, your rucksack is your *vital* possession. Without it you're nothing.

I went straight to a hotel and made a phone call to the bus company. In faltering Spanish I told them my pack was missing and they said they would look for it. If they found it then it would be put on the next bus out.

'When's that?' I asked frantically.

'Tomorrow,' came the reply.

Had they understood? It was too much to take. I was almost in tears. The likelihood was that it'd been loaded on the wrong bus and was now halfway to God knows where.

I booked into the hotel, working out that I had the cash to stay only a few nights at most. If my rucksack failed to show on the next bus then my trip was over. I would have to fly home. San José was nearby and I could fly back from there. With

37

little money and no credit card, there was nothing I could do but sit in my room in a deep depression. I dreaded getting an email from Paul. I would have to tell him I couldn't make the crossing. I felt awful. I was the only person who'd agreed to go with him, and if I had to pull out he might cancel the whole adventure.

The next day I turned up at the bus station: no rucksack. I slouched back to my hotel. It was lost, without doubt. Still, something made me hang around, but there was no luck the next day either. The situation was getting hopeless. It seemed my trip was going to end in a crashing anti-climax. I decided to give it one more day. I arrived at the station at the appointed hour and watched as the people and then the luggage were unloaded. All of a sudden there, among the sacks and the bin liners and suitcases, was my battered old pack. I've never been so delighted to see something that didn't have leaves and petals in my life. I let out a whoop of delight that startled most of the other travellers. Their looks said 'Who is this crazy gringo who gets so happy to see his luggage after a few hours on a bus?' I must have looked even weirder when I hugged it like a long-lost relative. I found the ticket salesman at the station who'd helped me over the past few days and shook his hand vigorously before heading straight to my favourite *pastelería* to celebrate with a cake.

Back at my hotel, I checked through the contents: everything was there, seeds, film and all. It's the sort of thing that never happens while travelling; once something has gone that's it, you never see it again. I started to feel good about this expedition. It felt fated, destined to be.

Panama City was vibrant and alive, more so than usual. It was carnival time, and the whole city was gearing itself up for a weeklong festival of colour, debauchery and noise. I booked myself into the Central Hotel, a seedy, crumbling, turn-of-the-century joint in the heart of town whose rock-bottom rates attract a cross-section of backpackers from the totally skint to the totally desperate for drugs, which are as easy to get as a beer in some places. It's the sort of place cockroaches go when all the other hovels in town are fully booked. In any Western country the place would have been condemned; the walls were peeling and tilting and crumbling, the façade worn and rotten, the furniture was ruined, ripped and mouldy. Yet for all its flaws it had a seedy, dilapidated charm. The colonial design meant some rooms were blessed with a balcony, and it was in one of those, belonging to a Canadian guy, I waited to rendezvous with Paul.

In the room with me, apart from the Canadian, was a new friend I'd made, a huge Dutchman called 'The Dude'. I wanted him to meet Paul because he was also interested in the Darién Gap. Some friends of the Canadians, two girls from New Zealand whom I didn't know, were in an anteroom off the main bedroom. At first I was unable to see what they were doing, just that they were kneeling on the floor and talking loudly with their heads down.

Probably lost a contact lens, I thought, so I ambled in to give them a hand.

'Can I help you look?'

One of the girls looked up. 'For what?'

I could see they weren't looking for anything at all. They were in fact perched over a thick piece of card on which were several neat lines of white powder.

'Do you want to do a line?' one of the girls asked, a rolled-up note held in her hand like a cigarette.

I shook my head.

She shrugged her shoulders, knelt down, holding up her hair so as to stop it falling onto the card, and snorted one of the lines emphatically. I watched mesmerized, never having seen anyone do this before. The girl then sat up, placed one hand on her left nostril and loudly sniffed several times through the right one before handing the note on to her friend.

'Who you waiting for?' she asked, continuing to sniff.

'A guy named Paul,' I answered, watching the other girl suck the white powder vigorously up her nose.

They smiled at each other and started talking. Then the first girl bent over for a second line, chatting all the time.

'We're going to walk across the Darién Gap,' I added.

She stopped just above the card and looked at me, the note still held at her nose. The rictus grin on both their faces faded, their constant gabble abruptly stopped.

'You're fucking mad,' they said simultaneously.

If anything, these sorts of warnings were making me more determined.

Paul arrived, looking tanned and healthy. After we shook hands, I introduced him to The Dude, who told him he was interested in the crossing. Unlike the two of us, he owned a new copy of the Lonely Planet guide in which it said about the Darién Gap, 'Don't even think about it,' or words to that effect. The Dude gave Paul a beer, then threw over the book for him to have a look at.

Paul picked it up and leafed through it nonchalantly. 'That's interesting,' he said. 'Does anyone want another drink?'

The Dude's eyes lit up with admiration. Paul knew his stuff. The New Zealand girls, however, still thought we were crazy.

We agreed that we would head down to Yaviza, a village some two hundred miles from Panama City, and wait a day for The Dude to arrive. There was a credit card problem he needed to clear up first, or so he maintained. After a few more beers, and a couple of Coca-colas for me, we went to sample the carnival.

The streets of Panama City teemed with people; car horns blared and the incessant shriek of thousands of whistles being blown simultaneously made my ears ring. It was 6 March and the last night of celebrations, so everyone was seizing the chance for one last decadent fling. Detritus from three days of excess littered the streets: cans, cups, cartons, wrappers and

41

streamers. Drunks propped themselves up against walls, others urinated down side streets, while those still standing danced and sang. We joined in the high spirits, singing and shouting at the tops of our voices. Combined with a few shots of rum, the excitement of our impending adventure made me giddy. Paul and I bought panama hats from a stall and wore them. Later we discovered that we'd featured on a local news bulletin; two gringos in silly hats acting like idiots were obviously newsworthy in Panama.

★ ★ ★

PAUL: Before the carnival I bought a few items from the local market I thought essential for jungle travel: a machete for three dollars, an aluminium cooking pot for five dollars, a straw sleeping mat for one dollar, iodine, matches, some string and other bits and bobs. More importantly, I also had my lucky one-dollar watch, bought on the Mexican border. Expensive outdoor equipment was unnecessary. The Indians who lived in the area managed without and so would we. We intended to eat as they did. Just in case, I packed a small amount of dried food for emergencies. That was all we needed.

In spite of all my planning, the night before we left for the Darién I felt a sense of dread, partly because I lost the others in the mêlée of Panama City's carnival. The final fireworks cracked like thunder high above me, showering sparks across the midnight sky. Smoke and the smell of gunpowder drifted by. I started to make my way through the jubilant crowd back towards my hostel, and soon I had left the throngs behind and was walking through the deserted suburban streets of the El Cangrejo district. I knew that within the next day or so we would be embarking on the adventure of a lifetime, but now, by myself, I felt scared.

Tom had at least turned up, though, and was raring to go. With such enthusiasm we couldn't fail, though I wasn't completely sure he knew what he was about to do. I wasn't even sure he would show up in the morning to leave for the Darién. I wondered whether I would have dared to take on the Darién alone. Was I obsessed enough to do that? However, for now, all the talking, all the planning, was over. I knew I would be OK once I started moving. Before embarking on my other trips I'd often felt like this; it was a normal and expected feelings of apprehension. One I simply had to overcome.

★　★　★

TOM: The next morning we left. Or at least we tried to. We couldn't find a bus to take us to the Darién, and for an hour we wandered aimlessly around the bus station.

'Where are the buses to the Darién?' I asked a driver.

He shrugged. Then he hollered something I didn't understand to a taxi driver. The car pulled up and the driver explained that he knew where to take us. We sped across town in typical breakneck fashion. He dropped us off at a smaller bus station. Paul paid while I got our packs from the boot. It wouldn't open. I became paranoid in case the driver drove off with our luggage — I'd lost my pack once and I couldn't face it happening again — so I thrust my foot in the passenger door. Not that that would have stopped him driving off, but there was no trouble. We collected our bags and went to buy our tickets.

'*¿Puedo tener dos boletos hasta Yaviza?*' I asked at the counter.

I turned and handed Paul his ticket. He looked surprised.

'Bloody hell,' he said, 'I didn't know you spoke Spanish.'

It occurred to me that I barely knew the guy, nor did he know anything about me.

'*Un poco,*' I said.

'You what?'

'That means I can speak a bit. I took a course in San Pedro.'

His eyes lit up.

'That's excellent, because my Spanish is crap. I took a three-day course in San José but I can barely remember a word.'

It was a little perturbing to discover that the man whose idea it had been to walk deep into the jungle where no-one would be able to speak English didn't know a word of Spanish. I supposed it didn't matter as long as I could manage a word or two.

The bus didn't leave for an hour so we went into the small café inside the station and ordered doughnuts dripping with fat — heart attacks in a snack. It gave each of us a chance to find out more about the other, though soon, inevitably, we began to trade travel stories.

'I once hitchhiked across the Sahara,' Paul said without a hint of bragging. His manner was very dry, very laconic, and I thought he was winding me up.

'What, the desert?'

'Yeah.'

'But there are no cars.'

'No, but there are one or two trucks a day.'

I picked up another cholesterol-booster and stuffed it in my mouth.

'What happens if none of them stops?'

'You just hope one does. I once had to wait two weeks for a ride.'

This bloke is hardcore, I thought. Next to his, my travels to find flowers and trees seemed like the ramblings of a greenhorn. He told me other stories until the bus pulled up, a garish vehicle that looked like an explosion in a paint factory. It seemed to halt at every stop on the outskirts of Panama City, crawling along in the traffic. At this rate it would take us weeks to reach the Darién. At each stop people got off, but none got on.

Despite the early hour, the carnival was still in flow. People thronged the streets, some of them finding it hilarious to throw water at each other and at passing vehicles. I heard a woman's voice shout 'Hello, tourist' in Spanish from the side of the road at one stop and I turned to wave, only to be hit square on the chest by what seemed to be a condom filled with water. It exploded on impact. I was soaked. I went to close the window but it was already shut. Its glass was missing. As the bus pulled away I could hear the sound of laughter melt away behind me. This ritual carried on until we cleared Panama City, Paul and I ducking in our seats to avoid being pelted with water bombs. It added spice to the journey, I suppose.

Soon we cleared the city and hit open countryside, alone on the bus save for the odd drunk sleeping off the effects of the previous night's revelries. At last, we were on our way towards the Darién.

4

LAST OF THE LOLLIPOPS

PAUL: The Pirogue glided gently against the flow as the long poles sought the bottom of the shallow Turia River. In our battered dugout the going was slow, but the boatmen had offered to take us upriver towards Púcuro for $40; an outboard motor would have cost $100. It was 11 March 2000. That morning we'd pushed the canoe off the riverbank at Boca de Cupe, the last outpost of Panamanian army and police. We were now beyond the protection of both law and government. The adrenalin ran high.

The jungle either side of the river was lush, canopy reaching above canopy, a vivid, intense green. Birds called out, appearing fleetingly, a flash of red and blue and green and yellow as they darted from tree to tree. Passing the occasional clearing we caught glimpses of butterflies, large multicoloured swarms or thick clouds of yellow ones. The banks of the river were tangled masses of trees, lianas reaching down to touch the water. There was no path and no sign of human life, save the odd cluster of huts, hamlets without names.

A few hours later we veered towards the left bank and entered a tributary where the water was shallower but less muddy and turgid, until it became as clear as a fresh mountain stream. The trees leaned closer, became claustrophobic, while the vines seemed to grasp at us. Tom, transfixed, called out the names of the plants we passed. Water rats and other mammals plopped into the river from the bank, then scooted across to the other side. Kingfishers, their blue and green colours glinting in the light, perched on branches; hummingbirds hovered at the lip of large flowers, the sight of which sent Tom spinning towards ecstasy. The solitude made it seem a magic world. This is what had drawn me here, to see this beautiful, unknown and unspoiled jungle.

My reverie was broken when, through the undergrowth, I saw a dilapidated sign that looked as though it'd been standing there for years. 'El Darién' were the only words I could make out. I nudged Tom and pointed to it. His gaze switched from the mass of foliage along the bank towards the rusting sign. He looked at me. Nothing was said, we both knew its significance.

★ ★ ★

TOM: As soon as I saw the sign my heart began to hammer against my ribcage. All the stories we'd been told, all the warnings we'd been given that we'd so blatantly dismissed, crowded into my mind. This was it, this was the Darién. Had the boatmen not been so relaxed my unease would have been worse. Had they shown any signs of nerves or fear then I felt certain I would turn into a quivering jelly. Instead they acted as

48

if they took gringos like Paul and me on this trip every day, talking to us, throwing stones at birds, acting without a care.

The last four days had built to this point. Our first stop after getting off the bus was Meteti — nothing more than a military base with a small town tacked on the side. After a night there we went on to Yaviza, a bone-shuddering two-hour bus ride over potholed roads. We saw no tourists, but I did spot some lovely terete-leaved oncidiums among the vast teak plantations we bumped and thumped past.

At Yaviza, once again, there was a military base where it was compulsory for us to see the commander in charge of operations. Two armed men led us past a helicopter pad and dug-in bunkers into a dark office. We were met by an imposing figure in fatigues, guns on his hips, sunglasses hiding his eyes despite the murky light. He asked where we were going. There was a map on the wall and we tried to show him our route. He looked at where we were pointing.

'No,' he said, 'that is dangerous. The border is bad. They come over and kill people. Do you know of the civil war?'

'We know, *señor*, but I want to go to Colombia and see the orchids.'

We pointed to another route. The word he kept repeating was *peligroso* — dangerous.

'What about this way?'

'*Peligroso.*'

'Or here?'

'*Peligroso.*'

'Or this way?'

'*Peligroso.*'

'How about this way, then?'

'*Peligroso.*' Always the shake of the head. He took off his sunglasses and rubbed his eyes. Then he looked at his watch. 'Look,' he said, 'you can pass through at your own risk.'

'*Gracias, señor,*' I said.

In a flash we were out of the door.

We tried to find a place to stay. The village was preparing for its annual carnival, which raised our spirits somewhat. Once we got a hotel we decided to stay for two nights because the locals promised cockfighting the next evening, and that was something I wanted to experience. In the Philippines I'd missed my chance to see 'razor-bladed' cockfighting. It was not something I approved of, yet I was keen to soak up the atmosphere and see what happened. Before I left England I had written a list of things I wanted to do and see, and watching a cockfight was on it.

Our hotel was right next to the local *discoteca*, which, from the sound of the thumping bass that echoed around the village, was already overflowing with the carnival spirit.

★ ★ ★

PAUL: A circular, concrete road runs through Yaviza. It's a dilapidated town that clings to the banks of the Río Chico and Río Cucanaque. The houses are carefully raised on stilts above the rain-sodden ground, all of them showing signs of tropical decay. Yaviza has eked out a living as a trading town, exchanging the raw materials of

50

the jungle for goods and cash. A ruined Spanish fort commands a view of the river, a symbol of the town's tenacity in the face of the tough jungle environment. The crowded streets buzz with activity, colourfully populated with Indians and the black descendants of runaway slaves.

In the heart of town we found a room at the Tres Americanas hotel. Tom and I sorted through our gear. By luck rather than planning we had everything we needed; the few items I had bought in Panama City complemented his tent, mosquito net and other bits and pieces.

During my research I'd come across a website edited by one Patricia Upton, who had extensive knowledge of the Darién from years past. Although I knew this information was outdated — the Darién of ten years ago is nothing like the Darién of today — it was all I could find, so I emailed her to find out if she had any recent information about the area or knew of somebody who might. I received several messages from people who'd skirted around the Darién or edged towards it but had never committed themselves to a crossing. Finally, before I left Panama City, I got a memo from two Americans who'd managed to get across a couple of months before. I hadn't yet shown it to Tom. Now I dug it out of my pack and handed it to him.

'Have a read of this and tell me what you think.'

I had no idea what he'd make of it. It began: 'We made it. We would not do it again, nor would we have done it if we had known the extent of the danger currently afoot in

51

Colombia.' The email detailed their journey through the Darién, how they were warned at every turn that they would not live to see the Colombian border. In order to hide their gringo roots and avoid accusations of being CIA drug operatives, they adopted German accents. After leaving Púcuro they picked up a guide and his friend, who led them past Paya to Arquía, across the border. They travelled alone to Unguía because they were unable to find anybody who wasn't terrified of the paramilitaries. Eventually they made it to a Colombian army outpost and caught a boat across the Golfo de Uraba to Turbo and safety. The email ended with a warning: 'In Púcuro we were told that three Americans had visited five months ago and had travelled as far in as Paya before returning and exiting the Darién by air. I can't imagine anyone else being as brainless, obsessed and fortunate as we were.'

My first reaction was disappointment: we'd been beaten to the crossing. But then I became more positive. If they could do it, so could we. The originator of the memo intended it to be a warning; all I saw, however, was proof that it could be done. It provided us with a plan, a route map, to make it through the Darién. My hunch was that we should pick up a guide in Paya to steer us away from danger and over the border following the same route as the Americans. That meant we could avoid any paramilitaries.

Tom read it and became even more excited — if that was possible.

'It's not put you off, then.'

'No,' he said defiantly. 'If they can do it, then so can we.'

I liked his frame of mind. He was twenty-three, five years younger than me, and he seemed fearless. His attitude was exactly what we needed. Immediately, I thought, 'We're committed, and nothing will stop us.' I went outside onto the balcony for a cigarette. I watched the sunset, convinced that in ten days' time we would be through and on the other side.

★ ★ ★

TOM: That night, as the music pounded incessantly, I showed Paul the equipment I had. Much to his delight, I produced a $20 Chinese tent, medical bags and my prized possession, a mosquito net. Combined with the equipment he had brought, there was nothing we couldn't cope with. Paul showed me an email he'd received a few days before leaving Panama City from two Americans who had made it across the Darién Gap only a few months ago. It made for a thrilling read and proved we could do it. That it was dangerous was obvious, but the positive aspect was that these Americans had found a way through.

The next day we waited for The Dude. We didn't expect him to show, and he fulfilled our expectations. To while away time, we wrote and sent our last postcards knowing that the next post office would be over the Colombian border. To myself I made a few notes on the back of a postcard: 'I think about the parents a lot and wonder about the risk a lot but with my lucky charm Paul, I feel very optimistic about the coming 'excursion'. No rain please!!'

The expedition still felt unreal, distant almost. We both felt that at some stage someone would order us to turn back. However, we were determined to try. We always had the get-out clause of turning back at either Púcuro or Paya should our nerve fail. I wrote a postcard to my parents, Gran and my sister:

> *Greetings from this extremely non-touristy area, last tourists here (two of them) in January, with the intention of crossing the Darién Gap to Colombia, we (a friend from London) are going for it, but we have the expectation of being turned back. Yaviza (Panama) to Turbo (Colombia) is the plan, 8 days or so. This is a heavily militarized zone and we've been checked 5 times on our way down from Panama City to Yaviza and once here in Yaviza were taken to a dark room with the military chief; all very friendly but with aim of dissuading us from entering Colombia. Never have I seen such a large amount of troops with guns all over the place. Will email Bristles [sister Ann] as soon as possible either from Colombia via Darién or after a plane flight, back to Panama City via Puerto Obaldia and on to Turbo, which is far safer. Idiots we are searching for adventure!!!*
>
> *All the best and best wishes.*

Tired of waiting around for the festival to start — the cock-fighting arena was still being built — we decided to make a start the next morning. The road had ended; there was only overgrown path or logging track to walk on now. We spent the first few hours hacking away wildly at the vegetation with a blunt machete — sapping work in the sweltering heat but enormous fun. Despite these obstacles we made good ground and soon we reached the small village of Pinogana. After a brief rest we set off again, hoping to reach Boca de Cupe by nightfall.

As we walked across an open field just outside Pinogana, two black women approached us, both carrying logs. As they came closer one of the women threw her logs to the floor and started to freak out, screaming wildly.

'They will kill you, they will kill you!' she kept repeating. 'They have done it before and they will do it to you!'

Paul and I looked at each other. Who were 'they'? She carried on shouting. Finally, she stopped. Shaken by this outburst, I turned to Paul.

'What do we do?' I asked nervously.

He looked ahead.

'Let's go on.'

On we went, hitching a lift for a mile or so in the back of a logging truck, which gave us time to rest, albeit a short time. Then we hacked onwards. It was tough but exhilarating to make such progress, and even more fun to splash across the rivers in our path. The memory of the screaming woman faded as we covered ground easily. Further on we picked up a guide who said for $30 he would take us to Boca de Cupe. We walked for the rest of the afternoon until the light began to fade.

'We must be nearly there,' I told Paul.

Then the guide turned to me.

'*Señor*, I need more money to take you to Boca de Cupe.'

'What?'

'Thirty dollars is not enough.'

Paul asked what was wrong. I told him that the guide wanted more cash to take us to the village. 'We've paid him. Tell him to get lost,' Paul said.

'Sorry, *Señor*,' I explained, 'but we have no more money. We have given you all we have.'

With that he simply shrugged his shoulders and walked off into the woods, ignoring our shouts of protest.

'I don't believe that,' Paul said, furious. 'He was just trying to rip us off.'

I looked around. It was about to get dark, we were in the middle of impenetrable jungle and we had no idea where we were heading.

'Let's try this way,' Paul said, pointing to a path ahead.

We set off walking and the path started to veer to the left. If we continued to follow it we would probably end up going back the way we came. All the time the light was disappearing. Soon it would be hard to see a hand in front of your face and we'd have to camp out.

'Let's go down there,' Paul said, pointing at another path.

We wandered down it, but yet again we seemed to make no progress. We had to face it: we were lost.

'I can't believe he left us here alone in the woods,' I said. 'We'll have to camp here.'

'Hang on, Tom, can you see him?'

I followed his finger, and through the gloaming I could make out a figure.

'If that's our guide,' Paul said, 'I'm going to break his neck.'

It was a passer-by. I asked where Boca de Cupe was and he pointed to a path. We took it and ten minutes later we arrived at our destination. It made the cheek of our guide even more breathtaking.

There was yet another military base where we had to announce our arrival. Just outside the town, it loomed menacingly, silhouetted against the dusk, a concrete station surrounded by three dugouts. The ground around it was cleared to prevent a sneak attack. Strewn everywhere were sandbags, some covered with tin roofs to form huts, with yet more bags on the ceiling. Heavy machine guns were at each post. Men wandered to and fro in their fatigues, guns slung over their shoulders. The base looked primed to repel an attack. Despite the frenetic activity, the soldiers were friendly and ushered us towards the military checkpoint where the man in charge didn't even bother to warn us. Word must have been passed down by radio after our arrival in Meteti.

It had been a hard day's walk but we'd seen owls, leaf-cutter ants, butterflies, lizards, coloured frogs and more, as well as the lovely *Brownea* tree in flower and oncidiums — our first orchids in the forest. That night we slept in a dusty wooden shack owned by a family, though the noise of the generator next to the house afforded us little sleep, despite our exhaustion. There would be some respite the next day because walking would be practically impossible: the jungle was too thick and Paul had forgotten to sharpen his machete before leaving Panama City. So the next morning we negotiated a boat ride to take us where the road didn't go, further into the Darién.

★ ★ ★

PAUL: Our boatmen needed a rest. The sweat poured off them in the blazing Equatorial sun. They were small wiry black men; Tom and I towered above them, in their tatty long trousers and Wellington boots, which everyone down here seemed to wear. As we relaxed on the riverbank I shared the last of my cigarettes, hoping I would get the chance to buy some more in Púcuro or Paya.

When we set off again poling became harder and the water shallower. Put your hand in to the elbow and your fingertips could touch the muddy bottom. Our progress was often halted when we hit small rapids and were forced to get out of the boat to haul it over; the water rose to our knees, and sweat dripped off our noses with the effort. It was 3.30 p.m. and our boatmen were tired. They could go no further: they had to be back in Boca de Cupe by nightfall. 'We'll have trouble with the local police if we arrive back after darkness,' one of them explained.

They dropped us by a small cluster of reed huts owned by Kuna Indians. Luckily we managed to find a few villagers willing to guide us to Púcuro for a few dollars; they even offered to carry our packs as part of the deal. We set off at pace, hoping to make our destination before night fell. They took us to within five minutes of Púcuro before turning back. We made it to the village just as the light started to fade.

As we arrived, a group was gathered in an open space, some standing, others sitting. They gave us wary glances, though some curious children scurried over to greet us, fascinated by our pale faces. We sidled up to the group, said our hellos and asked if they knew somewhere we could sleep. One man offered to put us up. We said we wanted to go to Paya, and perhaps beyond. This produced a lively reaction, much shaking of heads and a few loudly expressed opinions about our sanity. With my poor Spanish I was unable to follow the conversation, though I got the drift.

'Apparently three Indians from Púcuro went missing a week ago,' Tom explained. 'They've found the body of one of them.'

I nodded. Someone else piped up. Tom translated again.

'He says if we want to, he will introduce us to the dead man's family.'

We declined the offer. Neither Tom nor I said anything to each other; it was clear what was going through our minds, though. Should we go on to Paya?

We wandered around the village, found a dusty shop and bought some stale bread, matches, salt, rice and sardines. Our house for the evening was a two-storey building with a rickety ladder leading up to a bedroom where the family slept. We were confined to the lower storey and the hard, bare earth floor alongside the family dogs. Their sniffling and barking kept us awake. We talked about our meeting with the locals and what our next step should be.

Though I knew something of the situation in Colombia, it had become increasingly murky. The civil war had been rumbling since the 1960s, making it one of the longest-running conflicts in the world. Against a backdrop of poverty and widespread unrest, several guerrilla groups had emerged, the largest and most notorious of which was FARC (*Fuerzas Armadas Revoluciónarias de Colombia*), followed by the ELN (*Ejercito de Liberación Nacional*) and the now defunct M-19 (*Movimiento 19 de Abril*). Many other minor groups existed. Set against this lethal cocktail of political infighting between a corrupt government and the guerrillas were some of the largest and most powerful drugs cartels in the world. It was an explosive mixture. Paramilitary groups had sprouted in reaction to the guerrillas' increasing power. In 1997 the AUC (*Autodefensas Unidas de Colombia*) was set up by a group of drug lords looking to protect their valuable crops and position from the guerrilla movement. Since then their power had increased unabated. But which of these groups should we fear most?

FARC's grip on the Darién Gap had tightened over the past decade. It was now almost fully under their control, providing a reasonably secure route for goods, gold and drugs to be smuggled from Panama into Colombia to yield funds for their ongoing campaign against the government. Given their hold on the area, any outsiders who venture into the Gap are immediately viewed with distrust, assumed to be paramilitaries if they are Colombian, or CIA operatives trying to trace the flow of drugs that one day end up in the USA, or rival drug smugglers trying to export and import, though given the area's danger even criminals have started to give the Darién a wide berth. Fail to fulfil any of those criteria and the chances are a person will be kidnapped anyway; more than three thousand people are abducted every year in Colombia. It's almost the national pastime, seen by the various factions and renegade groups as an easy way to extract money, or, as is sometimes the case with FARC, as a bargaining tool to secure the release of their members held political prisoner by the government.

Tom and I discussed the relative dangers of the groups we might encounter. On my travels I had met a girl who was stopped by FARC on the Pacific side of Colombia, between Cali and Buenaventura about three hundred kilometres down the coast from the Darién. She and her friends had got away with giving them their penknives and nothing else. I told the story to

Tom and emphasized we were only backpackers, therefore of little use to anyone. It would be different if we were oil workers, for example, because they would fancy their chances of getting some money for us in return. As for the paramilitaries, well, they were simply best avoided.

The missing Indians were a worry, the first tangible proof of the dangers the Darién posed to innocent parties. Yet I reckoned if we moved fast it was possible to avoid trouble. Tom agreed. He was still very enthusiastic, which bolstered me. We complemented each other: there were times when I was terrified, though I said nothing, and Tom was really keen to push on, which girded me, and there were occasions when the opposite was true.

'What about guides, Paul? Do you think we'll need one?'

'Well, they haven't proved all that reliable so far. We don't want to get stitched up again once we're near the border. We don't need a guide to get us to Paya, though, we can walk that ourselves.'

There was a pause. The dogs snuffled somewhere in the darkness.

'I tell you what, Tom, if we find a guide when we get to Paya then we'll go for it. If we can't, then we'll turn back.'

He seemed happy with that plan. The decision made, I drifted into a light sleep.

The room we had been given was in the old immigration house. For years it had stood unused. There was an immigration book, its pages pristine and empty apart from a thin coating of dust and two handwritten names on the first page: James and Matthew, the two Americans who had beaten us through the Gap by a couple of months. This evidence of their journey authenticated their email. We wrote our names next to theirs.

The next day we were diverted by a group of villagers who seemed to be holding some sort of meeting in the village's assembly house. After it ended we tried to find out what it was all about. We were told one of the Indians who went missing the previous week had come back, albeit drunk. This was a relief. Perhaps the group was a drinking party which had gone off on a week-long bender. No mention was made of the one who was supposedly killed. Then someone else told us that it was seven people who went missing, not three. Who was right? Had it been a misunderstanding on our part, something lost in translation, or was it just the rumour-mill exaggerating things? It was confusing.

That night — after a day's rest from walking — we'd just sat down to eat when a stocky, dark, smooth-skinned young man came and sat on the stool opposite. He was not a Kuna Indian. He introduced himself as Carlos, a Colombian. He chatted constantly, glancing here and there though never directly at us, flicking at the dusty floor with a stick as he spoke. He seemed as if he was hiding something, but then eye contact was something we had rarely experienced in the Darién so far. With my limited Spanish I picked up only the general drift of what he was saying.

Nothing seemed to be a problem for him. He could take us.

It was refreshing to meet someone who was offering to help us progress, not just telling us to turn back, but we did not want to squander our cash needlessly. There was also the question of trust. Tom and I agreed that we wouldn't say yes or no to Carlos yet. He shrugged his shoulders. He knew that we'd need a guide eventually: crossing from Paya would be impossible without getting lost and it would be good to travel with someone who knew the area well. But a decision could wait for Paya.

* * *

TOM: The next morning we paid our landlady for our room, even though she tried to demand extra cash. 'Gringos have more money,' she said. We gave her short shrift. Just as we were leaving Juan Rivas, the village's immigration officer who was mentioned in the Americans' email, approached me and whispered a few words in my ear.

'You can get guides in Paya and you can cross to Colombia,' he hissed.

This buoyed my spirits and lifted Paul's when I told him. His whole face lit up. It was reassuring news after all the warnings.

As we left the village, the locals came out of their huts to wave us off. It was quite a farewell. I felt like Dorothy setting off on the Yellow Brick Road. We paused to take some pictures, then set off. We had another tough day's walking ahead of us according to Paul, though the rest had done us good. As we left the village behind we walked through a *plátano* (banana) grove and into the jungle, eventually finding a path. We must have walked all of ten minutes, if that, when we came across a small clearing. There, sat on a log, wearing a gaudy and expensive-looking wrist-watch, was a smartly dressed, almost Western-looking man, his face cleanly shaven.

'You like to change money?' he asked. 'You need Colombian pesos?'

What the hell was this well-turned-out guy doing operating a one-man bureau de change on a log in the middle of the Darién Gap?

'We have no money that needs changing, señor.'

'Good rate, good rate,' he said eagerly.

We shook our heads.

'I see you are going to Colombia,' he added. 'Do you need guides?'

'No, we're fine.'

As if by magic, two men appeared. One of them was Carlos, the guide who had offered us his services the night before. He joined the conversation.

'I know the route well,' he told us. 'I travel it every month or so.'

Again we said we might discuss it in Paya. We left the moneychanger there on his log, though when we turned around a few seconds later he'd vanished; Carlos and his friend, however, were right behind us. We ignored them and carried on walking but they followed us all the way for the rest of the day, walking behind us, in front of us and alongside us, often in sight, sometimes hidden.

The walk was punishing in the furnace-like heat. Up and down hills we strode, sweat pouring from us in streams. In the afternoon there was a sudden and violent downpour, forcing us to take shelter. When it stopped we set off again, steam rising from our wet clothes. Carlos and his friend disappeared during the last couple of hours of the walk, perhaps frustrated at our slow progress. They were the only human beings we saw on our journey that day.

★   ★   ★

PAUL: Paya was smaller than Púcuro, though it had a concrete path running through it. A neat cluster of wood and reed huts on the banks of the river, it was less friendly than the village we had left that morning. We were met by the chief's son, who took us to a little shop where we bought biscuits and Coca-cola. Then he took us to the assembly house where he said a woman would put us up for the evening.

While we waited for our meal, Carlos and his friend, Francisco, approached us again. The negotiations started and lasted for almost two hours, the main sticking point being payment and whether we would give him anything in advance. After our experience on the outskirts of Boca de Cupe, when we had paid money up front only for our guide to leave us in the lurch, we refused to take that option. Finally, we shook hands on a deal of $50 a day to take us all the way to Arquía, over the Colombian border, on condition that they also provided us with food.

That night we both slept easier, despite our bed again being a dirt floor. Like the Americans, we had found guides who would take us over the border and give us safety in numbers.

★ ★ ★

TOM: The next morning the atmosphere was tense. Nothing was said between us. I could see that Paul was as discomfited and uncertain as me. Paya was our very last chance to turn back. It was also where we had half expected our journey to end, that the military would refuse to let us pass and order us back into Panama, but the military base was deserted, nothing more than an empty shell. This was both uplifting and scary: uplifting because it meant fewer procedures to go through and no questioning; scary because the area was so unstable that the army had upped and left.

As we ate breakfast, a man named Vicent Pizarro paid us a visit. The day before we'd made a few enquiries about immigration papers for Colombia. Vicent collected our passports and an hour or so later returned with a piece of headed notepaper bearing the words 'National Immigration of Panama, Ministry of Government and Justice'. The logo and calligraphy looked official enough, the scrawled handwritten message below it less so. 'To whomever it may concern,' it read. 'Please let Thomas Guy and Winder Paul-Denniz pass freely with good health and

67

without hindrance into Colombia. They have passports and visas with which to enter. No more. That's it.' Or at least that's how I translated it. Where they got the idea we had visas is anyone's guess. The question of immigration was a troublesome one, and this seemed to be the solution. Again, it gave us a certain amount of reassurance. 'It's our ticket over the border,' Paul said delightedly. If not wholly satisfied, we were also feeling less doubtful about the guides' reliability. I had asked around the village and the consensus was that Carlos could be trusted.

Next stop was the shop, where I took the opportunity to buy a few treats, biscuits and a bag of lollipops, which I shared among us, keeping a few back for later. Then, just before leaving Paya and plunging further into the heart of the Darién Gap, I passed a note I had written in Spanish for Juan Rivas through the slatted walls of the assembly house, where the villagers were in the middle of what seemed to be an important meeting. I was told to wait until the meeting was finished, but we had to leave. Persistence paid off eventually. After five minutes of thrusting the letter through the slats and hissing, 'Please take this, señor,' an unseen hand snatched it impatiently from me. 'Take it to Púcuro,' I implored, before adding a 'por favor'. I got a grunt in reply.

The note read: 'Dear Juan Rivas, Thank you for your kindness. Paul and I will write to you in Púcuro when we arrive in Colombia. Thank you, Juan, and the people of Púcuro, and good luck in your life. Tom and Paul.' We'd agreed to write this as a safety policy. There was an outside chance something would go wrong and we hoped that if Juan heard nothing from us in the next fortnight or so he would raise the alarm.

As we left the village, Carlos and Francisco abruptly announced that they had forgotten the salt, forcing us to turn back. As they went off to find it, Paul and I sat waiting on the concrete path.

They took a while to return. Our guidebook said that Colombia was two days' walk away at best, which meant it might take us three. The sun was getting high, the temperature was already soaring and it was time for us to push on or valuable time would be lost. I was getting stage fright, worrying that we were about to do something dreadfully stupid. My main worry wasn't what lay ahead in the jungle, it was that our guides might rob us once we were out of sight. Paul said nothing, but the look on his face told me he was agonizing over making this last push. Had he admitted at that point to second thoughts about the crossing then I would have agreed with him instantly. But, rather than admitting these doubts, we made amiable small talk about the weather and our guides. Up until now we'd always been on the move; there was always one village ahead to reach, always an opportunity to turn back if we became scared and decided the prospect was too daunting. Now that luxury was taken from us: Paya was the end of the line. I wanted to say, 'Are you sure about this, Paul?' I felt sure he wanted to say, 'We can always turn back, Tom.' But we both kept our peace.

Carlos and Francisco eventually returned, and we set off.

★ ★ ★

PAUL: Five minutes into the walk and we were deep into the jungle, twisting and bending through the branches that hung over the vine-choked paths. Unlike Carlos and Francisco, who'd brought a .22 rifle, Tom and I had to stoop. We were dressed in shorts and T-shirts — like backpackers, in other words. It might have been unsuitable dress for the terrain, but anyone crazy enough to walk into that jungle wearing fatigues or any other outfit would almost certainly be asking for trouble.

As we climbed a steep hillock we passed two Indians travelling in the opposite direction. They greeted Carlos and obviously knew him. The conversation was hard to follow, though the little information we managed to glean indicated they were talking about a mutual acquaintance who'd been killed by the paramilitaries. One of the men also told Carlos that people were looking for him. He was unperturbed. Shortly after bidding the men a hearty goodbye we were on our way once more.

We continued our ascent to our first jungle camp in a small clearing on a mountain ridge. It had been a good day. Carlos and Francisco had not demanded more payment or left us stranded, so we felt more comfortable. The clearing was large enough for the four of us. As we prepared camp we spoke to Carlos about the Americans, and he admitted to having been their guide. It seemed logical, because all day we had followed a litter trail: fresh, empty packets of American food discarded on the floor. He produced a blue tarpaulin and, referring to the Americans, said it was given to him by 'Diego'. This was confusing because we knew them as James and Matthew and had seen those names written in the book. Then I worked it out. Next to their names they had put their home towns. One of them was San Diego.

Carlos kept up his chatter. Francisco, who was older, perhaps by a decade or more, said little. The Americans had impressed Carlos with the efficient way they had approached the crossing.

'They had a water filter,' he told us admiringly, 'with a plastic pump and a small cooker.'

We looked sheepishly at the plastic lemonade bottle we had filled at the river. We had decided against buying purifying tablets; instead, we had iodine, which acts as a purifier but gives a rank taste. We knew there would be highland streams where the water would be clean enough to drink, and anyway, the whole idea was to live like the locals, not to rely on Western contraptions.

We asked Carlos if he had taken any other people across the Darién. He shook his head.

'Just you and the Americans. But now that you have come I hope that many more tourists will pass through. I can make a lot of money,' he added with a grin.

The next morning, after breakfast and breaking camp, we set off briskly but became diverted by the scenery and the trees and flowers. Carlos found some bamboo and cut it in two to show us how to find water. After dawdling in the morning we upped the pace as the day drew on, stopping at nothing as we hurtled down the other side of the mountain. I spotted a reed cross as we rushed past. I wondered who'd died there, but there was no time to discuss it with Tom because we were covering ground at such speed. When we reached an ideal spot on the banks of a clear-running river and dropped our stuff in a heap, I brought the subject up.

'Did you see that cross?'

'Yeah. I did wonder who had died,' Tom said.

'I wondered *how* they died.'

Tom laughed and shrugged his shoulders. Then we fell silent.

'Suppose it could have been one of the local Indians,' I said. Then, before we gave it too much thought, 'Come on, let's pitch the tent.'

We had another companion that evening. Victor, a shorthaired, spaced-out character with woeful shoes, had also selected the spot for the night. Penniless, with only an avocado for food, he was utterly lost and had been stuck in this clearing pondering his next move for days. Stumbling across such a strange character in the middle of this jungle was bizarre, but it was good to meet someone so relaxed and friendly in such a supposedly inhospitable environment. As we all dined on the plump *pavo* bird Francisco had shot earlier that day — it was a bit like eating a roasted turkey — he told us the story of how he came to be stuck in this clearing in one of the world's most dangerous places.

'I come from Medellín in Colombia,' he told us. 'I was in Turbo one night in the middle of a heavy drinking session and met a ship's captain. This captain said his ship was going to China and I told him that was interesting. He said he would offer me passage. It seemed a good idea at the time, after a night of tequila. But the next morning it was not such a good idea. I wanted to leave Colombia, though. I have had enough of that place. So I decided to go where every man dreams of going: America. I want to find work.'

'Then how have you ended up here?' asked Carlos.

'I intend to follow the river into Panama and beyond,' he replied.

Carlos laughed.

'If you do that then you will die.'

Victor nodded. It was obvious he was a lost soul. Tom and I feared for him, though Carlos and Francisco thought he was unhinged and viewed him with suspicion. They went down to the river to wash, murmuring to each other, flicking distrustful looks at Victor. How they could view this pitiable character with such contempt bemused me.

As we parted company the next morning, I picked out a tin of meat from my rucksack.

'Take this,' I said, handing it to Victor. He gave me a grateful look, uncertain what to say. 'Tom, tell him that we wish him good luck in America.'

Tom translated and Victor smiled, revealing a

set of rotten teeth. He shook my hand vigorously.

Then it was time to move on. With luck we would hit the Colombian border later that day and I was in no mood to hang around.

After walking an hour or so our guides were sidetracked by another *pavo* bird in a tree. Francisco released a cascade of loud cracks, none of which appeared to hit the target. 'I've hit it many times,' he protested, 'but it is a very strong bird. I can get it.' Much heated discussion followed about the best way to achieve this. Suddenly Francisco fired another shot. There was a flurry of wings and a tremendous rustling of leaves as the big bird fell out of the tree at last and hit the earth with a thud. We thought it was dead, but suddenly it sprang to its feet and started to run away from us, flapping its black wings wildly. The guides set off in pursuit, shouting to Tom to try to cut it off further down the hill. I slumped down on my rucksack, irritated by this pointless delay. What on earth were we doing so close to the border making so much noise?

★   ★   ★

TOM: The bird fell from the tree like a coconut, yet it got up again, so I set off in pursuit, though I was diverted by a splendid scarlet passion flower which was begging to be photographed. Fun had been the main aim of the morning rather than serious walking. I wasn't bothered because we'd made such good progress for two days without a whiff of danger. Our confidence

74

was so high that fooling around seemed entirely appropriate. Paul did not agree. He thought little of our bird-hunt, and he made his feelings clear.

Carlos, Francisco and I returned empty-handed. I could see from the look on Paul's face that he was not about to sympathize.

'Can we get a move on, please?' he said. 'I want to reach Arquía some time this year.'

I translated for Carlos, and he nodded as if to say, 'You're the bosses.' We collected our things and started to walk.

'How far is it to the border?' Paul asked.

'Not far now, perhaps forty-five minutes,' Carlos replied.

Was that all? We were almost through the Darién Gap! We turned to each other and beamed. Colombia was just around the corner. I was disappointed at seeing so few orchids. Just making the crossing would be enough.

Excitement turned to apprehension when we came across Payita, a burned-out village to which the Americans had referred in their email. The huts were charred ruins claimed by the jungle, vines and weeds sprouting here and there, an impenetrable forest of regrowth, contorted branches and vines waiting to ensnare rucksacks and razor-sharp grass forming hidden tripwires.

Ten minutes later we came across a beautiful clear stream. Despite having washed the night before, Carlos announced he and Francisco were going to have another bath. They stripped down to their Speedos and waded into the water.

'It's noon and we've hardly travelled half a

kilometre,' Paul complained, checking his cheap Mexican watch. 'Why do they need another bloody bath?'

He kicked off his shoes and went and sat on a rock on the other side of the stream. To cheer him up, I delved into my rucksack and found the four remaining lollipops I'd bought from the dusty village shop in Paya.

'It's the last of the lollipops, chaps,' I said.

I gave one to Francisco and one to Carlos, then walked over to Paul and put both hands behind my back.

'Which hand?'

'The right,' Paul said, a smile playing on his lips.

I opened my right hand to reveal a blue lollipop. Those were the best. Paul's smile broke into a grin as he took it from me. I went and found my own perch. The day was bright and beautiful; the sun glistened on the stream. It was good to feel it burning on our backs as we dipped our feet in the cool, refreshing water.

★　★　★

PAUL: Carlos said it was only forty-five minutes to the border, though I didn't believe him. I estimated another three or four hours at least and I wanted to arrive in Colombia by sunset, but Carlos and Francisco seemed relaxed about being in the area, despite being so near to the border where the paramilitaries were supposed to patrol. Surely if it was as dangerous as people said then they would be more nervous?

As I sucked on my lollipop, my bare feet dipping in the water, I looked around. Once again the isolated beauty struck me. The sky was luscious blue; deep green vines and weeping trees stroked the surface of the water; humming-birds searched hungrily for nectar in the flowers. I had never been somewhere so remote before, just me and my pack, miles from the nearest distraction. Everything was perfect. Still, I stirred myself and tried to get the others moving. There was no time to hang around, tempting as it was to drink in the magical aura of the place.

★ ★ ★

TOM: After finishing his lollipop Paul rose to his feet, eager to get on. Seeing this, Carlos and Francisco left the water and dried themselves off. Carlos then held us up again by disappearing off into the jungle for a fifteen-minute shit. Paul was becoming more frustrated. Eventually he came back and we set off again, in single file, the final stretch ahead of us. Unusually, I went ahead of Paul, behind the two guides.

All of a sudden Carlos flung himself to the ground. I stopped, and Paul walked straight into the back of me. I could hear shouting. Then two men ran out of the bushes in front of us yelling so loudly I couldn't work out what it was they wanted. They were dressed in full camouflage gear, their guns pointing straight at our heads. My legs just gave way beneath me and I sank to my knees on the open forest floor, my hands up above my head. One of the men pointed his

AK-47 straight at my head. It took me a while to understand what he was saying: he wanted my rucksack. He managed to undo the waist and chest straps of my backpack, but struggled with the shoulder straps of the Karrimor fifteen-litre front pack. He was fumbling with them like a teenage boy with a bra strap. I tried to help him but I was met with a volley of abuse in return for my efforts. I left him to it, closing my eyes, trying to make sense of what was happening.

5

BRAS AND GUNS

TOM: I can't remember speaking to Paul for the first twenty-four hours. We sat in absolute silence, side by side on our hastily constructed beds. At night an armed guard sat two feet in front of us; during the day they watched us from their bivouacs, no more than ten feet away.

Thoughts of my family monopolized my mind that first night, as darkness fell and the jungle came to life. I hadn't seen my parents in twenty-eight months. We'd spoken once in that time, by phone while I was in Australia. Now there was every chance I wouldn't see them again. It was as if Paul and I had walked off the end of the earth. Apart, possibly, from Juan Rivas, no-one knew we were here; no-one even came through here. I wondered what had happened to our friendly guides Carlos and Francisco. We had last seen them spreadeagled on the ground at the place of capture. Had they been killed, taken away like us, or even released? Again and again I cursed myself for being so stupid, blithely walking into danger in the face of so many warnings. And for what? I had seen barely a single orchid. I thought again of family, friends and the gum trees at home, none of which I was expecting to see again.

I clung to the hope that our captors were neither paramilitaries nor revolutionaries. Yet who they were wasn't relevant; what they were going to do with us was. I felt sure they'd kill us. It was simply a matter of when. Sitting in our cell as dawn rose slowly and the heat of the day began to fill the small space, I felt I was on Death Row: incarcerated, claustrophobic from fear as well as from lack of space, as if the air itself were heavy, all the time waiting to die, dreading every second that passed as it brought me closer to the end. I felt as though I was sinking into a black hole. I had never felt so helpless or bereft.

I must have drifted off briefly as dawn arrived because I remember waking, slowly, at first unaware of where I was until it struck me suddenly, like cold water poured down my back, and the reality of our situation became appallingly clear.

Our hut was simply an A-frame roof on poles with an open door at either end allowing us to see out. Sat on our beds, to our right we looked out onto the fire where cooking was done; to the left was one of our captors' bivouacs, pole beds covered by ponchos. A couple — a stocky, menacing, moustachioed man, his mouth a collage of blackened stumps and teeth, and his large-breasted, heavily made-up and raven-haired wife — shared that shelter. If we ducked down we could see under the rim of the roof to the other three bivouacs, which allowed us to watch a lot of what happened around camp.

I told the guard I needed the toilet. He

grunted and motioned to the doorway. I relieved myself with him at my shoulder, surprised I could even go given the circumstances.

I soon began to get a sense of the camp's layout. We were at the top of a steep bank leading down to a tiny stream, on the other side of which was another precipitous bank, maybe twenty feet high. Looking up the camp there were three other bivouacs, and beyond that was freedom, hence the reason we were stuck where we were.

The camp was slowly coming to life. A fire was being prepared to cook breakfast. A male guard was gathering wood, with what I took to be his wife or girlfriend acting as the cook. I wondered what we would eat, having finished off Paul's supplies the previous night.

Back in the hut, Paul stirred. It looked as if his night's sleep had been as appalling as mine judging by the deep gashes of black under his eyes. He looked awful, though to be honest at that point my thoughts were centring solely on myself. I didn't blame him; I'd agreed to accompany him. Apportioning blame hardly seemed worth my while. Thinking of some way out of the mess we were in would be far more constructive.

★ ★ ★

PAUL: Guilt. That was the overriding emotion that first night. I'd led Tom into this quagmire. I had risked not only my life, but his, too. I felt that I knew most about the Darién; I was older, more experienced in travelling, and therefore I

81

should have been the sensible one. Tom just followed me, believing implicitly in my flawed judgement.

I was furious with myself. What a bloody mess. I had been driven to make the crossing. I'd accepted its dangers, welcoming the excitement and the adrenalin. Enjoying them even. It was what I wanted. Now the danger was real, unavoidable, and to be confronted. I should have made the decision to turn back, leaving the Darién well alone.

Then I thought of my parents and my brothers. What would they think? I was single and young with no-one to think about other than myself. Or so I'd thought. I hadn't considered the consequences if something went wrong. There were other people who would suffer, my parents and brothers foremost among them. My selfishness had let them down. I became aware of my responsibilities to them. If this went on for a long time, with them unsure of my fate for God knows how long, then the emotional stress I'd cause them would be far worse than anything I was about to face. At least *I* knew I was alive. The guilt was overwhelming. I'd made the decisions that resulted in this; the responsibility was all mine. I didn't know what to do or how to react. I felt helpless and very, very scared.

I tried to analyse our predicament. An unknown and hostile group had captured us. What did they want? Why were they holding us and waiting? Once they found out whatever it was they wanted, would they dispatch us with a bullet to the back of the head? No-one would

82

know what had happened to us. They had complete control of our lives and it was a disturbing feeling.

I could think of nothing to say to Tom, nothing whatsoever. Well, apart from, 'Fucking hell, what have we done?' Neither of us spoke about what might happen to us because we knew one major possibility was being killed. All I could do was sit in our shelter and stare aimlessly into the jungle.

We were guarded at gunpoint that first night and watched intently the next day. They didn't let us out of their sight for a second. There was no communication between us and them, save the occasional glance to get permission to go to the toilet. Who were they? It was impossible to tell which group they belonged to, whether or not they were the sinister paramilitaries we'd heard so much about. I looked in their eyes and saw fear — they had no idea who we were either. For all they knew, we could be CIA, drug runners, anybody.

On the second morning El Jefe stood near our hut, smoking a cigarette. As soon as I saw him smoking I knew I would ask him for a drag. It was simply a case of when. I watched him intently, trying to inhale as much as I could passively, but there was little wind. I've never wanted a cigarette more in my life. The craving became so bad that when he turned to look at me I simply said, 'Un cigarillo, por favor.' Without blinking he reached inside his camouflage uniform and pulled out a pack, walked over and offered me one. I took it, nodding gratefully, repeating *gracias* over and over. As he lit it for me, I sucked it in deeply, savouring the sweet taste. The pleasure was fleeting; stubbing it out was like extinguishing hope. The last fag before facing the firing squad.

★ ★ ★

TOM: Click-click-click. The sound was rhythmic, insistent. I'm no expert on guns but even I knew it was the sound of a magazine being turned, bullets being loaded and unloaded. 'Bloody hell,' I thought, 'they're gearing up to shoot us. We're dead.' I could see the moustachioed man from where I sat. As soon as the ritual was finished, it would begin again: he would click the bullets into place; then he would load the magazine by pulling back the bolt on the AK-47 and letting it go with a snap, bringing the round into the barrel. This display, for our benefit, continued the whole day, interrupted only when food was served. On the few occasions when my mind strayed from the hopelessness of our situation to something less morbid, the gun ritual proved a salient, awful reminder. Why try to rack your brain when it's going to be plastered over a tree trunk at any second?

Another sleepless night followed. I wasn't sure if I dreamed it, but I remember one of the women, the wife or girlfriend of the gun-cleaner, exposing her breasts in the night as she guarded us. The women tended to walk around in just their bras because of the heat. It was too

84

terrifying to be titillating. As she sat there two feet in front of my nose, she pulled the straps of her bra from her shoulder and began to massage talcum powder onto her breasts and nipples. After a few minutes she pulled her bra back up. The next morning a new guard replaced her.

'Paul,' I hissed, 'did you see her — '

'Rubbing powder on her tits,' he said nodding, a smile playing on his lips.

It was the first moment of humour we'd shared. I felt better for it.

Morning was always welcome because it gave us the chance to observe what was going on in the camp. From my bed I could see a small vine stem that had broken off a plant, become embedded in the floor and begin to propagate itself. From my rucksack I pulled out a tape measure and walked out of the hut, every pair of eyes upon me. I bent down and took a closer look. Yes, it was definitely growing. I measured it: eight centimetres. There were no orchids around here so this stem would have to do. Some single-plant husbandry might help divert me from our situation. As I returned to the shelter I saw everyone's eyes were still on me, a look of bemusement on their faces. One of them, the incessant gun-loader, even came across and had a closer look at the plant himself before walking away, shaking his head.

This little discovery lifted my spirits. Back on my bed I decided we needed to try to occupy ourselves.

'How about Twenty Questions?' I asked Paul.

'OK,' he said, brightening up. 'You go first.'

For some reason, the name Damon Hill entered my mind.

'Are you male or female?'

This continued until lunchtime. It was the first time we'd communicated at length for forty-eight hours. Occasionally we even smiled, but whenever we managed to forget where we were, and those moments were brief, there would be a click-click-click and our smiles would vanish.

We continued our game after lunch. All the tension, all the fear, not to mention the excellent sweet banana soup we had eaten, were playing havoc with my stomach. It was so bloated it was painful. I began to worry that I'd succumbed to food poisoning.

'Are you an actress?' Paul was asking.

'Hang on, Paul,' I said.

All of a sudden I farted like I had never farted before. It sounded like a tractor starting up on a frosty morning, the noise made more thunderous by its ricocheting and echoing off the trees in the clearing. It seemed to last for an age. A deafening silence followed. 'Queenie', tiara still on her head, was staring at me with disbelief and shock written across her face. I looked at Paul. He was the same: mouth agape, eyes wide.

'¡Perdón, señor!' I shouted out.

Queenie started first. She let out a high-pitched scream as if she was being attacked and doubled over holding her stomach. Then the others joined in. Soon they had all gathered at the fire in hysterics. 'Perdón, señor,' one of them said, imitating my voice, and they all cracked up again. Paul was roaring with laughter too, and so was I. It was unbelievable. Talk about the universal appeal of toilet humour. For fully ten minutes the uproar continued unabated, punctuated every now and then by an imitation of my words, which just set them all off again. Finally it stopped, and we carried on our game of Twenty Questions. But it felt like a load was lifted, and not just from my stomach. For the first time we'd shared something. Until that point we'd been viewed with suspicion, fear even. They were as wary of us as we were of them. But the slice of schoolboy humour broke the tension.

The high spirits continued even when the *comandante* returned from one of his many forays into the woods. God knows what he thought when his troops started sniggering whenever one of them said '*Perdón, señor.*' We started feeling slightly more confident about our situation.

Twenty Questions soon began to bore us. We needed a new game.

'Why don't you ask for our pen back? We could make a deck of cards,' Paul said.

'Out of what?'

'Do you have any paper?'

I looked in my rucksack and found the instruction manual for my confiscated camera.

'What about this?'

'That'll do.'

'How are we going to cut it up?'

'Good point.'

'I could ask for my penknife back.'

'There's no way he'll give us that back. You

might as well ask for an AK-47.'

'I'll still give it a try.'

I leant forward and shouted to my friend, the gun-cleaner, '*¿Puedo tener mi navaja y la pluma por favor, señor?*'

He looked at me blankly for a second before walking over to El Jefe, who came over to our shelter and asked what we wanted. I repeated that we wanted our pen and penknife. He turned and walked away without saying anything.

'Worth a try, I suppose,' I said to Paul, who shrugged.

Then El Jefe was at the door of the shelter again.

'Here you go,' he said. He handed me a pen and, to our astonishment, my red Swiss army knife.

We were ecstatic. I started drawing all over the camera instructions and within twenty minutes we had a set of cards. With the scissors, Paul cut out a square from the sheet he was sleeping on, and with the pen he began to colour in squares on it. All we needed now was some draughts. He went out of the shelter and collected a handful of twigs which he whittled into tubes and then sliced into discs. By the time we went to sleep that evening we were playing draughts. For a few hours, death didn't feel so close.

The next morning we woke with renewed vigour. My vine had grown two centimetres. We started a marathon of cards and draughts. When we stopped for a break I chanced my arm with El Jefe again, this time asking for a sewing needle so I could stitch a badge I had bought in Púcuro onto the back of my jacket. Once again he agreed. The needle snapped just as I was completing my first stitch.

'*Señor*,' I cried out, 'could I have one more needle, please?'

'*Mierda*,' I heard him mumble. 'Shit.' But he brought it. 'That is your last,' he said emphatically.

Though when that broke, I got another.

That evening I was at a small waterfall downstream having a wash. Watching over me was one of the guards who had come bursting through the bushes brandishing a gun a few days before, a short, wild-eyed man with a protuberant jaw. He looked like a nutter. He took the opportunity to wash himself, too, stripping down to his shorts and scrubbing his body vigorously with soap. They took their hygiene seriously. A few of them had been mumbling darkly about Paul's failure to wash. He'd grown a scruffy beard and it was clear they wanted him to clean up. When I told him that his reluctance to bathe was causing concern, he just shrugged. I could sympathize. It was hard to care about your appearance given the circumstances.

I decided to try my Spanish on the guard.

'Get many tourists here?' I asked.

He stopped scrubbing and shot me a dark look.

'Ask El Jefe,' he said, and returned to his washing.

★　★　★

89

PAUL: As we became more confident I noticed more and more going on around us. When I was not playing games with Tom, I started to name our guards. I doubted if they would willingly let us know their real names, and we were hardly in a position to ask, so we based them on any defining characteristics or what little of their personalities we could glean.

The first was easy: 'Tank Bird', a butch woman who made up the trio of women along with Queenie and the gun-cleaner's partner.

'She's built like a brick shithouse and has a face to match,' I remarked to Tom.

'You wouldn't want to meet her down a dark alley after a few cans of Coke,' he added.

'She's not so hot in a dark jungle,' I quipped.

In her defence, though, she did make a wonderful sweet banana soup, even if it did play havoc with Tom's bowels. His fart was a defining moment. It broke the ice; it almost broke the hut. Tom had continued to fart openly, though the joke had quickly worn thin. I wanted him to stop. It was becoming antisocial.

On our fifth morning I slithered down the steep bank to the stream for a wash and a shave. The combined effect of heavy rains and continual trampling by the six guards left a treacherously slippy, boggy trail down to the stream. In these conditions my simple suede desert boots were of little use. I slipped and slid my way down, followed by Mrs Gun-cleaner, AK-47 at the ready. She was going to wash and watch me. The stream was only a few yards from our shelter but we were always guarded with absolute vigilance.

At the stream there was little room to move; it was barely a trickle, despite heavy overnight rains. One moment it would be a raging torrent, but when the rains ceased it would be back to its pathetic self. I was in desperate need of a shave and my washing companion kindly lent me her mirror. My beard was becoming a little ragged and the unkempt look did me few favours. I was starting to regain my composure, and I noticed that the guards took a great pride in their appearance and cleanliness. It made sense to do the same, as Tom reminded me.

I removed the whiskers with my final blunt razor and some shaving foam borrowed from Tom. I examined my handiwork in the mirror and looked up to see if Mrs Gun-cleaner approved. She was standing there in a striking combination of lacy red panties and bra, offset by Wellington boots, an AK-47 and a surly stare. I could make out a large lovebite on her right breast. God, I thought, I've landed myself on the set of a Russ Meyer movie: *Bras and Guns*.

As I stood there awkwardly, uncertain as to where to look, her boyfriend appeared at the top of the bank. He gave me a look that said, 'Are you staring at my bird?' In return I gave him a lopsided smirk back that I hoped said, 'Yeah, but I'm not thinking what you're thinking, mate.' Standing at the top of the bank, he towered over me. His furrowed forehead and imposing broad shoulders indicated he was not someone to mess with. He was dressed smartly in an American woodland leaf uniform and carried an AK-47 with folding stock. How he kept his uniform so clean and pressed in this jungle environment was a mystery. In the top of his boot I noticed there was a pink comb and pink-backed mirror, which slightly undermined his hard-man image. He pulled the comb and mirror from his boot and began to do his hair. His girlfriend looked on admiringly. This is the bit in the film, I thought, where he strips off and takes her roughly on the riverbank.

I came back from my bath refreshed and feeling a bit light-hearted. I told Tom what had just happened. From that point on the couple were known as Mr and Mrs Comb.

★　★　★

TOM: My vine was flourishing in the hothouse jungle conditions: it had reached thirteen centimetres in length. Its resurgence, however, was attracting the unwanted attentions of our captors, who seemed to resent the interest I paid it. As I tended to it that sixth morning, The Nutter — as we'd named the short, simian-looking guard who'd rushed at us out of the bushes — and Mr Comb stood around talking about how they would destroy it. The day before I'd noticed how Mr Comb, on his way to the small store where they kept the *plátanos*, the small bananas that had been the staple diet for the week so far, had mimed stamping on the plant to get a laugh from The Nutter, who, it seemed, was easily amused. I decided to try to build it some protection. With some string I had

92

in my pack and a few sticks I'd collected from the jungle floor, I constructed a little cage around it. It would not deter anyone intent on its destruction, but knowing the vine had some protection made me feel better.

As we played cards in the afternoon, El Jefe paid us a call. He sat down across from us in our shelter. We'd been waiting for some form of interrogation. He produced an exercise book and opened it at a clean fresh page, pen at the ready.

'Tell me your name.'

'Tom Hart Dyke,' I replied.

He gave me a vacant look, so I repeated my name. He started to write laboriously. His handwriting was awful. What he wrote looked nothing like my name. I tried to spell it phonetically but was rewarded with another blank stare.

'Shall I show you, *señor?*' I asked tentatively, and motioned that I would write it.

He gave me the pen and paper and I wrote my name in big, clear letters. He read it carefully.

'And your friend's name?'

I turned to Paul and told him he wanted his name.

'Paul Winder,' he said slowly.

'Pow?'

'No, Paul,' I said loudly, as if pronouncing for a child to follow. 'P-A-U-L. Paul.' I pronounced it 'Pah-ool'. But still it was not getting through to him.

'Pablo,' Paul said suddenly.

'Aah!' said El Jefe. He wrote it down, with my help for the spelling of 'Winder'.

'Bloody hell,' said Paul, 'this is going to take all day.'

There was no reaction from El Jefe. He didn't speak gringo lingo. This was reassuring.

We'd agreed that if the chance arose we would mention our parents. Our chance had arisen.

'*Señor*, our parents will miss us very much if you do not let us go free,' I said.

He smirked, as if it was news he wanted to hear.

'What are your parents' names?'

We told him, and half an hour later they were written down. The same thing happened when we told him our addresses. This appeared to be a fact-finding mission because when I said I lived at Lullingstone Castle, my parents' estate in Kent, he didn't probe any further.

'What are your jobs?'

'I'm a gardener,' I said.

He nodded and wrote it down.

'And Pablo?'

'Tell him I work in an office,' Paul said.

'What sort of office?' he replied.

Paul paused. 'Should we tell him the truth?'

'I think it'd be best to.'

'OK, tell him I work in a bank.'

As soon as I told El Jefe a smile spread across his face. He underlined the word 'bank'. Then he asked what we were doing in the Darién.

'We are tourists, *señor*. I am looking for orchids.'

He didn't bother to write this down. He closed the book.

'That is all for now,' he said, and got up to leave.

'Ask him who they are,' Paul said.

'*Señor*, who are you?'

'What do you mean?'

'What do we mean?'

'Ask him whether they are FARC or paramilitaries,' Paul prompted.

I asked. Again, he smiled.

'There are many groups in Colombia, Tomás.'

'But which one are you?'

'We are the guards of the forest,' he said.

'When can we leave? Our parents will miss us.'

'Maybe tomorrow,' he replied, and then he left.

Paul was expectant. 'What did he say, Tom?'

I told him they were guards of the forest and that he'd said we might be allowed to leave tomorrow. We both saw that last statement as excellent news; perhaps these people weren't guerrilla group and *were* some form of police. And perhaps they would let us go now that we'd told them we were just tourists. Perhaps. It was the most optimistic we'd felt all week. Game-playing took a backseat that afternoon as we discussed the veracity of El Jefe's words. We both agreed not to get too carried away, that we might not be released, though given the dismal cloud that had been hanging oppressively over us it was difficult to avoid day-dreams of freedom.

Later that afternoon, new faces arrived. At least six guards turned up, swelling hostile numbers around the camp to twelve. It was difficult to make out what was going on, what they were saying, but the excitement was tangible. The Nutter was jumping up and down like a child on Christmas Day. A couple of the men were carrying a dead cow, which caused further glee. Something was definitely afoot. Slabs of meat were roasted above the fire and fed to us. They tasted delicious. Some of the new recruits came over to our shelter for a closer look at their bounty. One young recruit was fascinated by our game of draughts. He stood and watched us silently for more than five minutes.

'*¿Jugamos, señor?*' I asked when we had finished.

He nodded eagerly, so I set up the pieces and we started to play. On his second go he took a piece of mine that, while on a diagonal line to one of his pieces, was four squares away. 'Right,' I thought, 'I'll let it slide.' The next go, he did it again. As long as my pieces were on a diagonal to his pieces they were fair game for capture, whether they were on the next square or not. Colombian rules, obviously. Within two minutes he'd wiped the floor with me.

★ ★ ★

PAUL: The atmosphere was tense; something was about to happen. There was talk of us leaving the next day. Everyone seemed feverish, on edge. One of the new men appeared to be a commander. His webbing belt was festooned with hand grenades. He gave me a dismissive glance as he walked past our shelter on his way to consult El Jefe. Several other younger soldiers appeared, including a teenage girl, no older than sixteen or seventeen. Apart from the soldier who was keen to play draughts, they all kept their distance, though it was obvious they were curious. They kept stealing glances in our direction and whispering to one another.

That night, after our beef feast, a meeting was held between everyone in the camp. Only Tank Bird was left to guard us. I could hear them discussing plans higher up the slope at El Jefe's bivouac but it was impossible to tell what was going on. Tom and I could only guess. I was too nervous to sleep, but I drifted into a light slumber.

Suddenly there was a loud hiss in my right ear. I jolted upright, my throat tightening, my heart leaping. 'Shit,' I thought, 'what the fuck was that?' My temples pounded. Someone was stood over me. It was Tank Bird. What did she want? She was whispering something I didn't understand.

'Tom, what is she going on about? Tell her to bugger off.'

'Paul, she wants you to give her a present.'

She was no more than a few inches from my face but I couldn't see a thing. It was clear that she didn't want the rest of the camp to know that she was talking to me.

'What does she want, Tom?'

'She wants your boxer shorts.'

'What?'

'Your Daffy Duck ones.'

'Is she winding me up?'

'I don't think so, Paul. She's deadly serious.'

97

'Tell her to fuck off! They won't fit her. She's built like a tank.' Then I added, '*Mañana*,' to stall her. She was obviously nervous about speaking to us without asking permission and was taking the chance while the others were in their meeting. I just wanted to get some sleep.

Luckily for my pants collection the meeting broke up that second and she sulked off into the night.

'Jesus, Tom!'

'Looks like you've got an admirer, Paul.' He was laughing.

'Very funny.'

It was a fitful sleep that night. It's not every day that a woman demands your boxer shorts at gunpoint.

★　★　★

TOM: The next morning we were woken early and told to gather our belongings: we were moving. They started to destroy everything around the camp: their bivouacs, our shelter, the remnants of the fire. My vine did not make it. Mr Comb came over and with great glee smashed the cage with his foot and stamped triumphantly on the plant. Everyone was terse, intent solely on destroying any evidence we had been there, so I decided it was best not to protest. If they were going to release us, it would be wise to keep quiet and wait to see what happened.

★　★　★

PAUL: Brusquely, we were ordered out of our jungle beds in the dawn light. No-one had told us we would be moving but the meeting and commotion of the previous night had given us a clue that something was up. In a daze, I packed my few belongings and waited for further orders. Everybody in the camp was busily doing the same. One of the guerrillas brought us over a bowl full of *plátanos* and meat and another portion was placed in a plastic bag for lunch.

The new, grenade-laden El Jefe — the other having left — calmly issued orders to his soldiers. They reacted efficiently and without objection. Several of them left ahead of us to act as an advance guard. Now it was our turn. I shouldered my pack with a heavy heart; it seemed unlikely they were going to release us yet.

The grim-looking Mr Comb was assigned to guard us. Several others in our group went slightly ahead and one guarded the rear. They motioned for us to move. Mr Comb undid the safety catch on his AK-47, pulled back the bolt and then released it. It jolted forward with a sharp metallic ring, carrying a round into the chamber. He flicked the safety catch back on. To fire the weapon all he needed to do was slide the catch gently down. The whole procedure was performed in an exaggerated, deliberate manner, as if to say, 'If you run for it, boys, then there'll be a bullet following you.'

We climbed a steep hill through the back of the camp, in the opposite direction to the way we had entered seven days before. I didn't know where they were taking us, or for what reason, though I knew the further we moved away from our initial point of capture the more lost I would become. It was essential to concentrate, to at least have an idea of which direction we were travelling in. In the early morning it was easy as the sun was rising directly into my face. We were walking east.

At first, we followed a jungle path. Then voices ahead indicated other people, locals perhaps. The guerrillas didn't want us to see them, or them to see us. Orders were passed down and Mr Comb waved us down a steep embankment. We followed a ravine through dense under-growth, scrabbling for grip and grabbing onto thorny vines to prevent us slipping down the deep gully. 'God, if it's going to be like this all day we won't survive,' I thought. Fortunately we arrived at a river soon afterwards and crossed it, relocated the path and started to walk high into the mountains.

The morning air was cool but my thigh muscles burned with the exercise. We moved in a northerly direction. Rays of sunlight splintered through the jungle canopy. After about an hour we reached a ridge and I was pleased to see that the jungle vegetation was thinner here. Maybe I could see a reference point. To my right, I caught a glimpse of Lago Unguía and felt sure we were moving in the direction of the Alto Limon range of mountains in Colombia that straddle the border. This fuelled my growing belief that this group were one of the guerrilla factions. I guessed FARC, but wasn't sure.

We continued to trek higher, always guarded carefully but never harried or cajoled. As the sun rose, so did the temperature. Even though it often made navigation difficult, I was grateful for the protection afforded by the rainforest canopy. It made the heat bearable. Still, the sweat poured from me, the salt stinging my eyes. I felt reasonably fit but I was exhausted from the emotions of the past week or so. I willed myself on.

We walked all day, resting occasionally. Whenever we stopped, the Comb couple took out their delightful pink paraphernalia and preened themselves. They didn't mind if Tom and I chatted away to each other. Twenty Questions made yet another appearance. It passed the time. The guerrillas found it amusing.

'All you do is play games and eat,' one of them said to Tom.

At one stopping-point we heard a 'rat-tat-tat' sound, like drilling.

'What's that?' Tom asked one of the guerrillas.

There was a babble of Spanish.

'They say it's a helicopter shooting into the forest,' Tom told me.

'Fuck!'

The new *comandante* was an older man, in his late forties, I guessed. He was gangly but in good condition, his muscles taut. As he walked he kept up a constant stream of Spanish. He never seemed to shut up. I asked Tom what he was going on about.

'He's telling people where we're going. He told me he knows this jungle like the palm of his own hand,' he said.

All of a sudden we came to a stop. Everyone started to look around. Had we come across more locals, or a rival group?

'What's happening, Tom?'

'We're lost. They're all moaning that the *comandante* has got them lost!'

It was difficult to keep from laughing. They were not the best-organized bunch and this new El Jefe did not seem any more efficient than the last. My mind ticked over trying to find a nickname for him.

Eventually, they found the right direction. We stopped marching upwards and walked along a ridge before descending down a steep muddy path the rains had made treacherous. We slithered down for almost an hour, ending up covered in mud and debris. Suddenly we emerged into a wide grassy valley. The claustrophobia of the jungle was behind us and I breathed in the wide-open vista, relieved to see a cobalt-blue sky and to escape the confines of the forest. It was only one week since our capture and it had all been spent under the jungle's dark, brooding canopy. Now, in the light, I felt freer.

The advance guard had already established a camp and we were shown where to pitch our tent. Or rather, a pole and poncho. I collapsed in a pile on the grass and could think of nothing except resting and finding some water to drink. After setting up our camp, Tom and I went for a wash. The rest of the slaughtered cow was brought into camp and food was quickly prepared. But all I wanted to do was sleep. It was the first good night of rest since our capture.

The next morning the guerrillas were busy curing the meat over a large open fire. We lolled around, unsure as to whether or not we would be walking that day.

Earlier in the week I had begun to carve sticks to pass time. I hadn't known what to do with them, so I'd brought them with me. Now I had an idea. It was a glorious day, the sun was high, and the ground was a luscious green.

'Tom, how do you fancy a game of cricket?' I asked.

'Great idea,' he said quickly.

I found twigs to act as bails and went to find a suitable branch to act as a bat while Tom found a lime tree and collected some of the fruit to act as balls. I fashioned a bat using the penknife, and while it wasn't willow, it would do. I pitched three stumps following a lengthy inspection that would have done Geoffrey Boycott proud, and decided to bat first. Tom marked out his run. His first ball looped high in the air and spun sharply off the pitch.

'Bloody hell. Shane Warne!'

'Who?' said Tom.

Tom and I alternated batting and bowling. We bowled full tosses and bouncers, and knocked limes for fours and sixes. I even ventured a Richie Benaud impression. We imagined we were at Lord's in front of a full house, though our audience was less friendly than the members of the MCC. Only just, though.

While this went on, the guerrillas kept their distance, eyeing us suspiciously. Slowly, though, curiosity got the better of Tank Bird and the wiry *comandante* and they sauntered over demanding to know what we were doing.

'*¿Quiere jugar, señor?*' we chorused.

He shook his head. No, they would rather watch than play. We tried to explain that this was a game we played back home but stopped short of trying to explain the rules on the basis that if half of England doesn't understand them then guerrillas in the jungle of Latin America might have a problem, especially with the lbw law.

Tom glided in gracefully, like Botham in his pomp. It was a full toss at just the right height. There was only one thing to do, and I smacked the bastard as hard as I could. I caught the lime as sweetly as possible, slap-bang in the middle of the bat, a textbook cover drive. The fruit exploded spectacularly on impact. Lumps flew through the air, all heading in one direction: mid-off. It just so happened that that was where the *comandante* had stationed himself for the best view. The largest piece flew straight into his face, hitting him in the eye.

'Shit!'

I looked away, horrified. What had I done? I looked back and saw the *comandante* fishing bits of lime out of his face with his fingers. I toyed with the idea of telling him he was supposed to catch the ball, not wear it, but decided against it. He walked away, shaking his head, still flicking lime off his face. He didn't speak to us for the rest of the day. Tom was grinning like a kid who'd been caught apple-raiding.

* * *

TOM: We moved to a new temporary camp higher in the mountains by a cascading stream. As we moved from the gloom and doom of the jungle floor, my mood improved. This had nothing to do with expectations of being freed. The promise of 'tomorrow' was still being dangled in front of us but it was less tantalizing when we realized they were simply stalling for time. No, my giddiness was to do with one thing and one thing only: orchids. As we climbed into the mountains I knew this is where I would find the flowers that had lured me into the jungle to begin with. The air movement and moisture in the cloud forests would prove a breeding ground.

After we found camp, I went to bathe in the stream. As I washed, I spotted a fallen tree lying across the stream. I let out a yelp of delight and waded downstream. I could see it was dripping with flowers. From the corner of my eye I could see the *comandante* pick up his gun and walk across, followed by some of the others. I didn't stop. It was the most orchids I'd ever seen collected in one place in the wild, amazing sprays of *Pleurothallis* orchids and oncidiums, in red and yellow form, two to three feet long and with hundreds of flowers per spike. I was screaming out their names in delight. I turned around to tell everyone what I'd found and was met with a bank of stern faces. Nearly all our captors came over to find out what the hell I was doing.

'*Señor*,' I said to the *comandante*, who looked

nervous and twitchy, 'can you see all the orchids?'

From his face, I could see he was no horticulturalist.

'Look at the oncidiums!' I shouted, pointing up at the trees.

There were a few murmurs and shakes of the head. Satisfied that I wasn't going to make a run for it, they went back. After one last, lingering look at the log, I reluctantly pulled myself away and wandered back to camp, still drunk on what I'd seen but cursing the guerrillas for taking my camera. What a photograph the log would have made! Kew Gardens would have gone into a frenzy at the sight of it.

When I returned, Paul took me to one side.

'Brilliant orchids,' I told him.

'You've got to watch it, Tom. I've never seen anyone move so fast, especially waist-deep in water. If they know you're so quick they'll keep a really close eye on us.'

He had a point. When it comes to orchids I have little sense or reason. If I see them, I go and look at them. It's as simple as that, a reflex action. But we needed to watch our step and try to appear as harmless as possible.

6

RANSOM

TOM: 'This is bollocks!'

Paul was kicking the undergrowth furiously.

'*¡Pablo muy enojado!*'

The *mestizo* teenage girl in combat fatigues was right: Pablo was *very* angry. We'd spent two days walking for eight hours each day only to reach a damp, mosquito-ridden gully. Then we were ordered to camp next to a stagnant pond that smelled of raw sewage. It was used as a toilet and was downstream from where the guerrillas bathed, so a layer of scum of soap and disinfectant gathered on top of it. We wanted to camp on higher ground by a path, but our pleas were ignored and we were ushered to a slope at the bottom where it was dark, dank and unbearably muggy. Very little sunlight penetrated the jungle canopy. The angle of the ground was awkward, for it meant that if you lay with your feet at the top of the slope the blood rushed to your head and made you feel sick, while lying down the other way made you feel as if you were stood up.

Four days earlier, when we'd left the first site, we'd been informed that our release was pending. 'Tomorrow,' they said. While 'tomorrow' never actually arrived, it had given us hope that something would be imminent. This feeling had been bolstered the night before we arrived at 'Dank Dell', as Paul and I called it, when we were given eggs and bread to eat. One of the women, another new arrival with barely any teeth — we christened her Tooth Bird — had told me we would be leaving soon. She'd made walking gestures with her fingers, like they used to do on the old *Yellow Pages* adverts.

'Where?' I asked. 'Freedom?'

She nodded.

Our spirits were so high that evening that around the fire when they asked us to sing them an English folk song, we agreed without hesitation.

'What should we sing, Tom?' Paul asked.

'I've no idea. 'Michael Row the Boat Ashore'?'

'I don't know the words.'

We sat there in silence, desperately trying to think of a song. All of a sudden, Paul started singing in a wobbly, flat tenor.

'There were ten in the bed and the little one said, roll over, roll over. So they all rolled over and one fell out . . . '

I joined in during the 'roll overs'. The few guerrillas around the fire started to clap along, but they soon became bored when they realized the song was just one line repeated and our musical talent was nil. We quit when only six remained in the bed. I felt duty bound to think of something else.

'Ten green bottles, standing on the wall . . . '

No-one joined in and there was no request for an encore.

To hide our discomfort, one young guerrilla started to sing a mournful ballad in Spanish. Everything was relaxed; the tension seemed to have eased. All we had to do, we were informed, was meet 'The Boss', who from the comandante's physical description, his hands held under his breasts as if cupping a couple of footballs, appeared to be a woman.

Arriving at Dank Dell sent our spirits plummeting. No mention was made of freedom. The air was fetid, flies swarmed around us, and there was no chance of getting clean in that turbid water after four days of arduous walking. The promises were empty, but the aura surrounding Paul and me was by now so harmless that the guerrillas were confident of leaving their unattended guns strewn over the floor of the camp. As Paul walked past the pile to our proposed camp, he made sure he stood on as many as possible.

His frustration had been fermenting for some time. He had become irritated with me during our walk to Dank Dell when he overheard me telling our captors that my sleeping bag cost $500.

'Tom, for God's sake don't tell them things like that. We're supposed to be penniless backpackers and here's you admitting to having a sleeping bag that costs as much as the average Colombian annual wage.'

He had a point; I needed to watch what I said. The problem was that I loved to talk to them. Paul could withdraw into himself and think, content with speaking to me alone. I could not bear being on my own or having to think, so I spoke to whoever would listen.

Their lies, the way they raised our hopes then dashed them, the state of this new site, all of it was proving too much for Paul. I didn't know what to say to him; after all, we still barely knew each other. When the *comandante* came to tell us to pitch our tent, Paul let fly with a volley of abuse.

'Tell him to fuck off. I'm not putting up a tent here.'

'*Señor*, Pablo says he will be ready to put the tent up in ten minutes,' I said.

'I've had enough of this. How the fuck can they expect us to camp here? It's a shithole,' Paul ranted, swatting flies away from his face.

'He says thank you for the excellent way you have treated us, *señor*.'

Satisfied, the *comandante* left us.

I decided Paul was best left alone until he calmed down. Eventually he did, and we put up the tent. That afternoon I found him sat inside it, his eyes puffy and reddened as if he'd been crying.

'Sorry about that outburst earlier, Tom, it's just getting to me,' he admitted. 'It's just difficult, you know, missing your parents, not sure whether you'll see them again. I just can't see how they can keep us here like this for no reason. What do they want?'

I didn't know. Our mood swings were immense and exhausting. I had suffered, too. On one night of our long walk to Dank Dell I had been unable to sleep, and all because of my bank card, which the guerrillas had confiscated. During the first week my fingernails had grown long, but I bit them to the quick that night sweating over the thought that my account was being leached of all its reserves and that I would be left penniless. It was ludicrous, of course, given that there were few opportunities for our captors to use a bank card in the jungle. However, in my fevered state I imagined they had access to the Internet and were at that moment embarking on a giant spending spree, buying guns and grenades and God knows what else. The next morning I was astonished at my own stupidity. These violent mood swings between giddy, optimistic highs and Stygian depths of doom and despair were gruelling.

At Dank Dell we sat and waited. At dusk that first night I watched as they prepared for bed. The teenage girl, her long dark hair tied in bunches, struggled with her torch. It was broken, and she slapped it against her hand to try to get it working. Eventually she gave up and began to scour the jungle floor for glow-worms. Once she'd collected a handful she unscrewed the torch lens, dropped the worms in the top, screwed the lens back on and, hey presto!, her torch emanated a weak glow. She shook it vigorously and the beam from the agitated worms grew brighter. I was impressed, until I realized it allowed her to find her way to the toilet holes, conveniently dug directly behind our tent.

★ ★ ★

PAUL: For two days we festered at Dank Dell with little to do or distract us from the menace of our situation. After attempting to wash in the trickle of water that ran through the centre of the camp, I sat down in a melancholy mood. I didn't really want to speak to anybody. My mind drifted back to England, though soon my peace was disrupted by one of the teenage guerrillas. She was young and fresh-faced, a *mestizo*, a centuries-old mix of Spanish and Indian. She flirted with everyone, captives included. She'd been incredibly curious about Tomás and Pablo in the few days since she'd joined us.

Smiling playfully, she sat next to me and produced a pen and pad.

'Draw and write something for me,' she said.

'¿Qué?'

'Draw or write,' she replied, miming on the page.

So I started to write, and she watched me closely. I scribbled scattered thoughts across the page, mostly about what I wanted to do when I returned to England.

'What are you writing?' She was looking admiringly at my handwriting even though she was unable to read a word of it.

'Oh, about England,' I said, but it was difficult to explain due to my meagre Spanish.

She sat close, leaning into me as I wrote. Then I started to draw things for her: a horse, a dog, a cat, then a house. It pleased her, and for a moment I was lost in her smiles.

The *comandante* soon arrived on the scene, winking and nodding at me like a character from a *Carry On* film. I raised an inquisitive eyebrow back, then he started his mischief in Spanish. I could not understand what he was saying, though the implications were clear. If I needed a date I was sure I didn't need to go through a kidnapping to get one; however, I was also sure that whatever the *comandante* was saying, it had little to do with the innocence of dating. He pinched her playfully. It seemed a bit creepy, this man in his forties flirting with a girl easily young enough to be his daughter. Not that she seemed to mind, though.

★ ★ ★

TOM: I wandered around the camp during the day, talking to the guards, playing draughts and cards. Anything to stay away from the pocket of filth in which our tent was pitched. By this stage they knew we were not stupid enough to make a run for it.

One afternoon the young draughts fanatic — whom Paul had named Señor Dama, after the Spanish word for the game — and I were playing a game in the teenage girl's tent while Paul drew pictures for her. It was oppressively hot and humid, very sticky under the cover of the poncho. We played more than a dozen games until I felt myself starting to wilt.

The next thing I was aware of was waking up on a ground mat. My shirt was stuck to my back with sweat. Lying close beside me was the teenage girl. Paul and Señor Dama had gone. I must have fallen asleep. Slowly, I got to my feet, trying not to wake her, but she stirred and gave me a sleepy smile. I got out of the tent and stood up, yawning. Señor Dama nudged The Nutter and pointed at me, and they started sniggering. 'Tom's with the girl,' he said, and they giggled like schoolchildren. They had obviously interpreted my nap in the tent as something other than the heat taking its toll. 'Bollocks,' I thought, 'those two will spread rumours about this all around the camp now.'

Not that anything had happened. As if.

★   ★   ★

PAUL: The *Comandante* always seemed to be chatting and telling wild stories, acting them out as he spoke. But his mouth couldn't keep up with his brain. Or maybe it was the other way around. As I watched him this particular time, he crouched low to the ground, his automatic rifle gently cradled in his arms, its barrel running parallel to the ground. His head twitched constantly as his eyes went from soldier to soldier. A small audience of his troops sat around him in the little clearing of our camp, immersed in this piece of theatre. Their eyes followed him as he stood upright and opened his arms, gesticulating and waving his rifle gently in the air.

'They were on a hill, we could see the smoke from their fire. That was the mistake they made,' he whispered, moving his head forward, his hands miming the rising smoke.

Then he crouched down again and moved like

114

a cat across the clearing, all the time whispering descriptions, re-enacting the hunt.

'We couldn't see who they were so we crept within striking distance of them.'

I couldn't really understand it all, but I didn't need to: it was being performed. He leapt up, chattering loudly, and burst forward. It was the ambush. His mouth raced, words spilling uncontrollably from his lips. He was lost in the excitement of his story. Then he paused to catch his breath.

'We gained them and tied them up, staking them to the ground. They didn't see us until the last moment,' he declared proudly.

He was re-enacting the capture of two Peruvians who'd been making their way through the Darién in search of work in the United States. They'd been held for a few days, questioned to see what they might have to offer.

'They had nothing, they were poor and of no use to us, so we let them go.'

This gave me hope; then again, we weren't penniless Peruvians.

As I watched this charade I thought of a nickname for him: Jackanory. It suited him perfectly: always talking, telling stories, promising freedom and then nothing happened.

Which is exactly what happened for three days at Dank Dell: nothing. The camp was appalling and did nothing for our state of mind. We just sat there waiting for this boss to arrive, with nothing to do except play draughts and cards and moan to each other about the camp's conditions. According to Tom, the boss was a woman, which sounded interesting at least. I pictured some sort of Amazonian warrior who would have us all quaking in our boots.

Finally, on our third day at the camp, she arrived. Except she turned out to be a he, a tall, surly-looking black guy who towered over the others. The idea that he was a woman was obviously just one of Jackanory's embroidered tales, like the time he told everyone how he knew the jungle like the back of his hand before getting us lost. This new arrival had stature. We could see him at the top of the camp discussing us with Jackanory, and the lax air that had existed for the past few days evaporated. Everyone had snapped to attention now this guy had arrived. A girl followed in his wake, bowing to his every need. As he walked down towards us, I saw he was carrying an M-16 with a grenade launcher. He was one scary-looking soldier. Jackanory was so full of bullshit it was difficult to take him seriously. No such problem with this bloke.

He came and sat opposite our tent and took out a pad and pen. I braced myself for a more in-depth interrogation, but once he'd started, even with my scant Spanish, I realized all he wanted was the same information El Jefe had sought: names, addresses, nationalities, parents' names and addresses, reasons for being in the jungle. The only question he asked that was different focused on other places we had travelled to.

Tom seized on that and launched into a list of all the countries he had visited, even making some up, it seemed. In total he reeled off thirty-four of them. I shifted uneasily in my seat. The less we told them, in my view, the less they would have on us.

'I went to Cambodia, it used to be a war zone there,' Tom enthused, as though he made a speciality of being in such places.

Our inquisitor had been getting bored, going through the motions, writing down the details, but he perked up when he heard these details of Tom's travelogue, even more so when he mentioned the war in Cambodia. I winced. In fact, my hair stood on end. Like his mistake with the sleeping bag, I feared Tom's willingness to tell the guerrillas anything was not the best tactical move.

'Tom, for fuck's sake, think,' I hissed. 'Just slow down. Stop talking about things like wars and all the bloody places you've been to. They'll pin something on us.'

Afterwards, he apologized profusely. I told him not to worry about it, but I wanted to get through to him that we should only offer them information when they pressed for specific answers. Tom's view, like most travellers, was that a smile would always be returned with a smile. Normally I would agree, but this was hardly a normal situation. M-16 and his cohorts were planning something for us, though what we didn't know. I hoped, however, they would soon realize their mistake, acknowledge we had no value and presented no threat, and just release us.

TOM: Paul was upset that I blabbed about Cambodia being a war zone. I had been too honest, but M-16 said when he took our parents' addresses and telephone numbers that he was going to call them straight away. I didn't want to tell any lies.

When he asked me why I was in the Darién, I told him I was in love with plants. He stared at me as if I'd said I was in love with him.

'¿Qué?'

'Señor, I love orchids and I am here in the jungle to photograph them.'

He shook his head as if he didn't believe me.

'That's done it,' I thought. 'If he wants proof, I'll give him proof.' I went to the tent.

'Tom, what are you doing?' Paul asked.

'I'm going to give this lot a lecture about seeds,' I replied.

I went and grabbed the Velcro bag I used to hold all the seeds I had collected. Back outside, I let rip in my best Spanish.

'This region is great for finding and collecting all sorts of exciting plants, and that's why I'm here.' I opened the Velcro bag. 'For example, señor, I've found an unusual palm from the Palmae family.' I held up the giant striated seed. 'It is very similar to *Caryota urens*, the fishtail palm, from Asia, which I've also seen in the Darién. But, better still, I've collected two huge seeds.' I displayed the rounded, hard, mother-of-all seeds, collected from the same site where we had played cricket.

At this point, M-16 began to frown at my excitement.

'These are from a *Pandorea jasminoides* climber,' I continued, 'which has large, scented, pink flowers, from the Bignoniaceae Latin plant family.'

Actually, this plant is from Asia and Australia. I hadn't a clue what I'd collected, but I figured that in this situation the best policy was to overwhelm him with jargon. By now an audience had gathered round to find out what the gringo was up to.

'Finally, *señor*, I've many seeds from the calabash tree. That's the common English name; in Latin it's called *Crescentia cujete*, again like the *Pandorea* from the Bignoniaceae family. This seed I collected from Púcuro. Its young fruits make tasty eating' — when pickled, that is, but I didn't know the word for pickled — 'and a drink can be made from the cooked seeds. Some people even use the leaves to treat toothache.'

Given some of the dental disasters the guerrillas were home to, I felt that might provoke some interest.

'*Señor*, I would have more seeds to show you today that I've collected over the past two years of travelling but I've sent them home to my mum in England to be put in a fridge for storage until I return to my country. For example, red-coloured magnolia seeds from Universal Studios in Hollywood, USA; giant, tough salak seeds from Indonesia; and the minute, jetblack seeds of a blue penstemon from the Copper Canyon in northern Mexico. Upon my return all these seeds will be germinated in my small but warm greenhouse. We need greenhouses in England because it's cold, *señor*. We even have frosts!' I imitated a shiver and went 'Brrr!!' There were a few giggles from the back. 'Moreover,' I added, 'I can study these plants as they grow. I have more love for my plants than for my Korean girlfriend, *señor*!'

I could see smiles, some nervous, on the faces of the guerrillas. Some of the others said simply, 'This man has a girlfriend?' The girl I was referring to was my one and only ever girlfriend, Lin, whom I'd met while gum nut collecting in Mildura, Australia.

I stopped, and put my seeds back in their bag. M-16 simply closed his notebook, stood up without saying a word and walked away, shaking his head.

* * *

PAUL: M-16 returned, took out his wallet and showed me some foreign notes: Italian lira, German marks and French francs. I wasn't sure what point he was trying to make, but it was good news: they must have encountered experienced tourists before, perhaps taken a small bribe and let them through. Now, because so few travellers had passed through in the last few years, they had taken a more suspicious view of us. However, there was hope.

He pulled a one thousand lira note from the wallet and asked me how much it was worth.

'One thousand lira! Not much, *señor*, maybe

half a dollar?' I told him in my faltering Spanish.

The others gathered around us laughed, apart from the note's owner, who looked crestfallen. Until now he had probably lived under the illusion that the thousand on the note indicated a lot of money. Perhaps a quick-thinking adventurer had convinced him of this, and extricated himself from an awkward situation for the price of a chocolate bar. In spite of his disappointment, the meeting ended amicably. I was pleased no enmity had arisen. We just had to stay calm and relaxed and engender the same spirit within them.

The next day we were on the move yet again, travelling back the way we had come. Several members of the group left us at this point, including Tank Bird, much to my relief. My boxer shorts were safe.

We charged through the jungle, spirits higher in the hope that soon our nightmare would be over. An afternoon storm crashed around us in the misty hills, and rain poured through the canopy. The path quickly became a bog. Then we left the jungle and came out into another steep-sided valley which had been partially cleared for agricultural purposes. The rain ceased. A small hut in the distance indicated the presence of civilians, so we skirted around this. Tendrils of cloud drifted softly by and the fecund, verdant forest brimmed with life. The misty scene was like something from the cover of *National Geographic*. I marvelled at our surroundings. At least, I joked to myself, I was getting to see far more of the Darién than I'd intended. Then we were following a stream almost bursting its banks after the rains. Still soaked, we climbed back up the far side of the valley and were rewarded for our speed with succulent pieces of sugar cane. We struck a makeshift camp for the night, and the next day Mr and Mrs Comb departed elsewhere, along with Jackanory, who waved heartily to us both as he went. Only The Nutter remained of the group that had first apprehended us.

Our next camp was a marked improvement on Dank Dell. This time we were on high ground, on a ridge next to a clear-flowing mountain river. It had a more permanent feel to it. Raised beds were constructed, a small raised fireplace built and the area cleared of trees and undergrowth.

I took this opportunity to wash my meagre possessions. The river cascaded through a series of rocky pools, sparkling like crystal and teeming with little fish. I dived into one of the pools to refresh my weary body after the toil of jungle marching, then I basked in the warm sunlight, the river cutting a roadway of fresh air through the canopy. I began to read my South America guidebook, paying extra attention to the pieces on the Darién. It had been handed back to me, together with Tom's alarm clock. We did not know why, and we did not question it. The 'gifts' excited us initially, though Tom soon discovered there was little use for an alarm clock in our situation. But the book was welcome. I was still sure this whole mess would soon be over. Tom caught a few of the guards speaking about 'liberación' and indicating a walk to freedom

122

with their fingers. The fear of death receded somewhat as the atmosphere eased. Part of me was even starting to think about what a cracking tale I would have to tell in the pub when I got home.

M-16 had vanished as quickly as he had appeared, while in Jackanory's place a new *jefe* arrived. He was the spitting image of Will Smith, the actor, though a foot smaller at least. No need to scrape around for a nickname for him, then. With him was his girlfriend, a woman of mixed race, her coffee-coloured skin giving her a Western look. Her name was Maria. Both watched us warily from a distance, unlike the teenage girl, who seemed fascinated by us. She'd taken a particular shine to Tom, though that might have been because he spoke Spanish, so it was easier to communicate with him. But then Tom spoke to them all: The Nutter, Señor Dama, and the other young recruits who made up the eight that were now guarding us.

★ ★ ★

TOM: After the shit and stink of Dank Dell, river site was a blessing. Like Paul, I had felt the tension and uncertainty of our situation pulling me down. Sat around the fire at one of the temporary camps on the way here I had confessed to the young girl, who now seemed to be part of the group, that I was homesick.

'I miss my parents,' I told her.

'So do I,' she replied mournfully.

'I haven't seen mine in two years,' I said.

'I haven't seen mine for many years.'

I was taken aback. I had always considered the guerrillas merely as obstacles to our freedom, never as humans with families. This girl was younger than my sister. I wondered how she had come to be involved with this bunch of idiots, but decided to save the question for another time.

The day after we arrived at River Site, things started to happen. Will Smith approached me and said he wanted to talk to me later on. Later in the day he returned, with M-16, whom we had not seen since leaving Dank Dell. Paul sat at the entrance to our tent while we walked down a path to the riverside ten feet below. I sat down on one log, my back to the river, while they sat on another opposite me.

'You are a drug runner for the CIA,' Smith said as an opener.

'What?'

'Your passport shows you came from America. We think you are a drug runner.'

'*Señor*,' I said, 'I am a gardener.'

'You're part of a cartel, Tomás. What route did you take from America?'

I told them I had gone through Mexico, Guatemala and El Salvador, back to Guatemala, then to Belize and back again to Guatemala, through Honduras, Nicaragua, Costa Rica and finally Panama.

'I have seen lovely orchids,' I added, even though I had seen very few. I wanted to reassert my plant-collecting credentials. 'Lovely butterflies, too.'

M-16 shook his head. They changed tack.

'Listen, we want you to leave the forest.'

My heart thumped. Were they going to let us go?

'But we want Pablo to stay here,' M-16 added.

'I don't understand,' I said.

'You go to England and speak to Pablo's friends, his work and his family, and tell them we want money. You collect the money and then come back here, contact us by radio, and we exchange Pablo for the money. In two weeks it can happen and you will both be free.'

This was a kidnap. It sounds stupid, but that was the first time I'd realized it. Until that point I'd thought we were merely being held until they cleared up who we were. Once they discovered we were backpackers they would let us go.

'How much money?'

'Three million dollars.'

I was speechless. I started laughing.

'Three million dollars?'

Both of them nodded. 'Three million dollars and we release Pablo.'

I stopped laughing. This was not funny. They were deadly serious.

'Pablo does not have that money,' I said.

'Yes he does,' M-16 said. 'He works in a bank. You told us that.'

Shit. In hindsight, telling them that piece of information might not have been our best move. However, I still couldn't believe they wanted so much money.

'This isn't like the film *Ransom* with Mel Gibson,' I said in disbelief.

There was silence. Obviously they hadn't seen it.

'I can't get that money,' I insisted.

'Yes you can. It will only take two weeks.'

I wasn't sure what to say to that, so I told them I needed to think about what they'd said.

'OK, Tomás, speak to Pablo. Take some time to think about it,' Smith said.

They stood up to go.

'You will change your mind tomorrow,' M-16 added with certainty.

★ ★ ★

PAUL: I watched from my raised bed high on the riverbank. M-16 and Will Smith were questioning Tom. The other guerrillas were shifting nervously around, chatting about nothing in particular. Their ears were cocked but they didn't want to appear to be listening in. Occasionally I could hear raised voices, though the rushing of the river tended to drown them. Something serious was happening. It struck me as odd that they didn't want to speak to me as well, but then Tom did speak the better Spanish; I had taken three days of lessons in Costa Rica and that was all. I tried to relax, hoping our ordeal was being resolved beside the river.

Half an hour later Tom returned.

'Well, Paul, we know what they want.'

'What?'

'Three million dollars.'

'Fuck! Really? What bullshit!'

Tom explained their plan. It was clear now:

we'd been kidnapped. Any chance of a quick release was gone.

Tom went off to pray — the guerrillas had told us it was Easter — while my brain reeled with confusion. I felt angry with them for forcing us to make a decision like this. By the time Tom returned I had steadied my nerve and thoughts.

'Tom, we can't agree to this,' I said. 'Whoever's left behind is dead.'

'But what will they do if we don't agree?'

'I don't know, but we can't accept any part of the plan. That's tantamount to saying that getting that sort of money is possible. Which it isn't. Let's face it, neither of our families can raise that amount quickly.'

'It doesn't have to be me who goes, Paul,' Tom offered. 'I don't mind staying.'

'Tom, *neither* of us is going. First rule of adventure: never split from your partner until you are absolutely forced to.'

He seemed to accept that I was right. I could tell he was uncomfortable with the situation, and I couldn't blame him, but I tried to fortify him.

'We just have to smile broadly and tell them we aren't going anywhere. Make the whole thing into a joke and be as polite as possible. To confront them over it would be crazy. But the important thing is to show a united front. If they sense any weakness in one of us, they'll exploit it.'

Our joint survival, I felt, hinged on this. Over the previous weeks they'd been so relaxed that the whole thing had almost become a party. Automatic rifles were left strewn about within

127

easy reach. Tom was great at charming them, chatting and joking, improving his Spanish, introducing them to games and plants.

All night I tossed and turned. Was refusing them the right thing to do? We were hardly in a position to bargain; they were in complete control. But the prospect of being left alone with them was terrifying. Then again, the Darién trip had been my idea; I was responsible for it, and for its consequences. 'Just charge on in and to hell with the warnings' had been my Darién motto; Tom had joined me because his natural brio urged him to. Maybe it would be better for us to split after all. At least one of us would be guaranteed safety. We knew that the person who went home wasn't going to come back with the money. No-one at home, either family or the authorities, would let that happen.

They allowed us to think over their plan for the next two days, then another meeting was arranged. Think is all we did. Everything was in their favour. They had all our documents and could very easily prove they had us. It couldn't be that difficult for them to use these to contact the authorities in Panama or Colombia. However, the more I thought about it the more confused I became about their tactics. Surely they could use our belongings to prove they had kidnapped us and ransom the two of us for even more money? All was not what it seemed. I decided we had to remain cool and calm, to hold out against them, to test their resolve. After all, they'd engaged in talks in the first place and their treatment of us so far had been good. If

128

they wanted to engage in a battle of wills, I was quite happy to join in, though they could easily win it with a serious threat of violence, or by staging a mock execution. Still, I was determined to stand firm.

★　★　★

TOM: After leaving us to sweat on the offer for two days, I was called back down to the river.

'What is your decision?' Will Smith asked.

'Sorry, señor, but I don't want to go. We both go home or we both stay.'

'*Siempre en la Selva*,' Smith snarled. 'Then you will always be in the woods.'

M-16 produced my passport from his pocket, opened it and showed me the page that had an American stamp on it.

'You are both drug cartel dealers,' he asserted. 'You travel the world selling drugs.'

'I never met Paul until Panama City, señor.'

'Why did you meet him?'

'To travel into the wonderful forests of the Darién.'

'Liar,' he shouted back. 'You are a drug dealer.'

'We are not, señor.'

'Liar,' he shouted again. 'You are a drug dealer.'

'I'm a gardener.'

'Drug dealer!'

'OK, Tomás,' Will Smith said, 'you come to Colombia to get plants but why does Pablo come?'

'He skis, señor. He is on his way to the mountains in the south so he can go skiing.'

This was, in fact, the truth. Paul had planned to go skiing in the Andes after the Darién crossing.

'He is a drug dealer too!'

These accusations and protestations of innocence continued for some time.

'Look, Tomás,' Will Smith said eventually, trying to calm things down, his voice a whisper, 'there is a guide around that corner who will take you back into Panama.'

'What about Paul?'

'You will be back in two weeks. Pablo will be safe with us here. Then you can both go free.'

'Where am I supposed to get the money?'

'Pablo works in a bank. They will pay for him to go free. His parents miss him, is that not true?'

I had to agree it was true. I didn't know what else to say.

'Then they will also give money for his freedom,' M-16 added.

This was getting too much for me on my own. I felt myself weakening.

'Let me speak again to Pablo,' I said.

They agreed, so I walked back to the tent and told Paul we would die in the forest if we refused their offer.

'Screw them,' he said defiantly. 'Come on, I'll come down with you.'

We returned. The thought of their reaction when we announced we were purposely going to defy them was too much for me, and as we sat

130

down I excused myself, saying that I needed a dump. Really what I needed was some time to think. I went and sat behind a bush. I was shaking uncontrollably and almost in tears. I'd had enough. I decided to tell Paul that I would stay instead. There was no way I would allow myself to leave and bear the guilt of deserting Paul. No, I would stay, even if it meant dying. A bullet in the back of the head would be quick and painless and I would not have to live with Paul's abandonment and death on my conscience.

I walked back to the log, sat down and turned to Paul, M-16 and Smith watching me intently.

'Listen, Paul, I want you to go. It was my lust for orchids that got us into this. It's my fault.'

'You've got to be joking! This is not your fault, and I'm not going anywhere without you. If I leave you here, you're dead. Screw these bastards. They're not getting a penny.'

I didn't have the energy to disagree. M-16 was watching this with a smile on his face, aware that I was cracking. Even though he couldn't understand what we were saying, he could tell I was upset and that Paul was angry.

'Pablo,' he said to Paul, 'you can go instead. Tomás's parents miss him and you can get some money from them.'

I translated for Paul, staggered by the way they'd switched so quickly. 'You bastards,' I thought. 'A minute ago it was me you wanted to send.' I felt angry, and with that anger came the determination to resist their demands, whatever the consequences. When I'd finished translating I

131

gave Paul a look that said, 'Let's give them nothing.'

'Tell these arseholes that we can't go back because we have no money,' Paul replied, 'and neither do our parents.'

More words were exchanged, but it was clear the meeting had reached an impasse.

'We will wait for you to decide who goes,' M-16 said as he stood to leave, as if we would change our minds eventually. 'Tomorrow, we leave early.'

★ ★ ★

PAUL: '*Siempre en la Selva.*' Will Smith had been emphatic, and I took the threat seriously. It wasn't a direct death threat but the implication was there. The whole camp was surprised and perplexed by our decision. They looked at us and shook their heads as if we were crazy. The girl asked Tom why he didn't want to go home. They refused to believe that one of us would not jump at the chance to leave.

I thought about escape, fantasizing about diving into the flooded river below. The rainy season was fast approaching and soon the banks of all the rivers here would be broken by raging torrents. It was no more than a quick run and jump from our tent. At night they probably wouldn't notice us missing for a few hours. If I took one of my plastic bags and filled it with air it could become a makeshift buoyancy aid. Enthused with the idea, I began planning it in detail. But the heavy rains never came, and a

132

good job too. I hadn't checked the bags, which were now full of ragged holes torn open by jungle thorns. We would have drowned in seconds.

But that sort of action was quickly looking like our best option. They wouldn't let us go for nothing. It did occur to us that Juan Rivas might raise the alarm but he would surely be too scared to contact any authorities. More likely, he would pretend never to have seen us. We discounted any chance of him helping us. Our only hope was to escape, or to pray fervently for a diplomatic solution, to hope the guerrillas contacted the outside world with a ransom demand and our freedom was negotiated. Escape was unfeasible until the right time, the right camp. If we ran without knowing where we were going they would find us and shoot us. God knows how long a diplomatic solution might take. Tom and I agreed we would never give in to their request for one of us to go. It was clear they expected us to cave in. They would just wait, so we agreed to do the same, to frustrate them, even to act as if we were enjoying the ordeal in the hope they would give up and let us go. It was a long shot but it was our best one until we came across a chance to escape, which depended on us working out where we were and in which direction we should head.

Gallows humour set in. After another day of inactivity at the River Site we were on the move again, wading up the river and back into the mountains. For some reason a song entered my head: 'Always Look on the Bright Side of Life' from *The Life of Brian*. I taught Tom the words and the tune, and as we marched through dense jungle towards the cloud forest we sang non-stop for an hour.

Upwards we trekked, guarded by Will Smith, Maria and the teenage girl, the latter two giggling at our singing. Scouts moved along the path further in front of us and to our rear. Tom took every opportunity to pick up plants along the way, filling his cooking pot with them and explaining to me the difference between an orchid and an air plant. It went in one ear and out the other. We came across yellow and green frogs so vivid they looked computer-generated.

Our progress into the mountains was hampered by the constant attack of biting flies. Bigger than mosquitoes, and around the same size as the average bluebottle, these hellish insects often assaulted in swarms and issued a nasty sting, like a bee's. Tom and I named them 'bastard bees'. It wasn't only us they went for; Smithy and the rest were waving them away as we climbed. At one stage Will Smith caught one in his hand and pulled off its legs. Then he placed the struggling insect on Tom's shoulder. It rolled off.

'It's drunk!' he said.

We travelled through an open cultivated area, stopping only to fill our water bottles with crushed sugar cane juice before tackling a steep incline. The sun beat down without mercy, pounding my head with its powerful rays, and I craved to be back under the canopy. Soon we reached a vertiginous slope, scrambling up it for an hour or more, tugging at tree roots and vines clinging to the mountainside. Without them we would have tumbled back down the rain-muddied slopes. Finally we reached a ridge and the going eased. I was eager to reach the peak and sneak a glimpse at the topography, but they purposely walked us around the summit rather than over it, until we eventually halted at a small tree-lined camp in the process of being cleared. The Nutter and some of his comrades were already at work felling trees and building shelters.

As I marvelled at how quickly a camp could emerge from a tangled mess of trees and foliage, I sucked the mountain air deep into my lungs and held it there until I thought they would burst. Looking across to what I believed to be the west, I saw a passenger jet write its vapour trail across the blue sky. A better way to travel across the Darién, I thought to myself ruefully.

7

GUERRILLAS IN OUR MIDST

PAUL: Base was established high in the Altos de Limón region. I guessed we must be about two thousand metres above sea level, perhaps near the highest point in the whole range. The nights were much colder now. Mist and cloud wafted through the trees and around the camp. The damp was constant and all pervasive; it seeped into our bones.

The guerrillas worked phenomenally hard during the first day or two to build the camp. When we arrived there was little to distinguish the area from the rest of the cloud forest, yet within twenty-four hours the area had been cleared of foliage and raised beds had been constructed along with thick reed roofs and walls to rebuff the torrential rain, which arrived most afternoons and transformed the pathways into trails of sinking mud. The raised beds were essential: raindrops the size of ten-pence pieces pounded the ground and exploded like water bombs, splashing two feet high and splattering mud over everything within their range. Once the living area was established, their next task was to fell an area of jungle to allow the sun's rays through. Without such a source of heat the camp would have been even damper, clothes impossible to dry. Wearing wet clothes made the situation more miserable.

Our tent was positioned in the middle of the camp, backed by thick jungle and surrounded by a crescent of bivouacs. Smith's and Maria's sat by the stream and the fireplace to the right of our entrance; in an anti-clockwise direction, around us were Home Boy I and Perty — so named by Tom, rather worryingly, because he'd noticed his nipples were constantly erect — Home Boy II, and next to him was The Nutter and the shy teenage girl. Señor Dama's hut completed the semi-circle. A kitchen area and covered fireplace were built to cook meals. The final addition to the camp was a small covered table with benches across from our door, a station where our night guard sat. Will Smith started to cultivate a small garden of herbs and vegetables, which gave me the impression we might be here for longer than a few nights. I looked forward to a change in the diet. We had been introduced to *arepas*, a cake made from maize, but the endless bowls of *plátanos* and meat were getting tiresome.

Neither Tom nor I knew for certain what our captors' next move would be. We assumed they'd contact the outside world with a ransom request, which afforded us a rare few moments' amusement during those first days at Cloudy Base, as we came to know our new camp in the sky.

'I can't believe they think they'll get three million dollars for us,' Tom said.

'You never know,' I replied. 'A quick

whip-round in the pub at home, parents' life savings, pawning my maps — they might rustle up fifty quid or so.'

An established routine emerged as we waited for their next move. We would rise at dawn, woken by a cry of '*tinto, tinto*' when the bitter Colombian coffee was ready. It might have been the colour of mud and of a similar consistency but we were glad of the injection of energy it provided. Then it would be breakfast, *plátanos* and rice, and a cigarette, after I procured a pack the last time the guerrillas had collected supplies, presumably from a village where the locals were willing to exchange goods for cash or protection. Tom and I would then idle away time until midday and lunch, playing cards or Twenty Questions, though we had become bored with that, having exhausted all the famous men and women we knew. The number of times Tom was Geoff Hamilton was well into double figures. 'Are you Geoff Hamilton?' was always my opening gambit.

'Bloody hell, Paul, how'd you guess that?' Tom would exclaim.

'It's the twelfth time you've been him.'

After lunch and another cigarette there would be more time to idle away until around three, when Tom and I would commandeer the fire and fry ourselves some sliced *plátanos* as a daily treat. Perhaps we would have a nap before dinner at around five, smoke a cigarette and play a few games of cards, and when night fell, at about six, we would turn in for the night. Twelve hours were spent awake, twelve hours in our tent asleep, or trying to sleep.

With so much unused time, my thoughts turned to making myself as comfortable as possible. Given that the guerrillas had put a price on our head and had decided we were of immense value, I felt as though our status had grown and therefore our confidence increased. Maria offered to wash our clothes and everyone was being polite, trying to please us. With this in mind I took a few small liberties. The mountain stream was clean yet far too cold to bathe in. The guerrillas had chopped an extensive supply of firewood, so I used as much as I could to stoke a blazing fire — we aimed to be a drain on their energy and resources — and placed on it one of the large pots, filled with water.

'What are you doing?' enquired the teenage girl, perplexed yet also curious. No-one else seemed interested.

'The water is cold,' I replied, 'and I want a hot bath.'

After burning as much wood as possible to heat the water, I carried the pot over to the stream. The teenager watched every movement I made, fascinated by the whole ritual. I stripped down to my pants, picked up my bowl, carefully scooped up some steaming hot water, dipped it into the river to temper it and splashed it over my head. I repeated this several times. The warm water felt nourishing and soothing.

As I was drying myself off the girl came down to join me at the stream and stripped to her underwear. She was carrying a large pot of hot water. I watched her as she set it down and dipped her cooking bowl into it. But rather than cooling it in the stream she poured the scalding water straight over her head. She squealed in pain. I winced with her. Luckily for her the water wasn't boiling so no damage was done, but she looked at me with tears in her eyes, as if to ask, 'What went wrong?'

Refreshed by my bath, I went back to my tent and continued to carve the final pieces of a chess set I'd been working on to give to Tom as a surprise birthday present. I hoped he could play chess. His birthday was 12 April: the guerrillas' radio blared out music and intermittent bulletins mentioned the date.

★　★　★

TOM: Señor Dama departed with his pack after a long conversation with Smithy. We discussed where he might be going and decided that he must have gone off with our passports to get a message to the authorities that they had us and wanted three million for us. The guards worked furiously around the camp, chopping firewood, strengthening their bivouacs or felling trees, all except Smithy, who simply sat on his bed staring forlornly at his shoes, chin resting on his hand, as if waiting for something to happen. The only times he got up were to tend his vegetable patch.

On our second afternoon there he walked across to speak to me while Paul was washing in the stream.

'How are you, Tomás?' he asked.

140

'Very well,' I replied. 'This is a very nice camp, señor.'

He nodded. 'Good,' he said.

That, however, was as far as his small talk went. His face became more serious.

'When will you decide who is going to return for the money?'

'*Señor*, we told you. We can't go alone.'

He shook his head emphatically.

'We are waiting for you to go, Tomás,' he said. He turned to leave, then added, 'Don't tell Pablo we have spoken.'

When Paul returned, I told him immediately.

'I don't believe this,' he said incredulously. 'They're still waiting for us to decide? But we told them we're not going anywhere!'

'That's what he said, Paul.'

'Surely they've sent out a ransom demand. They can't just wait for us. What if we don't agree? Will they just wait for ever?'

I shrugged. I didn't know either. Though there was one thing I did know.

'I don't want them to send out a demand,' I said. 'We got ourselves into this. It was our cock-up. No-one should have to bail us out.'

'If they want to wait,' Paul said, 'then let's wait. It's a battle of wills. They think we'll crack first.' Paul carried on shaking his head. 'But it's a bluff, Tom. It has to be. I bet Dama has gone off with our passports.'

It was stalemate. Smith continued to sit staring at his boots while Paul and I tried to keep ourselves occupied. I worked on making our hut as comfortable as possible, widening the bed and

141

building a porch. I gathered rocks and stones from the river, arranged the larger ones in a rectangle shape around the outside, the smaller ones in the interior. It gave us somewhere to sit when the clouds swirled in and around the camp and the inevitable deluge followed. Because of the damp our rucksacks were starting to mould, so I decided to build a covered rack to hold them. Paul was happy to sit and do comparatively little, which annoyed me slightly because I was really trying to make a difference. But we were dissimilar in that respect. I needed to be busy; he spent his time in thought, sometimes with the aid of a cigarette.

To help myself get through each day it was necessary to erase certain memories: of my parents, my home and my greenhouses in particular. They became irrelevant. I once dreamed of Gran and her wonderful cream teas and that almost reduced me to tears. It was so vivid, and then I woke up and realized I was not at home eating iced buns; instead, I was in the jungle eating *plátanos* that cause the worst possible runs, yellow and stinking. So I blocked out such thoughts as much as I could. However, while you can stop yourself consciously thinking about your family and home, it is virtually impossible to control your dreams, and whenever I dreamed of them I felt like crying.

★ ★ ★

PAUL: For those first few days at Cloudy Base we received regular visits from a black guerrilla.

He would stride casually into camp, go over to Smithy and the pair would whisper to each other. In a moment of black humour, I named him Whispering Death, mentioning to Tom, only half in jest, that he was bringing messages and orders from elsewhere to execute us.

The second time he came to the camp, he hung around and ate before disappearing to what we presumed was another camp nearby. Tom and I thought he might be reporting information to Smith from one of the group's leaders, a general of some sort. This view changed on his third visit: he wasn't interested in us, he was interested in the fresh-faced teenage guerrilla. Tom and I watched as he whispered to her, making her laugh and smile. All of a sudden, the pair of them disappeared into one of the bivouacs. The Nutter nudged Homeboy I and smiled. We all smirked and giggled. Twenty minutes later both of them came out wearing sheepish grins, their clothes unbuttoned and creased. From that point she became known as 'Loose Teenager'. The name fitted her perfectly. She'd flirted and mucked around with everyone ever since we'd first met her. The day before her assignation with Whispering Death, while Tom and I were playing cards, she'd sneaked into our tent. When Tom went to lie down, she jumped from beneath our sleeping bags, frightening the hell out of him. Riotous giggles and guffaws had echoed through the jungle. Everybody else, it seemed, was in on the joke apart from the gringos.

'This shouldn't be funny,' I said to Tom that

night as we lay in the darkness trying to sleep. 'It's like being on a school trip sometimes.'

'Yeah,' he agreed. 'Get this: The Nutter told me today that Loose Teenager fancies me.'

'You're kidding.'

'No, he came up to me and said, 'She is a nice girl. She likes you.' '

'What did you say?'

'I didn't say anything.' He paused to think. 'Mind you, I suppose it'd give me something to do to pass the time.'

'Don't go near her, Tom. Stick to orchids.'

I refused to accept that no-one was making any effort to contact the outside world with a ransom demand. On our third day at Cloudy Base, Smith sat hunched on his bench rifling through a bag of documents and papers.

'Tom, can you see what Smithy is looking at? It looks like our documents.'

'What would he be doing with them?'

'I'm sure they are. Go on, ask him for them. Say we want to laugh at our passport photographs.'

I continued to pester him, and at last he agreed. A few minutes later, his persuasive powers as good as ever, Tom came back with the bag. Apart from our traveller's cheques, everything else was there: passports, various receipts, driving licences and the maps of the Darién. The passports all but confirmed that the guerrillas were still waiting on us.

The greatest fillip was seeing my maps. I decided to risk keeping them and hoped they wouldn't notice. Furtively, I slipped them under my pillow. If they asked where they were then I would look as innocent as possible, curse our absent-mindedness — 'We must have left them in the tent, señor' — and give them straight back. With Smith in charge, the atmosphere around the camp was so relaxed that I was becoming blasé. I felt confident we could get away with almost anything. We gave the bags back, remembering to tell Smith how hilarious our passport photographs were.

No mention was made of the missing maps.

Having them in my possession felt like a small victory. If I could calculate where we were then planning an escape route back to Panama was possible, though it would be difficult in the mountains. Whispering Death's occasional presence indicated that other camps were nearby, and we were still guarded at night, which made a getaway in the dark a perilous proposition. A compass would be essential, together with a full moon to light our way. At night it was as dark as a cave; it was unlikely we'd be able to travel more than five feet before walking into a tree and knocking ourselves out. In spite of these obstacles, I felt truly optimistic for the first time since our capture. Tom's mind, however, was not on escape. He'd found some orchids.

★ ★ ★

TOM: On the tough mountainous trek to Cloudy Base, I was taking orchids from everywhere, from trees and from rocks; I carried them behind my ears and in my hair to get them

145

to the camp. At first the guerrillas were merely surprised by my behaviour; after two or three occasions, however, they became annoyed and yelled at me to keep moving. It was difficult to obey them: when I spot an orchid, I need to see it up close, wherever it may be, be it up a tree or down a ravine. It's a reflex action; the orchid compels me to stop. No matter what the circumstances are, I find it difficult to moderate my behaviour where orchids are concerned. When I was being interviewed for my secondary school the first question I asked the headmaster was, 'Got any orchids?' One school had wild common-spotted orchids growing in the surrounding fields. I chose it. Luckily, the school was happy to have me too.

To my delight, Cloudy Base was dripping with flowers. During our first few days there I went as far as the camp border and saw and collected *Lemboglossums* and *Encyclias*, though the real prizes were revealed when the guerrillas began to chop down trees to create space for drying clothes. On the fallen branches and tree crowns were reams and reams of orchids, including *Sobralias*, a gorgeous epiphytic plant with glossy leaves that have pale but distinct veins. They start their lives in the tree but grow on and along the ground when the branch falls, though many die due to lack of light. But I found them before this happened. *And they were flowering!*

The rack for the rucksacks served a dual purpose: it was also an orchid nursery. Once I had a place to display them, things got ridiculous. I had access to so many orchids and I

146

wanted bigger and better species in the nursery every day. I wanted bigger plants, larger leaves, headier scents, vaster pods, greater variations. I was growing them on the roof of the nursery, on its side, along its bottom. Then I started putting them on and around our tent. I found fifteen-foot-long oncidiums which I wrapped around the rope supports of our tent so that they lined its borders, like fairy lights on a tree. Soon I'd hoovered up every type of orchid in the surrounding area.

The guerrillas would sometimes come across to inspect my collection. Will Smith was unimpressed.

'That's not an orchid,' he would say, pointing at a *Pleurothallis*.

'Yes, it is.'

'No, it's not.'

'*Señor*, it is. I've got them in my greenhouse at home.'

'You have orchids? Why? For medicine?

'No.'

'For money?'

'No. I just like them.'

There was a pause as he took this in.

'But that is not an orchid,' he repeated.

'*Señor*, it has parallel leaf veins, three petals, three sepals and a column. That means it's an orchid.'

He walked away, shaking his head.

They soon realized I was a fanatic. It affected some of them. The Nutter brought me a picture-perfect red bromeliad I'd never seen before in my life. 'But where are the orchids, you melon?' was my first thought, but I didn't want to hurt his feelings and for the purposes of my collection I made it an honorary orchid.

Once I'd collected all I could from the felled trees around the camp I felt the urge to go further into the forest. I tried to explain this to Smith. 'No way,' was his succinct reply. This was on 12 April, my birthday. Ordinarily, spending my birthday held captive by armed men thousands of miles from home would not have been a cause for celebration, yet the orchids managed to stave off any depression. I was determined to enjoy myself, and the best way I could think of doing that was finding orchids. So I decided to play my trump card.

'Please, señor, let me go. It's my birthday.'

I gave him the most imploring look I could muster. I could see his resistance was wilting.

'OK, you can go,' he said eventually, smiling, 'but we will have to tie you up to ensure you do not run away.'

'Yes, please do,' I said, proffering my wrists.

'Mierda,' he said, shaking his head.

'Señor, you can tie my hands, even my feet, I don't care — '

He held up his hand to shut me up.

'I will not tie you up. You can go with a guard,' he said, and walked off.

'Can Pablo come too?' I shouted after him.

He just waved his hand as if to say, 'Whatever.'

Before we left camp, we asked Smith if we could walk to the vista. Paul wanted to see the lie of the land and get some idea of our location, perhaps work out a possible escape route. 'No way,' said Smith once more, and this time he meant it. Despite this, Paul decided that he would still come along because it would look suspicious if he suddenly dropped out.

The taciturn Perty was chosen as our guide, and Paul and I spent well over an hour away, me trying to spot flowers, him trying to find a vantage point. It was a disappointing trip until the return journey to Cloudy Base, when all three of us stumbled upon a large, fallen tree limb next to the footpath. It was plastered with orchids. I'd spotted the limb an hour earlier on our outward journey, yet its botanical riches weren't fully revealed until a closer inspection on our return. One plant stood out among the rest, and although it was in bud I knew what species it was: the infamous *Encyclia cochleata*. I felt faint. I'd dreamed of seeing this awesome flower in the wild for more than two years, and here it was. Had it been in flower Paul and Perty would have had to scrape me off the floor.

Perty did not seem too pissed off with my capering around with joy, but when we returned to camp, and in front of the others, he suddenly became aggressive. He called Paul and me 'maricónes', or 'poofs'; pointing to the cockleshell orchid I was attaching to my nursery he said what sounded like *igua puta*, son of a whore. Charming. You may insult me, I thought, but don't diss the orchid. It had the last laugh a week later when it flowered spectacularly. My joy was unconfined. 'Look, look, it's flowering!' babbled to everyone in sight, though no-one shared my excitement.

The orchid hunting continued. It was ironic that before being captured I'd seen three orchids in flower, a pathetic amount, but now I was a prisoner I was finding them everywhere. I suppose that's the trick: if you want to find the best stuff, get taken hostage.

A couple of days later, while on an extended 'shit run', I laid eyes on a newly fallen, decomposing tree that was covered in epiphytically inclined orchids, many of which had survived the crash to the forest floor. This tree was a few hundred yards from the centre of camp. I wanted to return to explore the site, and made this clear to Smith. As cautious as ever, he allocated Homeboy I, a fervent orchidophobe — I'd overheard him bad-mouthing my collection to the others — as my guide on the slippery walk to the tree.

When I got there I yelped with excitement: there were *Restrepias* everywhere. I collected three flowering plants that were either varieties of the same species or three separate species — without a field guidebook I couldn't tell. I'd never seen them in the wild before though. *Restrepia* flowers are large in comparison to the small plant, and the petals and sepals quivered dramatically in the highland breeze, the dorsal sepal and upper petals moving like whiskers in the cool forest air. For me, the lateral sepals, the lower portion of the flower, are the most exciting because they are united and form the largest part of the flower. The lateral sepals are sometimes speckled, blotched black or colourfully striped. All three of the flowers I collected, although variable in size and colour, possessed a rich red background. They were absolutely sensational.

Homeboy I didn't agree. He complained on the way there, during the collecting, and emphatically on the short stroll back, dragging his feet and swiping at nearby foliage with his machete. I tried to cheer him up by pointing out some beautifully fused lateral sepals. His abrupt response indicated he didn't appreciate my botanical lecturing.

'We're going back now,' he said, a nervous look on his face.

'But *señor*, can I have just five more minutes? There are more to be found.'

'*¡Majorda!*' Fuck off.

He stormed off. I felt obliged to follow him. It was one of my first orchid hunts and I didn't want to be barred from going out again.

Around the fire, where the others were gathered, Homeboy I started ranting.

'I'm going to miss Easter with my family,' he moaned. 'I can't play basketball. Instead, I've got to be here, doing work, my job. I can't even have my brandy or my whisky and get drunk. Why do I have to go with him while he collects flowers? Orchids serve no purpose!'

The hunts continued, and the orchid collection I built up was extraordinary. Among the gathered beauties were suspected odontoglossums, a miniature oncidium and an *Epidendrum pseudepidendrum*. Central to the display was a *Stanhopea*, though gallingly it was not in flower. But that was probably a good thing: the guerrillas might not have appreciated its powerful odour. Had Kew Gardens inspected my collection, I'm certain they would have seen species they had never come across before. Any collector in the world would pay thousands of pounds for some of the plants I had. Unfortunately, taking them back to England was not an option: collecting wild orchids without relevant documents or personnel is a criminal offence and thieves are hit with hefty fines or even thrown in jail.

But what harm was there in keeping them while I was in the jungle?

★ ★ ★

PAUL: '*¿Tomás, Jugamos?*' loose teenager would ask during the afternoon, checking with Tom to see whether the card school would be in action that evening.

'*Sí, sí, después la cena,*' came his reply.

At dusk we gathered under a reed shelter on a pair of benches at a table constructed from branches to play Beggar-my-Neighbour, a game Tom's family usually plays at Christmas. The guerrillas *loved* it. They watched while Tom and I played during our first few evenings at Cloudy Base. Loosey was the first to join in, then Smith and The Nutter. Finally, Maria completed the school.

The rules are simple. All the cards are dealt face down, then, in player order, they are turned face up on a central pile. If an ace is laid then the next player has four opportunities to follow this up with a picture card; if a King is laid then they have only three opportunities, and two for a Queen. The Jack is the most powerful card of all because players are allowed only one opportunity to match it. Whoever lays the last picture card gets the pile. One by one, people are eliminated; the person with all the cards at the end is the winner.

The cards were dealt. Tom snapped the first card down, and around we went. There were audible sighs and giggles because no-one had yet laid a picture card. The tension mounted. Then Will Smith turned up a King; three cards followed quickly, though there was no luck for Maria: she got nothing. Smithy took the pile.

He started again, then Maria, with The Nutter after her. He had a Queen.

'¡La Reina!'

Everyone cheered. Tom's first card was a dud, but he followed it with a King.

'¡El Rey!' went up the cry.

The guerrillas edged forward on the benches. I snapped down a card, then another, then a Jack.

'¡Jota!'

Heads were shaken at my luck. Was it me, or was there an envious look on Smithy's face? He had barely won a game, in spite of our best efforts to let him. It's difficult to throw a game of chance though. Under the table, I tried to shuffle my cards. They were in a good mood and I wished to keep it that way. Our whole strategy was placate, placate, placate. Our lives depended on our ability to appear innocent, harmless even. They were waiting for us to decide who should go home. They didn't realize we would never,

153

ever agree to that and that we intended to go home together. Once they realized that, all this laughter would end.

My Jack was matched immediately with an ace. Steadily, the hand was building into one that would be useful to win. Around the cards went again. This time The Nutter laid a Jack; Tom followed with a lowly card and The Nutter won the hand, giggling loudly. Loosey was the first to go.

'¡Está saliendo y que le vaya bien!' The Nutter shouted to her in a singsong voice. 'She is leaving and I wish her well!'

I was eliminated too, and was given The Nutter's trademark farewell. Everyone laughed as they lost. Everyone, that is, apart from Smithy.

I turned to Tom.

'How did we get ourselves into this situation, Tom? It's mad.'

He shook his head slowly in bewildered agreement.

'Thanks, Dad,' he said, looking to the sky. 'This game could be a lifesaver.'

Soon, Tom and The Nutter were the only players left in the game. Tom was running out of cards. Everyone waited, anticipating The Nutter's victory — an outcome I was praying for. Tom's last good card saved him; The Nutter couldn't match it. He sighed and scratched his head. The exchange continued, back and forth, until finally Tom laid his last card. 'El fin,' he said as he put it down, and then held out his hands to indicate he had no cards left. Realizing he was the winner, The Nutter jumped up in delight, breaking into a little jig, his wild brown eyes darting around, his protuberant chimpanzee jaw laughing madly. I was delighted neither of us had won.

★ ★ ★

TOM: Despite the relaxed atmosphere, a guard still watched us every night. One night I was woken by the brightness of the moon, not something that was a problem under the suffocating jungle canopy. I stumbled out into the crisp night air for a look and was left in awe: the fullest of moons glowed intensely, the white light bouncing off the trees and casting abstract shadows across the whole camp. It felt as if a spotlight were being shone on the mountain and nowhere else.

'What are you doing?' The voice was behind me. It was The Nutter.

'Admiring the moon.' It felt like an unsatisfactory response. 'I'm looking at insects in the canopy,' I added off the top of my head, flicking the top of a tent with my hand.

This seemed to satisfy him. Not the brightest, The Nutter. The night before Paul had unzipped the tent door and was in the process of putting on his shoes when the beam from The Nutter's torch bathed him in light.

'What are you doing?' he barked.

'I'm off to urinate,' Paul replied. 'What are you doing?'

There was a pause.

'I'm shining a torch,' he said.

155

This exchange kept us amused for weeks afterwards.

The Nutter was a fixture around the camp. He and Smith were the only ones who never left. The others came and went, disappearing for food supplies for days at a time until they returned, presumably from some distant village down the mountain. One afternoon Perty staggered into camp with the hindquarters of a cow draped over his shoulders. He was topless and the blood had coloured his torso red. He made a dramatic sight, the flesh, blood and sweat mingling on his bare chest. Having hauled the cow up the hill, he was close to collapse. Perty was the least communicative of the guerrillas. This might have had something to do with his unpopularity within the ranks. Few people spoke to him and he was treated as if he were of a lower class. When he was not working, he spent much of his time on his own, either singing or playing with himself.

'Are you OK, *señor*,' I asked one day as he warbled a tune while his hands were picking yet another fight with his balls.

'*Majorda*,' he replied, scowling.

He developed flu and was confined to his bed, a victim of the damp. One of the Homeboys also fell ill. On 19 April my left leg became swollen around the ankle. All night it expelled poisonous, murky blood despite the antibiotic tablets Maria gave me when I showed her the swelling. The Nutter came across for a look as I lay in bed, popping his head through our tent door.

'We will have to cut off your leg, Tomás,' he

said, his face an image of unrestrained glee.

The expulsions stained my ground mat and sleeping bag with blood. No-one knew what the problem was. They suspected an infection. It was Loose Teenager who first spotted the culprits.

'Worms here in Tom's foot,' she said, 'and another, and another,' her finger pointing to other tender sores and boils.

Maria rushed in with Will Smith. He counted them, and those that had gathered around me gasped. I was told to squeeze the boil on the left side of my right knee as hard as possible. A gob of pus and liquid blood shot out. *'Saliendo, saliendo,'* cried a few of the gathering. 'It's going, it's going.' But whatever was on its way decided to stay. I didn't have sufficient strength to squeeze it out myself.

I walked outside and lay down on the makeshift operating table on the edge of camp. A razor blade was produced and the hair was shaved from the infected area. Smith lit a cigarette. A chill of horror coursed through my body, turning me as rigid as an ironing board. Was he going to cauterize the boil? He inhaled and blew the smoke hard through his fingers to obtain a spread of nicotine on a page of his notepad. Added to this was a sticky petroleum substance. The crowd grew and prognoses were exchanged all round, forcing Smith to hush them for calm. I was both fascinated and revolted, not knowing what was coming next or how much it would hurt. Smith applied the paper to the boil. Paul's attention was grabbed, and he looked over from the fire area where he was seated. The compress was removed, painful in itself.

'There it is,' said a voice.

'*Saliendo*,' said another, as Smith started to squeeze.

I couldn't believe the amount of pressure he applied. As dirty blood rained out from the sore I put my hand up to cover my mouth and stifle a scream. Paul was now stood to my left, directly behind me. I could see him cringing, turning white as Smith's thumbs pushed inexorably closer together and there was a pop. The pain immediately started to ease. Smith held up the culprit like a minute trophy: I could see a white worm a centimetre long, shaped like a tadpole, with a menacing feeler and a translucent tail. The main body was lined with hairs.

There was no respite, and the ritual began again. Another five worms were mined from various parts of my lower limbs. The most spectacular was from the swelling beside my right knee. Smith applied his excruciating pressure and a one-and-a-half-centimetre-long monster exited at pace, landing on the ground a metre away. It was a blessed relief because the tricks adopted to entice it out, such as placing a burning cigarette near the skin, meant the worm 'played' inside my leg. On one occasion, Will Smith's face was covered with a jet of pussy blood as he attempted to eject one particularly stubborn wriggler. That was the only worm to evade his thumbs, though; the rest were thrown on the fire. The whole ordeal was agony like nothing I'd ever experienced. The strength in his fingers to get into the shinbone to squeeze out the worms was incredible. Two hours later, the score was totted up: seven worms had been expelled. Well, six and a half: one had had its head removed, its body left inside to die. It was a day I will never forget.

★ ★ ★

PAUL: The camp looked like the Chelsea flower show. Our tent was swathed in orchids, like a float in some horticultural parade. And as for the shed Tom built for his rucksack, well, that had long since been buried beneath mounds of flowers. Orchids obsessed Tom; once he saw one nothing could distract him from it, not even a gun pointed at his head. We'd been kidnapped, and still orchids were all he could think of. He tried to pass on some of his enthusiasm for them, chattering wildly about different species, his tongue tripping over itself in ecstatic bursts of description, the words an incomprehensible deluge. I sat next to him with a baffled look on my face as he tended his nursery. He would look up at me briefly and pause, then go back to examining another plant and continue his monologue. I was sure that at times he forgot what was going on around him.

I left him to it; they were little more than weeds as far as I was concerned. I admired his passion, however. Tom was different, unique, and I admired him greatly for it; he grabbed life and shook it for all it was worth. He was the ideal companion, and he made me smile in the most testing circumstances. But there were other things on my mind. I was looking for a means of escape. We were still within walking distance of Panama and safety, perhaps as little as three days. I walked with Tom around the camp on his orchid forages trying to work out where we were.

Whenever I had the chance and the sun was shining, I took my South America guidebook over to the felled area of the camp to bask in its warmth, planning destinations to visit in South America on future travels. Curiosity and boredom soon got the better of the two Homeboys and The Nutter.

'What is the book?' Homeboy I asked.

'A guide to South America,' I replied. I was picking up more Spanish as the days went by.

I pointed out the various countries and roughly where we were, though I was reluctant to appear too knowledgeable about this fact. Their knowledge of geography was poor. The Darién and Colombia were the only places they knew. I showed them the maps and photographs in the book, which they stared at, fascinated.

'Have you been to Bogotá?' Home Boy I enquired.

'No, you stopped me,' I replied with a wry smile.

The Nutter flashed back one of his wild grins. He had been point when we were ambushed, and he was proud of his work.

'Yes, you were walking,' Home Boy II continued.

He understood walking; they all did. All their lives they had been walking through this jungle. They were exceptionally proud of how far and how fast they could go.

'We were walking to Colombia,' I continued, acting out a walk with my fingers.

'Why?'

'Maybe I can find work there, and it is cheap to walk,' I lied.

They nodded in agreement, and I went on to explain why we didn't use motorboats because they cost too much money. I knew that was something they could relate to.

'The cities of Colombia are very beautiful,' Home Boy II said. 'We cannot go to them; we must stay in the forest. In the cities you can be comfortable, sleep in a bed, eat good food and drink. We will miss Easter this year. We cannot go to the villages to party. We have to work.'

I knew that that work was to guard and hold us.

For some days we had been warned that 'The Devil' was arriving; mention of 'El Diablo' circulated the camp. I didn't know what this entailed, though I was sure he must be important to be afforded such respect.

The next day, he swaggered nonchalantly into camp. The other guerrillas greeted him with reverence; they were all expecting him. He eyed us up, smiled, and then greeted us. He was built like a concrete bunker, very broad shoulders, as solid as a man could be with mean, scowling features. I doubted if anybody or anything could have knocked him down. 'El Diablo' suited him. Over his shoulder was slung a heavy machine gun, while his rucksack was laden with belts of bullets.

161

'Paul, do you see the size of his gun?' exclaimed Tom.

'Yeah, it looks like it should be mounted on a helicopter.'

'He's got to be some sort of boss, someone higher up the ranks who's come to sort us out.'

'Perhaps he got that gun because he's the only one capable of carrying it.'

Despite the joke, we had to admit he was one imposing soldier. We could sense the fear among his cohorts. Were this a school trip, El Diablo would have been the class bully, and the others gave him a wide berth. Where did he come from? Was there an agency leasing out hard men for hire? Rent-a-Guerrilla, perhaps? After arriving at the camp he did little but smoke and make lewd suggestions to Loose Teenager and Maria while the others worked, washing, chopping wood and maintaining their bivouacs. He was left to do as he pleased. The sole communal task he performed was cooking, which he did meticulously. He sat there stirring the pot for hours.

'I am a good cook,' he would say in his lugubrious Spanish drawl. 'My mother taught me well.'

Maria walked past him once as he tended diligently to the pot.

'You need to get yourself a real man,' he said, looking disdainfully over his shoulder at Smithy. 'Like me.'

He leered at her; she did her best to ignore him.

Whenever Loosey came near him he would put his hands to his face and mime as if parting something before waggling his tongue.

'I like anal sex,' he would tell her.

Wisely, she ignored him too.

The food he cooked tasted like shit. Naturally, we didn't tell him. We would take a bite, make 'mmmm' noises and nod our heads. He would smile contentedly.

'My mother taught me well,' he would repeat with a beatific grin.

I had given the chess set to Tom for his birthday, to his delight. Unfortunately, he proved too easy to beat and his mind could concentrate only on orchids. There was room for little else. None of the guerrillas knew anything about the game. I sat on the bench beside the table made of branches, admiring the pieces I had whittled, slightly disappointed that my efforts had been in vain. Then El Diablo approached me.

'¿Pablo, jugamos?' he asked.

'¿Sí, dama?' I had always played draughts with the guerrillas.

'No, ajedrez,' he replied.

'¿Qué?'

Then I realized: he wanted to play chess. This barrel-chested monster was claiming he knew how to play chess. I sensed an easy victory, like shooting fish in a barrel.

We set up the pieces and started. I was quickly on the defensive; he knew exactly how to play. His moves were measured and unhurried, a bit like his cooking, though the results were less disastrous. I was caught unawares; I'd been found guilty of underestimating my opponent. Within half an hour I had been cut to pieces. El

Diablo slapped his thigh, laughing loudly.

'Again,' I said, wondering if there was any Russian blood in his family.

'Later, Pablo,' he growled, and strolled back to his bivouac.

★ ★ ★

TOM: The camp was becoming less relaxed and more restless. It seemed as if we were about to move again. It would be difficult to leave my orchid collection behind, though I was determined to take the best specimens with me. For more than two weeks I had been free to collect orchids at will, interrupted only when the local grubs decided to feast on my leg. The swelling had subsided and the wounds had healed well, thanks to the burrowing thumbs of Will Smith. It was as I sat fingering the hardened scabs on my legs in the tent one afternoon that Paul and I were alerted by a cacophonous cackling noise. The Nutter's head popped through the door.

'Monkeys,' he said excitedly.

We scrambled outside and saw that a troop of howler monkeys was approaching the clearing. When they reached the point at which the camp started their chattering became louder and more high-pitched. 'Where the hell has our forest gone?' was probably the gist of their conversation. Following a brief pause, they started to circle the clearing, swinging athletically from tree to tree. The Nutter brought his gun up and levelled it at the troop, but Will Smith ordered him to put it down. Instead, he amused himself by imitating the noise the monkeys made.

Later that day, the guerrillas went off into a huddle, presumably to discuss their plans. Paul and I played cards, trying to guess what the conversation was about. When it broke up I was at the stream, sat on a tree trunk, brushing my teeth. The Nutter came down to join me, flashing me a gap-toothed grin as he sat down beside me.

'How are you, Tomás?' he asked.

I told him I was fine.

'What are you doing?'

'Brushing my teeth.'

'And how are your teeth?'

'OK.'

He was being very friendly. Unnaturally so, to be honest.

'Are we feeding you well?'

'Very well, señor.'

'And how is Pablo?'

'Pablo is good.'

I wondered where this was leading.

'Where is the money?' he said suddenly.

I shrugged my shoulders, unsure how to answer.

'If I was to be taken, then I am sure my parents would pay for my freedom,' he said, as if reciting a script. It didn't require a genius to realize The Nutter had been put up to this little charade.

'Where are your parents?' I asked.

He gestured as if he didn't know.

'One day,' he said, 'I was working in the fields. Some people wanted to see us. In the house where my parents were, there was a struggle. I heard shots being fired. I ran away and joined my friends in the jungle.'

'Are they dead?'

He said he didn't know, then his face brightened and he changed tack.

'You learn some good Spanish words with us, eh?'

'Yes, señor. ¡Majorda!'

'I like you, Tomás,' he said, laughing and patting my shoulder. 'If we caught two Americanos then we would swap them for you and Pablo.'

'Go on then,' I thought, 'don't just talk about it, do it.' But all I said was, 'Thank you, señor.'

'The money will come soon,' he said.

'But señor, we are just backpackers. I look for orchids.'

He laughed a fake laugh and patted my left thigh this time.

'We had tourists before,' he revealed. 'We made phone calls, and after years, the money, it appeared.'

As he said this, he looked up to the sky.

'From where?' I asked.

He brought his hand slowly down from above his head.

'It drops,' he said.

I presumed he meant that a helicopter or a plane had dropped the money. I hoped he didn't believe it just fell from the sky.

He turned to me and flashed his smile once more.

'El Jefe said he wants me to stay with you and

166

Pablo because I was with the group that found you,' he said.

'That's good news,' I replied, forcing a smile.

With that he stood up, patted me on the back again and returned to his tent.

The exchange left me bewildered. I related every detail to Paul and we agreed The Nutter was acting to orders. But why? All I'd learned was that if we did not go and get the money then the guerrillas expected it to fall from the sky in a couple of years' time, as it had apparently done in some other kidnap. Paul, as sceptical as ever, doubted the veracity of this other kidnap story.

'They just want us to think that if we don't go home it will take years to get their money rather than two weeks. No wonder it takes so bloody long if they don't tell people they've got us.'

'The Nutter said they would make phone calls.'

'Well, go on, boys — phone! They haven't phoned because they probably don't know how to.'

Neither of us knew what would happen next. But the twenty days we spent at Cloudy Base were at least bearable. We were being treated well. In a way, the prospect of moving was disconcerting. I would rather stay than find out what was around the next corner. But the next day at dawn we were told to pack. This time the camp was not dismantled so I took the opportunity to salvage twelve of my favourite orchids, tying them onto my rucksack straps.

This took a long time, and a few of the guerrillas came across to hurry me along.

'*Igua puta*,' one voice said as I worked as quickly as I could to secure the flowers to the straps. Did he mean the orchid or me?

8

TROUBLE AHEAD

TOM: Trouble ahead was two days late. I was attaching a spectacular, flowering *Miltoniopsis*, given to me by Loose Teenager, to my nursery at Snake Gully, our new camp, when I glanced to my right. El Diablo — whom Paul had renamed Space Cadet after he saw him smoking dried leaves of some description — and the hapless Señor Dama were escorting a short man in dirty pink tracksuit bottoms down the muddied path from the jungle to the camp clearing. A cloth was wrapped around his head — it looked like a tea towel — which covered everything apart from a letterbox opening for his eyes. He walked with a slight limp. He greeted Will Smith warmly.

'He's here,' I shouted to Paul.

'What happens next?' he said rhetorically.

My palms were sweating and my mouth was dry. For three days we'd been told that Trouble Ahead was coming. Or El Jefe, as the guerrillas called him. But he wasn't just an ordinary *jefe*, this guy was *El* Jefe, the stress very much on the first word to indicate he was *the* boss. More than a week had passed since we trekked down from Cloudy Base and set up camp in this dark, hidden gully and we sensed the guerrillas had become tired of waiting.

As ever, the nickname was Paul's invention. On the walk down from Cloudy Base he had commandeered Loose Teenager's shortwave radio and managed to pick up BBC World Service. He was so excited when he picked up the sound of a rich English voice, the warm tone ringing out in the jungle amid the crackle and hiss, that he punched the air and the lenses on his glasses steamed up. In Snake Gully we lost the signal until Smith threw the aerial into a tree for us. For a couple of hours Paul turned the dial imperceptibly left and right, head pushed forward and cocked to the left so his right ear could pick up the slightest change in noise, his face a still-life in concentration, until the English voice came tumbling out of the static once more. There was live commentary of the Whitbread Gold Cup from Sandown. A horse called Trouble Ahead was vying for the lead until it pulled up at the final fence and another horse, Beau, went on to win. Buoyed by English voices and the cheering of a crowd in the background, a sign from home that life was continuing as normal, and doing something as mundane and everyday as listening to a horse race gave us both hope. Paul named the new boss after the thwarted horse. It was a metaphor for our position: he was going to try to outwit us, but he would eventually fall and we would come through victorious.

He arrived on the last day of April.

Señor Dama wandered to our tent, as always positioned at the bottom of the camp encircled

170

by the other bivouacs.

'He wants to speak to you,' he said to me.

'Good luck,' Paul said, as if I were heading into an exam. Which I suppose I was: Spanish oral. I didn't want to find out the penalty for failing. We had already agreed to adopt the same tactic we had adopted during previous interrogations and maintain we were penniless backpackers.

Señor Dama led me through the camp. The guerrillas watched me, their faces hopeful. The arrival of Trouble Ahead was an event they'd waited for with some expectation, and when he was delayed without reason the disposition of the camp had become sullen and despondent, in contrast to the blithe, carefree mood in the mountains. In fact, since arriving at Snake Gully they'd all been behaving oddly. I caught Loose Teenager and Maria crying around the camp fire one night and became paranoid that they were sad because orders had come through for Paul and me to be shot. Immediately I was plunged into the same black hole of despair and fear that had swallowed me during our first week as captives. Paul tried to reassure me, pointing out that it was probably smoke from the fire in their eyes and that revolutionaries hardened by decades of armed struggle, if that's what these people were, were not sentimental types. I saw his point, though it occurred to me that Loosey in particular might not have been in this situation before; murdering hostages might be new to her.

The next evening they were crying again. Even

171

The Nutter's eyes were bloodshot.

'What's wrong?' I asked frantically. 'Why are you sad?'

'Nothing is wrong,' Loose Teenager replied morosely. Her tone did little to allay my sense of dread.

That night I had a vivid dream. I was sat in my uncle's rose garden on a gorgeous summer day drinking fruit punch with Gran. The colour of the roses was deep red; it was as if everything had been shot in soft focus, giving it a lush, cinematic quality. Waking up to discover it was a dream was crushing. In my anxiety I asked Smith for a machete, and he agreed. While working off my fear, I felled half an acre of World Heritage jungle. Sorry, Kew.

Paul's constant support and comfort prevented me from developing into a wreck.

'Come on, Tom,' he would say softly, 'it's all right, mate, no-one's going to shoot us. Let's play cards.'

I followed Dama. He pointed me towards the top of the camp where Trouble Ahead was sitting on a plank of wood that formed a bench. In front of him, spread out on the floor, were all our books, which Smith had taken back from us a day or two before, pieces of paper and our driving licenses. He was holding a notepad and pen. Close up, through the opening of his tea-towel mask, I could see he'd only one eye, the left, a piercing green orb. The other was missing, the lids stitched up, leaving a dark, gruesome gash. Tracksuit bottoms aside, he was a menacing presence. Without speaking, he motioned for me to sit down opposite him on a smooth rock.

'*Buenos días*,' I said, trying to be as polite and friendly as possible.

The Cyclops eye swivelled and flicked up and down, seemingly seeing everything. Either he grunted, or the cloth in front of his mouth muffled his reply.

'*¿Cómo le va?*' I tried. What's up?

'*¿Usted CIA?*' he growled in response.

'No, *señor*. I am a backpacker.'

'But no-one has mentioned you are missing on the radio,' he said.

'That's because we're backpackers, *señor*. We're unimportant.'

'No, you are CIA,' he barked. He spoke quickly and the cloth made it hard to understand everything he said.

'Honest, *señor*. I hunt orchids.'

There was silence for a few seconds as he took this in.

'You want to risk your life finding orchids in the Darién when you can travel to Medellín and visit the orchid fair in March and April?'

I was stumped by that, to be honest. Again, it was clear he was far more savvy than any of the others who had questioned us.

'But, *señor*, it is different here,' I replied, regaining my composure. 'There are many more species that grow in the jungle. There are twelve new species of orchid in the Darién and I wanted to find them.'

That bit came straight off the top of my head. As far as I knew, there could have been twelve million or none at all. He shook his head defiantly in response. I was failing to convince him. Time for show and tell.

From a tree next to us, I snatched an orchid.

'*Señor*, this is an orchid. It is an *Encyclia*. I am here to find plants like these and to take pictures of them.'

There was no response, just the eye boring into me.

'I tell you, *señor*, I find orchids. Look at the palm trees, the bromeliads,' I said, gesturing around us. I went on to name several of the trees dotted around the camp, using their Latin names. This bit was true. I did know all their names. 'I am a gardener,' I continued. 'I collect seeds and grow them in my small greenhouse back in England.'

I repeated this phrase in reply to all his queries. Eventually, he got bored.

'*Mierda*,' he whispered to himself.

Strangely, it was I, the hostage, who'd worn down my interrogator. Aware that few CIA agents are mad about flowers and trees, he switched his line of questioning.

'You are carrying drugs from the United States,' was his next accusation.

'No, we are backpackers,' I countered.

Then he picked up Paul's Lonely Planet guide from the floor. The page was opened at the chapter about the Darién. His finger pointed to a paragraph.

In addition, the Darién has become a major area of activity for guerrillas from the neighbouring Colombian province of Antioquia. In January 1993, three US missionaries, who had been working among the Kuna and who were known for their aid to travellers throughout the region, were kidnapped from the town of Púcuro; it's said they were kidnapped by Colombian guerrillas, reportedly affiliated with the Colombian Revolutionary Armed Forces (FARC). The FARC demanded US$5 million for the three missionaries. They were never ransomed or released, and they are now presumed dead.

I'd read the passage before, but I acted as if it was the first time I'd seen it. I wondered how he'd understood the passage given his lack of English. But his fingers pointed to words like Darién, other names of places in the area, references to FARC and amounts of money, all of which he could have understood and from which he could have worked out what the text was referring to. Then his finger pointed to a section about drug trafficking.

'But I'm here looking for orchids,' I reiterated.

His eye stared at me for a few seconds.

'Five million,' he said.

'¿Qué?'

'We want five million dollars for your freedom.'

This new figure amazed me and for a second it knocked the wind out of me so I couldn't reply. I felt a complete sense of despair.

'But we don't have that money,' I said weakly.

175

He nodded his head slowly.

'Señor Jefe, we have no money,' I repeated.

'What does your father do?'

'Señor, he owns a small shack, with a garden full of weeds.'

I made no mention of the fact that Lullingstone Castle is part of an estate that includes a fifteenth-century manor house, a Tudor gatehouse, a parish church of Norman origin and 120 acres, which used to be 7,000 but has now 'reverted' to the size it was, approximately, at the time of the writing of the Domesday Book. Not to mention the eighteen-acre fishing lake, an old herb garden, an ice house and a four-poster bed in which Queen Anne once slept. Thankfully, the 'castle' part of my address had obviously meant nothing to my earlier interrogators. At the word's mention, dollar signs would have popped up in the eyes of any English-speaking kidnapper with half a brain.

'What else does he own?' he asked next.

'He owns a scooter,' I replied, 'and a horse. Oh yes, señor, and a cat.'

Diligently, he noted down all these possessions in his rather neat handwriting, including the cat. Then, all of a sudden, he cursed, shook his head and scribbled out the bit about the cat.

'We have a very small house,' I added for good measure. 'In the winter season we have to wear Wellington boots because the roof has so many holes and we get soaking wet, señor.'

They all wore Wellington boots in the jungle,

so this detail was something I imagined they would relate to.

'What is your address?'

I hesitated, not sure whether to give him a false address or the real one. Given that I'd already told El Jefe at the first camp, I decided on the latter. He checked in his notepad; he'd copied it down earlier anyway from my driving licence. 'This guy's not stupid,' I thought.

'My *compadres* tell me Pablo has lots of money.'

'No, he is a poor backpacker like me.'

'Pablo is a member of a world famous skiing club,' he replied.

He must have learned this from our interrogation by M-16 at River Site. I had to say something in response, but what?

'*Señor*, it is so funny. When Pablo goes skiing he needs people either side of him or he will fall over. He skis like shit.'

My aim was to make him laugh; I wanted to ease the atmosphere. There was yet another ominous silence.

From the pile of books and objects on the floor, Trouble Ahead pulled a card. It was Paul's health centre appointment card. The time of his last one was written on it. Trouble Ahead showed it to me and pointed to a number in the top left-hand corner.

'CIA,' he said.

'No, *señor*, it's a medical card. For when Pablo is ill.'

Next he made mention of a Chilean traveller, how he'd been kidnapped and exchanged for a

million dollars. He also mentioned two Austra-
lians, though I didn't understand what he said
about them. Basically, the message he was trying
to get over was 'pay up'. I went into the routine
I'd adopted before.

'But señor,' I said, 'we have no money and our
parents have no money.'

Then he started to bargain.

'You can afford four million.'

'No, señor.'

'Three million?'

I shook my head. This went on for what
seemed an age. I didn't want to give him any
indication that our families could pay a penny.

'We have no money. Only a vegetable patch.'

'How big is it?' he shot back.

'As big as this area,' I said indicating the small
area we were sat in.

'And what do you grow?'

'Carrots, señor, and a few cabbages.'

He growled with frustration.

'You will write a letter to your parents,' he
said. He ripped a page out of his notebook.
'Write that you are well, that the food is good,
and that you are being treated well.'

I started, and immediately made an error: at
the top of the page I wrote El Darién, our
location. I carried on, writing all the stuff I was
ordered to include, with a few extra details
expressing my love for my parents, that sort of
thing. When I finished he asked me to read it to
him in Spanish. As soon as I mentioned El
Darién, he began to shake his head vigorously.
Pulling a lighter from his pocket, he burned the

178

letter. He ripped out another page and asked me to try again.

'No Darién,' he added tersely, then set about the soup Señor Dama had brought him for lunch, which he ate by lifting the veil from his mouth in order to get the spoon underneath.

I hoped it wouldn't fall off. I could picture his fury at my seeing what was under his disguise. He'd probably execute me on the spot.

I started writing once more, adding a few more details this time: 'We are in good spirits and are healthy . . . we are being treated well . . . the orchids in the jungle are lovely . . . the food is good, etc.' Then I read it back to him. When I reached the sentence about orchids, he flipped. Presumably he thought that reference could be used to identify our location. He shook his head and demanded that I hand over the letter. Once again he produced his lighter and burned it, except this time the paper stuck to his finger and as the flames rose he could not shake it off. He singed his fingers and blew on them to ease the pain. He was angry now and gave me another piece of paper, telling me to write without referring to orchids.

By this time I was also pissed off, so I wrote from the heart: 'Dear Mum and Dad. Our kidnappers are all idiots. They are a bunch of gits. Give them absolutely nothing. We are well. Don't worry about me. The orchids here are lovely. My friend Paul is with me and he is also fine. All my love, Tom.' Trouble Ahead asked me to read it back to him in Spanish, and of course, given what I had written, mine was a rather loose translation. 'Dear Mum and Dad,' I read aloud. 'Having a pleasant time with our kidnappers in this lovely place. The food is brilliant and the weather is great. Please listen to whatever demands our kidnappers make. They are all very excellent people and very friendly, too. My friend Paul is with me and is also doing well. Lots of love, Tom.'

I looked up to see Trouble Ahead nodding sagely.

'Very good,' he said, and took the letter off me. He said it would be sent to England to get my money. That was the end of my interrogation.

★ ★ ★

PAUL: I waited all morning for Tom's grilling to end. The camp was silent throughout; no-one even murmured. At one point Tom appeared and called me over, explaining that Trouble Ahead wanted to speak to us both. I stumbled out to the back of the camp but was sent back by Trouble Ahead, who hissed in anger. Eventually it was my turn, though I wasn't really sure what he could glean from me because of my terrible Spanish. Yet I knew I could use the language divide to my advantage.

Rain forced the interview site to be shifted. Trouble Ahead limped down to our tent and sat across from me under our poncho. I could see the others gather around, straining for a view, trying to eavesdrop.

'*Buenas tardes, señor,*' he said.

We shook hands and the thought flicked

through my mind that this was like going for a job interview, albeit a surreal one. And this time it mattered.

'*¿Cómo está?*' Nice of him to ask.

'*Bien, bien, señor. ¿Usted?*'

'*Sí, bien.*'

We ran through the questions we had been asked before: name, address, nationality, education. He asked what property and belongings I owned.

'*Mi mochila, es todo.*'

I wanted to say things he could relate to, and everybody owned a rucksack in the jungle. Most people lived out of one. However, soon I was running out of things to say in Spanish. I called over to Tom for help. Trouble Ahead scolded me for this, as if to say no conferring. All I wanted to do was draw out the process as long as possible to frustrate him. I needed the language books to translate everything. Trouble Ahead relented, and Tom brought over my Spanish dictionary and phrasebook.

He asked what my father did.

'He works in a small shop.'

'He owns it?'

'No, *señor.*'

'What is the address?'

I gave him the address of a hairdresser in Chelmsford.

He asked about my brothers and sisters. I told him we all lived in the same house and didn't own a car. Then he wanted a friend to contact. I denied having been to university, in case it implied wealth. He cross-referenced the answers

181

to some of the ones we had given at previous interrogations. Any new questions, and I took liberties. His handwriting was good compared to the others. Yet how sophisticated was he?

'It's very dangerous here,' he observed. 'Why risk your life?'

'*Es bonito, aquí.*' It's beautiful here.

He looked perplexed.

I scrabbled through my Spanish phrasebook for more things to say. I ignored the 'First Encounters' section — we were past that stage. The 'Nationalities' section was useless in the circumstances. I stopped at a section dealing with 'Cultural Differences' and had a look at a few phrases. '*¿Esto es una costumbre local o nacional?*' said one. Is this a local or national custom? What? Kidnapping? I wasn't sure asking whether kidnapping was a local or national custom was politic in the circumstances. Eventually, I conjured a reply. I said the jungle was interesting and tourists had passed through here before, though it probably translated into something totally different.

Next, I turned to the 'Language Difficulties' section.

'*Perdone mi español. ¿Habla usted inglés?*'

He shook his head.

'Why don't you carry weapons?' he asked.

I referred to my dictionary. It was a slow process, and it irritated him.

'*¿Usted, CIA?*' he accused.

'*¿Qué, señor?*'

'CIA. *Inteligencia.*'

I really hadn't understood the first time

because of his accent, but now I knew what he was getting at. Still I feigned incomprehension.

'*¿Qué, señor?*' I said, hoping my eyes would not betray my fear. Trouble Ahead could accuse me of whatever he wanted; he was judge and jury.

I felt like saying 'I know naaathing', though I stopped myself.

I fobbed him off with whatever I could. I thought it didn't really matter what I said; I could always claim there had been a language misunderstanding at any point. I spent as long as possible scanning through my dictionary, looking confused and sighing. There was nothing he could do about it.

'*¿Cuanto vale? Plata.*'

'*¿Perdón?*'

He was asking how much I was worth. He pressurized me to put a figure on my value. We bartered like hawks in a market. Eventually I relented and said he might get a thousand dollars.

'No, *cinco millón*,' he declared.

He insisted it would come from England, I insisted it wouldn't. He laughed and loosely threatened me, saying that if no money came I would always be in the forest. He drew my attention to the three missionaries kidnapped in January 1993 by pointing to the relevant passage in Lonely Planet. I took this as a threat. I decided against asking what had happened to them.

Then he wanted me to write a letter to my parents. I didn't like the idea yet I had little choice. I wrote that I was fine, that the food was good, that I had cigarettes, and that the jungle was damp and it was difficult to keep things dry and clean. 'Look forward to seeing you soon,' I added hopefully at the bottom. Trouble Ahead briefly explained his plan to transfer the letter to an intermediary, and then to someone in England who would deliver it to my parents. It sounded simple, but it mightn't get through. He seemed nervous about it. He wanted nothing about him or the jungle to be mentioned in the letter.

The interview was at an end. He stood up and walked away with my letter. 'Bye, bye,' he said as he left, like a four-year-old boy on his way into playgroup. It was the only English he spoke throughout his whole visit.

Tom and I discussed what we'd said and what might happen next. It sounded as if Tom deserved an Oscar for his performance. Trouble Ahead probably didn't know what he was letting himself in for.

'They're going about this in a very strange way,' I observed to Tom. 'How come it's taken six weeks to get this far?'

We were both happy with the way we had dealt with Trouble Ahead. We even laughed at how our value had leapt by two million dollars in the space of a fortnight.

'If we stay here a year, we'll be worth hundreds of millions,' I said.

But later in the day Tom started to fret again.

'I'm worried,' he told me. 'I'm sure they'll find

out we've lied and that we haven't told them everything.'

I tried to calm him down, to tell him there was no way they would find out the truth. Tom was brave — he could easily have said to the guerrillas that he was willing to leave me to get the money, but he didn't break. That night, though, he couldn't sleep.

★　★　★

TOM: I felt down. Even though I hadn't made any mistakes during my interrogation, I had failed to achieve what I wanted: freedom. Even worse, it occurred to me that with the letters they might actually get something out of this whole saga. I hated, despised the idea that they might profit from this. 'This is it now,' I thought. 'The shit is really going to hit the fan when those letters get to England.' I assumed the letters would be handed to a middle man, taken to Yaviza or Pinogana, places we had passed on our way into the Darién, and mailed from there. I hoped my parents would note the defiance in my letter and refuse to pay.

Paul had been hilarious during his interrogation. Trouble Ahead had been speaking so slowly, as if to an idiot, yet Paul always replied with '¿Qué?' like Manuel from *Fawlty Towers*. Afterwards, though, when he told me the story, he was petrified, shaking visibly.

That night my mind relived the day's events. I was unable to sleep. At two I got up and spent some time making small talk with our guard,

185

who changed every hour. I drank milky coffee and waited for the sun to rise. Around dawn, Señor Dama wandered off and I decided to stoke the fire, throwing on it a pair of socks I knew belonged to neither Paul nor me and watching them turn into a fireball. This was not what I had in mind. Dama returned and looked perturbed by the size of the blaze. The Nutter then spent the whole morning searching for his only pair of socks, asking everyone if they had seen them. I felt guilty as hell. The Nutter had just come back from a five-day walk to collect food. When he'd removed his shoes on arriving at camp, I'd seen that his feet and ankles were almost entirely stripped of their skin; what little there was was cracked and flaking. A black welt ran around the top of his calf where the tops of his boots had rubbed against the skin. It looked hideously painful. Now I had torched the poor bugger's last pieces of protection. Even though he was the man who had captured us at gunpoint, I had no interest in seeing him suffer.

After Trouble Ahead's visit the mood around camp transformed from lacklustre to electric. The guerrillas were convinced that the boss's intervention meant the money would arrive soon. '¡Cinco millón!' they would say to each other in astonishment. 'Think of the things we could buy,' I overheard Space Cadet saying in an awed whisper. This is the last thing we wanted to hear. If they were getting so excited about receiving the money, what would they do when it didn't turn up? I went back to felling trees at

186

high speed, though Will Smith soon put an end to that.

'No more, Tomás!' he barked. 'You are trying to expose the camp to outsiders.'

I denied this accusation vehemently. 'I only want to let in more sunlight,' I said, pointing to the sky, which was true because the camp was dark, secluded from the sun and my orchids were suffering.

'I said no!'

The machete was confiscated.

Even Loose Teenager recovered her good humour, despite the death of two of her three bright green budgerigars. She'd been given them as presents by various suitors who had wandered in and out of camp. The *perricos* could not fly because their wings were clipped, so they either perched on branches around the camp or sat on the guerrillas' shoulders. They were worshipped, treated with the utmost respect. Paul and I hated them. When no-one was looking, we threw stones at them. That stopped the little bastards chirping.

We were inside our tent when the first one came to grief. There was a commotion, Loosey screamed, and we ran out to see Señor Dama fishing a soggy green budgie out of the evening's soup with a spatula. He put it on the ground where it went through its death throes. Then it stopped. Señor Dama picked up a nearby cooking pot, placed it over the bird and started to tap the top of it with his knuckles.

'What is he doing?'

Paul was as bewildered as I was. All the others

looked on as if this was an everyday occurrence.

'He'll live,' Señor Dama said to Loosey, who was in tears.

He lifted the pot and the bird was still very dead. He replaced the pot and repeated his ritual.

'These lot are crazy,' I said to Paul, and we went back inside the tent.

The next morning, the second budgie bought it. Again, Loosey began to scream hysterically. We rushed out of the tent to see her pointing down the river.

'What's wrong now, Tom?' Paul asked.

'She's saying the *perrico* has been washed away,' I said, suppressing a smirk, unsuccessfully. It had rained heavily in the night and the river was swollen.

Paul snorted. 'We'd better get back inside the tent,' he said, realizing the others might not find it as funny.

So only one bird was left. Loosey made such a fuss of it, rarely letting it out of her sight. In the spirit of friendship, I went to stroke it once and it pecked my finger. From that point on I wished it nothing but ill.

★　★　★

PAUL: The morning after Trouble Ahead left, I woke to a tumultuous noise. The guerrillas seemed excited by the progress of the meetings. Maybe they thought the situation would be resolved quickly and that some money would be arriving. My instinct told me otherwise: this was going to take a long time. I felt nervous; perhaps Tom and I were stretching our luck too far. They built their hopes up so much. When the whole plan failed they might take their anger out on us. I sat in silence, cogitating on what the grisly outcome would be, watching everyone chattering wildly, overflowing with optimism.

A large supply 'drop' was made that day — perhaps Trouble Ahead was rewarding them. Soap and toothpaste were distributed, much to the delight of everyone, including us. *Hojaldres*, savoury flat bread like naans, were prepared as a treat, along with chocolate, soup and stew with all sorts of flavourings. Tom and I helped them make a batch of *hojaldres*, though they poured scorn on our technique. We ate until our stomachs were almost distended.

The joyful air around camp persisted for a few days. Tom and I had promised to dance and sing for them at some point, and we couldn't put it off any longer. Loose Teenager wanted a reprise of 'Bright Side of Life', and we gave in. With an expectant camp gathered around our tent, we went inside and donned our shorts *à la* morris dancers. I toyed with the idea of shouting a rock-star-style 'Hello, Colombia!' except I wasn't sure we were in Colombia, and Colombia, if that was what it was, did not look too ready to rock.

'This is the national anthem of Great Britain,' Tom said in Spanish. Then he turned to me. 'I don't know the verses.'

'Don't worry,' I whispered, 'just join in the chorus.'

I started to sing.

Some things in life are bad,
They can really make you mad,
Other things just make you swear and
    curse;
When you're chewing on life's gristle
Don't grumble, give a whistle,
And this'll help things turn out for the best.
And . . .

I looked at Tom to give him his cue.

Always look on the bright side of life
De-doo, de-doo-de-doo-de-doo . . .

Neither of us could whistle so we sang the
'doo-de-doos' while kicking our legs in the air
and at the same time flinging our arms upwards;
right leg out and right arm up, then left leg out
and left arm up.

Always look on the bright side of life
De-doo, de-doo-de-doo-de-doo.

On the second round of the chorus we almost
achieved synchronization, though Tom was now
improvising by bringing his knees up to his chin.
We kept the dance going throughout the second
verse.

If life seems jolly rotten,
There's something you've forgotten!
And that's to laugh and smile and dance
    and sing.

I gave my hips a wiggle here.

When you're feeling in the dumps,
Don't be silly chumps!
Just purse your lips and whistle — that's
   the thing!
And . . . always look on the bright side of
   life . . .

'Come on, everybody!' I screamed.

Space Cadet was the first to respond, moving his hulking frame in a less nimble imitation of our limb-flinging dance. He tried to sing along, though the result was incomprehensible. Smithy was laughing loud and hard, his arms wrapped around his chest. Loose Teenager had tears rolling down her cheeks, and The Nutter was jumping up and down like a kid in a playground who needs a pee. Only Maria wasn't laughing. Her features were set in a look of utter astonishment.

Tom was wigging out, singing the chorus again and again. I cut in with the last verse. Smithy could contain himself no longer. He literally fell on the floor, rolling about laughing. At least three of the others were imitating us. The camp was in uproar. I finished the verse, sat down utterly exhausted and tried to catch my breath, but Tom kept going, kicking his legs like a can-can dancer on crack.

I sat watching everyone, amazed that this rollercoaster experience had veered so abruptly from the fear of Trouble Ahead's arrival to the lunacy of this moment. Was it only forty-eight hours earlier I had been discussing the value of my life?

Tom was still jumping around, gesticulating and chattering in Spanish. Then I noticed the last *perrico* perched in a small sapling nearby. It jumped down behind Tom. He stepped back. His heel rose and came down. I cried out as the scene unfolded in slow motion, but it was too late. The bird disappeared under Tom's boot. The camp stopped, Tom spun round and looked down. The final *perrico* gave a little splutter and died.

There were ten seconds of silence. Tom looked terrified. Everything seemed to hang in the balance. Suddenly, the whole camp exploded with laughter. Even Loosey joined in.

I'd landed myself in a madhouse.

9

MONKEY STEW

PAUL: We'd been at snake gully for three weeks when the order came for us to move. Before we set off, the guerrillas gave back our cameras and their cases. They were tired of carrying them — unsurprisingly given the size and weight of Tom's camera and tripod. Trouble Ahead had confiscated our films, though. Tom bemoaned the many pictures of flowers he'd lost.

He rooted through the camera bags.

'Holy crap!' he exclaimed.

'What?' I turned round, and saw Tom holding his compass, looking at it as if it was pure gold. 'Where did you find that?' I hissed.

'It was in my camera bag,' he said.

I snatched it out of his hand.

'I can't believe it,' I said. 'We can escape with this.'

Until now, the main barrier to any escape attempt had been the claustrophobic jungle. Without a compass we'd have got lost in seconds and been caught. But now, if we could work out where we were on the map, we could plan an escape and use the compass to follow the route.

'We need to hide it, Tom. We can't let them know we've got it.'

I slipped it into my pocket, hoping to snatch a

few surreptitious glances at it as we walked and try to fathom in which direction we were heading.

★　★　★

TOM: It was a tough day of walking down into the valley. We camped at a miserable boggy site where the rain poured persistently, soaking everything: the ground, our tent, our clothes. We spent three wretched days there doing little except watch the deluge batter the camp.

Bored, I felt the urge for some form of liberation. I knew there were locals around: you could see plumes of smoke from fires rising above the trees. On my way to bathe with Paul, I walked off along a deep highland river, intending to blame Loose Teenager if anyone asked where I was going. She had told me there was a fruit tree in an adjacent field that bore fruits that tasted like 'ice-cream'.

After negotiating an awkward bend in the river, I stumbled across a well-worn path and continued past three horses into 'real' open air. I could breathe deeply in this open, sunny field and imagine for a few wonderful moments that I was free. It was exhilarating. Then I traversed a small tributary of the main river before reaching a boggy path that stank of horse manure. I waded through the mud until the path widened and opened into another field. Suddenly, there were locals everywhere. Eyes bore down on me from behind trees and shrubs and from the field. Three men sat cross-legged on the ground, smoking and staring at me without saying a word, shocked at the sweaty, exhausted, curly-haired and pale-skinned apparition that stood in front of them panting like a dog. I noticed their rucksacks were identical to those used by the guerrillas, so I decided to get back quickly.

In my head I rehearsed my excuse in case I was questioned about where I'd been. I picked a ginger-type fruit from an herbaceous plant as evidence to support my story and returned to camp. Paul was having his bath. Loose Teenager gave me an angry look, but it was The Nutter who challenged me.

'Where have you been, Tomás?' he barked.

'She told me about a fruit tree, señor,' I replied, gesturing towards Loosey. 'It is very good.'

'He is lying,' said Maria.

'No, no,' I protested, playing the wide-eyed innocent. I held up the gingery fruit. 'Look, I collected this.'

That seemed to stall them for now, but word spread about my jaunt and soon it reached Will Smith. He strode across to our tent.

'Where have you been?' he demanded.

I repeated my excuse.

'Don't do it again!' he screamed. 'The locals are fierce men. They will kill you.'

He continued to rave and rant while I protested and apologized.

'If you do not obey me, Tomás, I will have to tie you up. Including your mouth!'

PAUL: Tom was fidgety as we walked down to the river, hidden from the camp by dense undergrowth, ahead of Space Cadet and The Nutter.

'I recognize this place, Paul,' he said nervously.

'So do I,' I replied. 'I think the area just beyond the camp was where we played cricket that time.'

Now the clearing was being cultivated by the locals, which explained why we were being guarded so closely. They did not want us to see them, or to be seen by them.

By the time we got down to the river, though, Spacey and The Nutter were some way behind us. Tom took this as an opportunity to race up the river to have a look. I left him to it.

'Where is Tomás?' asked Spacey when he arrived.

I just shrugged my shoulders and continued to wash in the fast-flowing river. The Nutter looked around but could see nothing. Then Spacey became more insistent. Again I just looked at him and shrugged my shoulders, feigning not to understand. He came closer and I played for time.

'*¿Qué, señor?*'

By now he was getting angry, so I swept an arm in the direction of upriver and The Nutter went to investigate. Spacey was still unhappy and continued to question me about where Tom had gone. The less I responded, the more aggressive he became. He hopped onto a large rock embedded in the river and stood above me while I washed. I continued to smile and shrug. In frustration he reached out to grab me, but I swayed gently back just out of reach and his hand missed me. I watched as he started to overbalance, flapping his arms in a vain attempt to stay upright, but his bulk was too heavy and, letting out a yelp, he fell into the river. He landed with a thud, his knees hitting the stony riverbed. As he did so he knocked our *vajillas*, or small bowls, the soap and some clothes off the rock and into the river, and with these items he swept downstream in an octopus tangle of arms and legs. His head scrabbled to the surface every now and then for air before disappearing below the surface. Eventually he stopped himself some thirty yards away and clambered out of the water like a bedraggled muppet.

I started to laugh; fortunately he was too busy trying to find all the things that had fallen into the river to see me. I soon stopped when he started to make his way back up the river with a determined look on his face. Fortunately Tom had returned by this time. I began to explain what had just happened while trying to control my laughter. Spacey came back distracted by the loss of various items, especially both *vajillas*. They were valuable pieces of equipment and difficult to get hold of.

When Señor Dama found out later that day, he wasn't best pleased.

★　★　★

197

TOM: The next day, Will Smith gave Paul a brand-new radio and deputed to him the task of getting it working. He must have impressed him with the way he had found the World Service on Loosey's shortwave transistor radio. 'Whatever you do, don't give it to the idiot who loves flowers,' must have been their reasoning. 'Give it to the guy who works in a bank.'

'It's for the boss,' Smith explained. Presumably he meant Trouble Ahead.

'Where did you get it from?' I asked, marvelling at its size.

'Friends,' he said nonchalantly.

Generous ones, apparently: among the packaging was a receipt for $459. With it was a card for an electrical shop in Panama City and instructions with a section in English which Paul fished out while I unpacked the box. Trying not to look too competent, on the basis that they might suspect we were technological geniuses who worked for a multinational, and therefore very rich, electrical firm, we made sure we looked at every button on the radio as if we had never seen their like before.

While scouring through the packaging to find batteries I came across a booklet with a blank grey cover. I opened it up. On the facing page were the words *Fuerzas Armadas Revoluciónarias de Colombia*. I flicked on to the next page and saw a list of contents. 'How to be a Member' read one chapter heading.

'Paul,' I whispered, 'it's a FARC manual.'

He leaned over and had a look.

'Jesus,' he said, 'what is it? Some sort of guide?'

'Seems to be.'

'Does it say anything about hostages?' he asked.

I searched through the list of contents. Unable to see anything connected to kidnapping or hostages, I turned to the index at the back and found the words *secuestros por los extranjeros*, or the kidnapping of foreigners. Scrabbling through the booklet, I found the corresponding page, though by now Smith had spotted us.

'What have you got there?' he demanded, walking over to us.

I tried to read hurriedly but could make nothing of it.

'Give it to me,' he added, and snatched it out of my hands. He looked at it, put it in his pocket and walked off without saying a word.

'That proves it,' Paul said. 'They're FARC.'

The more we thought about it, however, the less certain we were. The manual could have been included in the packaging by mistake. Mere possession wasn't incontrovertible proof they were members of FARC. Surely a revolutionary army such as FARC would be more efficient than these poltroons? They could be a bandit group; they could have stolen the radio from FARC. Will Smith seemed indifferent when he saw we'd been reading the pamphlet. Did that mean anything? All these doubts played on our minds. However, it was probable that our captors were an offshoot of FARC. From that point on we decided never to mention the word FARC in front of them again to avoid arousing their suspicions. The guerrillas often became suspicious if they heard us whispering to each other. Once, The Nutter had stormed over to us and demanded we tell him what we'd been saying.

'We were talking about the beautiful forest and how much we love it here,' I replied.

'*Sí, señor*,' Paul confirmed, grinning and nodding like an idiot. '*Bueno.*'

The Nutter had cursed and gone back to the others.

Faced with any hostility from now on, we resolved to remain as placid, calm and polite as possible. We made up a few codewords. Instead of 'dollars', we said 'dough'; in place of FARC we substituted the word 'cabbages'; paramilitaries, whose name in both Spanish and English was similar, became 'peanuts'.

'What do you reckon, Tom? Do you think this lot are cabbages or peanuts?' Paul asked that evening, his left eye winking wildly.

'They could just be pricks,' I replied.

On the fourth morning we were having breakfast when there was movement in the camp. Will Smith was deep in discussion with the others. Suddenly, what had been a quiet breakfast scene became frantic and chaotic. The fire was snuffed out, bivouacs were dismantled, and everyone was running to and fro packing their belongings. The Nutter came down to our camp, picked up our pot and threw the contents in the bushes.

'You are moving. Now!'

He looked maniacal. When we were slow to move, he started stuffing our clothes and belongings into our rucksacks while the others took down our tent.

'What's wrong, *señor?*' I asked.

'*Paramilitarias,*' he said, wide-eyed and breathless, and continued to ram our stuff into our rucksacks.

In the mêlée my mind turned to the orchids I had salvaged from Cloudy Base. I went to save them, but the nursery I had been in the process of constructing was gone and my orchids lay scattered on the floor, trodden on and broken. I tried to pick them up, but this prompted a volley of abuse from The Nutter.

'Orchids require careful packing, *señor,*' I remonstrated.

'We're going!' he screamed at us. '¡*Majorda!*'

I asked Smith what was going on.

'*Hay personas que quieren encontrarnos para venganza,*' he said in a panicked voice, waving his arms around the camp. Some people were looking to avenge something or other. 'One of my *compadres* is missing,' he added, though who it was and when it had happened wasn't clear.

The guerrillas searched everywhere, including the bushes, to make sure we had left no evidence of our existence. In less than half an hour the camp had gone from being fully operational to non-existent. Once packed, we were shoved into the forest and told to walk quickly.

'Move!' they shouted.

We set off at running pace, though we kept stopping. Whenever we did, Paul and I were ushered into the undergrowth and told to stay out of sight. When the all clear was given, we would emerge and the pace would increase. Often we would veer off the path and smash our way through the jungle. We spent an hour doing this, then the guard in front stopped and we all bumped into one another, like human dominoes. Smithy turned round, his index finger on his lips. I turned and repeated the action to Paul, who did it to The Nutter behind him. The Nutter turned round, finger on lips, to quieten the guard behind him, then he realized it was Space Cadet. No-one dared tell him to shut up, so The Nutter thought better of it. When Smith decided the threat had gone, we moved stealthily on.

The palpable fear among the guerrillas transmitted itself to me and Paul; I couldn't decide whether my heart was beating against the walls of my chest out of dread or exertion. Our inactivity and lack of exercise at Snake Gully had left me unfit, so moving at such a speed was a real trial. Paul handled it better. He was always ahead of me during frantic journeys like this, his wiry frame more adept at struggling up hills and through forest, despite the disastrous state of his boots.

We camped at a place we called Dank Dell II owing to the murky, damp gloom that hung around what was nothing more than a big muddy ditch. Space Cadet, who was the easiest for me to interpret because he spoke so slowly, started to ask the others about the day's events.

'Why did we leave so quickly?' he asked everyone.

'Paramilitaries were looking for Tomás and Pablo,' he was told.

The rain pissed down constantly and the guerrillas once again used the area at the back of our tent as a toilet, so it stank. People sauntered in and out of camp, guards we hadn't seen before. They would look at us and joke about 'inspecting the merchandise'. The mood around camp was still good, but as time passed at Dank Dell II frustrations surfaced. Loosey and Maria spent a few days snapping at each other, arguing over the cooking and other petty matters. There was little love lost between them. Then, one afternoon, it developed into a fully fledged catfight. Both of them started by screaming their heads off, abusing each other at the tops of their voices. Loosey made a grab for Maria's hair and it came undone, unravelling to below her backside.

'Come on, ladies!' Space Cadet said, urging them on.

Maria fought back by grabbing Loosey's hair and soon they were yanking away viciously, turning around in a circle, heads bowed as each held the other's hair in a relentless grip. Earrings and gold chains lay scattered across the ground. Both of them were crying now as well as screaming.

'Stop it now, ladies,' Space Cadet said, worried that things were getting out of control.

Eventually, they broke apart. Loose Teenager was bawling her eyes out. 'My mum is dead,' she kept repeating.

I hated the camp. We were in the lowlands and the mosquitoes were on voracious form, flying devils that swarmed at dusk, feasting on any exposed area of skin. We had to keep the tent sealed at all times to keep them out, and when I developed terrible diarrhoea and worms started to appear in my faeces, the ambience of our tent was not what you would describe as pleasant. When I needed the loo at night I would ask to borrow a torch from the guard, but he would always refuse, so I would have to go off in the dark and would often end up stepping in excrement, belonging either to me or someone else, trailing it back into the tent. The rain never relented and I was banned from going exploring and orchid hunting, instead confined to our stinking tent.

One lunchtime, sat around the fire, I blew my nose and instantly felt diarrhoea running down my leg. It came out the bottom of my trousers. Space Cadet spotted what had happened and announced it with great amusement to the camp. Fucker. They all came over to have a laugh at the tourist, at first refusing to believe Space Cadet but then bursting into fits of laughter when they saw the evidence. They were incapable of believing something unless they had seen it with their own eyes, which did not bode well for our continuing attempts to convince them we were penniless backpackers. Loose Teenager, Perty, The Nutter, all of them revelled in my humiliation. Apart from Will Smith. He brought me some dysentery tablets.

★ ★ ★

PAUL: We moped around waiting for further information, the days broken only by endless games of chess and the regular meal and bathing times. My birthday on 18 May was fast approaching. It seemed it was going to be a sombre one. There was little to do but wait, play chess and hope that a supply drop came soon.

New personnel appeared and came over to have a look at us. They appeared friendly, and it soon became obvious that another camp had been established a little further down the valley. I decided it wasn't worth telling them that it was my birthday. I hadn't noticed them making much mention of their own birthdays to one another. Maybe it was something to which they attached little importance, unlike the Western world where we have the time and luxury to celebrate such dates. For Tom's birthday at Cloudy Base they'd brought pieces of chocolate which they'd made into a drink, but even then I hadn't had the impression that they fully understood the meaning of the day.

Much to my surprise, we received a supply drop: soap, toothpaste, tins of food, salt, sugar and other basic foods appeared. Most important of all, there was a pack of Marlboro cigarettes. They were the most precious part of the cargo, and I was delighted to get some real cigarettes rather than the local ones that stripped your throat. It was just what I needed on my birthday; at that moment, other than freedom, I couldn't think of a better gift. I lit one immediately and savoured the moment, then asked Tom if he wanted one. He said yes.

'It's my second cigarette ever, Paul.'

'Really?'

'Yeah. I had a clove cigarette in Indonesia.'

I held up a match for him to light his fag.

'And I've been drunk four times.'

He obviously had a thing for counting vices. He stopped talking and took a drag. Immediately, he went silent. I continued to enjoy my cigarette.

'I feel strange, Paul.'

He was swaying slightly on his feet, his face was white and his eyes were 'gone'. I thought he was going to fall over, and he squatted next to me to steady himself. I finished the cigarette for him.

After this, packets of cigarettes appeared much more regularly, almost as if there was a corner store somewhere. All sorts appeared: local ones, Western ones, even some filtered menthol ones. Tom got more used to them, and continued to keep a note of the number he had smoked in his life. I hoped he would soon get the opportunity to get drunk a fifth time.

★ ★ ★

TOM: When the time came to leave Dank Dell II after nearly a week of filth and squalor, I was overjoyed. It was a hard trek to the next site, though a beautiful one, too, through luscious forests and past cascading waterfalls. We camped beside a stream from which it was possible to drink. We spent almost two weeks there. Every day the guerrillas' radio blared out their favourite station, *Apartado Estereo*. I tried to occupy myself translating the lyrics of popular love songs: *Estoy enamorando de ti . . . estoy enamorando lo sé* — 'I'm falling in love with you, I'm falling in love I know it' — and *Yo no soy, yo no soy, el hombre aquel* — 'I'm not, I'm not, the man that . . . '

My mind drifted back to England; it was about the time the Chelsea Flower Show would be starting, and spring would be in full voice. The thought made me homesick. There was no better time to be in England; I could almost smell freshly cut grass, the fragrant lilac blooms and my eucalyptus trees. To console myself, I would go down to the stream and sit and draw in my exercise book, which I also used as a diary, conjuring up wildly elaborate designs for an arboretum in my garden.

The conversation around camp occasionally made me sick with excitement. Every now and then someone grumbled to Smith about the length of time it was taking for the money to arrive.

'It happens now,' he would maintain. 'They pay this minute.'

This would send a buzz around the camp. Every time I overheard, I reported straight back to Paul.

'Smith says our parents are paying this minute,' I said.

'Bollocks,' Paul replied. 'And where the hell would our parents get five million from anyway?'

Paul's theory was backed up when I asked to check our belongings and discovered they still had our passports and driving licences.

'They need to hand those over to prove they have us,' Paul pointed out. 'The letter won't be enough on its own.'

Despite Paul's scepticism, I had faith in Trouble Ahead's determination and couldn't prevent myself from getting carried away by the promise of our ordeal ending soon and my being able to go home to see my family, and to visit the Hampton Court Flower Show. While I didn't want them to get the money, sometimes I would weaken at the prospect of getting home, whatever the price. My mood fluctuated almost daily. There were times I wanted them to get nothing whatsoever; but if it was the case that negotiations were taking place, that money would change hands, then I couldn't stop my excitement at leaving from outweighing my disappointment that the guerrillas had got what they wanted.

Nothing happened. Guerrillas continued to wander in and out of the camp, most of them new faces. One of the guests proved skilful at catching animals in traps he constructed himself. He was a light-skinned man, tall and wiry, with a long, pockmarked face, sunken eyes and prominent cheekbones. There was something of the animal about him. Among his catch were deer and a gua-gua, a small spotted pig, which he skinned and gutted with relish at our camp. He slowly blended into the camp, assuming control. I asked Maria who he was. 'My brother,' she replied. Paul named him Trapper. Will Smith gradually became diffident and distant, less preoccupied with the thought of the money arriving any day.

From our experience so far, all two months of it, we sensed that a change of personnel was in the offing. One night there was much talk around camp of people leaving, once again generating immense excitement within me. Could this be the end? I smoked two of the guerrillas' menthol cigarettes to calm my nerves. I'd now smoked four cigarettes in my life. I felt like a chain smoker.

Then, out of the blue came the story-telling *comandante* from Dank Dell I whom Paul had named Jackanory. He strode into the camp, jaunty as ever.

'Send in the clowns,' I said to Paul.

'I knew we hadn't seen the last of that idiot,' Paul replied.

We greeted him warmly.

'*¿Cómo le va?*' he said, shaking our hands vigorously.

'Where have you been all this time, *señor?*'

'Walking in the woods,' he said.

We could see he was proud that we remembered him. He puffed out his chest and swaggered around the camp as if it conferred added status upon him.

Trapper's animal slaughter continued. One evening we were brought a meat dish for dinner. Most of the time the unfortunate creature was skinned, disembowelled and sliced and diced in front of the whole camp — the gua-gua's eyes were even hung in a skin sack filled with liquid above the fire for some strange reason — but that night the butchery had taken place offstage, away from camp.

'What is this?' Paul said, peering into his bowl suspiciously, sniffing hesitantly.

'I don't know,' I said, my mouth full.

'It's a bit chewy.'

'Tastes good, though.'

'There's black hair in it,' he said.

I carried on eating. Then, between his index finger and thumb, Paul pulled from his stew a small thin piece of grey rubbery flesh.

'This looks like a finger,' he said.

I agreed that it looked like a finger.

'It's a fucking monkey,' he said, disgust spray-painted across his face. He put his bowl down quickly.

'What's this?' I said to The Nutter, pointing at my stew.

'*Pavo* bird,' he replied.

'A special type of cow,' said Space Cadet.

'It's a fucking monkey,' was all Paul kept repeating.

After dinner, as I brushed my teeth, I asked one of the new guerrillas what the evening meal had been. He pointed upriver and performed a monkey impression. I decided against passing this information on to Paul.

★　★　★

PAUL: When we met Trouble Ahead we'd been promised Wellington boots. The guerrillas had even asked us for our shoe size. I knew they were standard Colombian jungle footwear and that if this ordeal was to last any length of time we would need them, but I didn't believe for one minute they would actually materialize. My desert boots were almost finished: both heels had gaping holes in them, the perpetual damp was rotting them and the soles afforded little grip in the wet, muddy conditions. So when Señor Dama appeared in camp with a large supply drop, including boots, I was delighted. I stared at them covetously while waiting for them to be distributed. The group examined several pairs, for the continuous walking had taken its toll on everybody's footwear.

Finally, I was given a pair. I tried them on and they felt good. However, before I could really test them out and revel in dry feet and good grip, Perty came across. He was unhappy with his size, so I swapped with him. Now that he was happy, I tested my pair gently in the mud, then I stamped around heavily, sending splashes of mud in all directions. Then I did a dance of delight. The guerrillas looked on as though I was mad. I ran down to the river and jumped into it, splashing around in the water. I was incredibly happy, like a three-year-old cavorting in puddles. Happiness is dry feet. I continued to play with my new present for another half an hour, walking around camp and to the river, stepping confidently down its steep and slippery bank, then back to the tent through the mud. The boots were the best and most useful gift I'd received in years.

But they presented us with a dilemma. Tom had got a pair too, but he still had $120 stashed in his leather boots. It was a useful hiding place, and the money would be essential when we landed back in the real world. A month or so back, Tom had thought long and hard about telling the guerrillas about the cash, worrying that if they found out then the consequences could be fatal. I argued we had to keep it for the future. Yet now we had new boots they might become suspicious if Tom kept his old, knackered leather pair. In the end, we kept everything, claiming that the leather boots would be needed when we got back to England. Tom tied them to his rucksack and made sure not to let them out of his sight.

★　★　★

TOM: One afternoon, after señor Dama had cut Paul's wildly overgrown hair with a blunt pair of rusty scissors — and made quite a good job of it, truth be told — Will Smith approached us.

'Can I have your rucksack, Tomás? As a present?'

'No,' I said. 'I need it, señor.'

'But you're going home, Tomás.'

What on earth could he mean? I knew not to let my hopes rise.

'But I am still here now,' I replied.

He shrugged, handed a tin of food to each of us and shook our hands.

'I am leaving,' he informed us, and with that he walked out of camp alone.

Part of me was sorry to see him leave. Under his charge the atmosphere had been bearable, and there had even been moments of laughter. He left Maria behind. She simply vanished over the next day or two, to where we didn't know. The Nutter — the man who had captured us, who had spoken so longingly of getting his money — left too, with only the smelly, stripy bag I had bought in Bangkok to show for all his hard work. When I gave it to him he looked delighted; he wore it over his shoulder in the self-conscious way a debutante wears a new Prada handbag. Space Cadet completed the exodus that afternoon — to Paul's mild disappointment. Now there was no-one to play chess with.

Jackanory was left in charge, bursting with pride. A couple more guerrillas came into the camp, albeit temporarily. One young guerrilla we'd never seen before peered through the door of our tent one afternoon as we napped.

'¿Qué?' he said, turning his hand in a clockwise motion, as if to say, 'Anything I can do?'

'¿Qué?' I replied.

'I'm twenty-two years old,' he replied, enigmatically.

Paul then had the idea that we might get him to get rid of a wasp nest in my rucksack which had been bugging us for days, and had prevented me from going anywhere near it. I passed on the request to him, and he agreed eagerly. We showed him where the rucksack was, and he examined the cone-shaped nest in the top and stroked his chin. He then asked for a bin liner from our packs, which he placed over his upper body and head. No holes cut for his eyes, just his arms sticking out the bottom. He stumbled over blindly and managed to lift the rucksack off the log it was sat on, but the strap caught on a branch. The wasps were alert to the danger. They left their nest and made straight for the young guerrilla. He flapped his arms around his waist to fend them off, staggering and spinning round and round, getting further tangled up in the bin liner. He looked like an incompetent ghost fluffing a haunting.

'Who *is* this guy?' said Paul, shaking his head.

He managed, eventually, to get the rucksack onto another log, took off the liner and started to count the stings. His stomach was worst affected.

'The wasps will go now,' he said, indicating the rucksack, though he did not say why.

We were sceptical. Sure enough, though, the wasps dispersed over the next few hours. Perhaps it was the thought of another bloke in a bin liner that made them seek sanctuary elsewhere.

Loosey, Perty and Señor Dama were still with us; Jackanory was in overall charge, though Trapper increasingly took most decisions, despite the fact that he never slept in the camp. It emerged that Jackanory was only with us due to injury. I overheard people speaking about him. 'He is with us to rest,' Señor Dama told Perty. 'He's not well.' Two other guards made up the camp. One of them was female, an expert at fishing, with very hairy armpits. 'Nena', Paul named her.

'Why do you call her that?' I asked him.

'After the German pop star.'

214

I had no idea who he was talking about.

'You know. She sang 'Ninety-nine Red Balloons'. It was number one for ages in the eighties.'

He hummed the tune.

'Never heard of it. Did the singer look like her?' I said, pointing at the new guard.

'Not facially,' Paul said.

'Oh.' I was baffled.

'Nena went on *Top of the Pops* once and she had these really hairy armpits.'

'Right.'

The name stuck.

On 1 June we left and endured one of the hardest days of walking yet. Señor Dama and Perty were sent a few days in advance to set up camp, or so we assumed. It was obvious we were being taken somewhere the guerrillas thought we could not be followed. Rather than walk on land and leave a trail, we were forced to wade along a river. The going was slow and ponderous; sometimes the water was up to our waists, at other times it rose to our chests. They were unhappy with the speed of our progress. 'Faster, faster,' they shouted, and pushed me in the back.

'I know you can walk faster!' Trapper shouted.

There was no sense whatsoever that he liked us, or that he saw us as anything other than walking dollar bills. He never played cards with us like Smith used to. The only time he acknowledged us was to insult or abuse us. The night before, as we sat eating, he had leered at us.

'You and Pablo have sex tonight,' he said,

215

laughing, accompanying his words with crude hand gestures.

'Señor, Pablo and I have sex every night,' I replied as seriously as I could.

His face froze. His eyebrows lifted so high they almost disappeared under his hairline. Then I laughed, and he smiled, uncertainly. I could see he wasn't sure whether I was joking or not.

10

DEEP HEAT

PAUL: We clambered through the steep, suffocating jungle from our holding camp to a ridge, guided by Sparky, the guard who'd arrived with Nena and who'd fixed the radio when it broke. On finding the ridge we came across a path and walked briskly along it escorted by Nena, Jackanory and Loose Teenager. The Wellington boots proved to be perfect footwear. The muddy track was easily negotiated and I revelled in my newfound grip and the novelty of dry feet. After a few hours we descended into a valley and stopped on the path before the order came through to move again, once the guerrilla scouts had given the all clear. We came out to a clearing — the site of our capture some two and a half months earlier.

Looking at it now, it was clearly a point of vulnerability, the perfect ambush point. The burned-out village of Payita is the spaghetti junction of the Darién; paths from all directions converged on this point. It was easy to bump into people. The other side of the river was open and the path we had walked down could be seen while the onlooker could remain hidden. They had seen us before we'd seen them.

Tom looked around carefully, scouring the

landscape for the point where we'd been forced to kneel, guns pointed at us. On our walks he'd already discovered that the plots he'd thought were graves were actually jungle beds, hollowed-out trunks of banana trees filled with weeds and plants on which weary travellers, villagers and armed fanatics could lay their weary heads.

But Trapper urged us on. We raced along the right-hand side of the river and waded across it. Brief flashes of sunlight and fresh air invigorated me, and then we were back in the forest. Trapper was in no mood to hang around. Even when we stopped for a brief rest and some lunch at a river bend an hour later, he soon broke it up and chivvied everybody along.

Trapper had first appeared a couple of weeks before. My first impression was of an unassuming guerrilla interested only in capturing game for food, but now he'd turned into an irascible martinet. Throughout the walk he barked orders at us to move faster as we fought our way upriver. We spent two hours wading through waist-deep water, presumably to avoid leaving footprints for any interested party to follow.

We travelled east along a ridge and south up the river. I grabbed every opportunity to sneak a look at the compass bearings as we clambered over logs and twisted around trees, usually when the line of guards was stretched out and no-one could see my hand slip stealthily into a hidden pocket in my pack. At times I lost myself in the thrill of the expedition: it was a true *Boy's Own* adventure.

A giant *Morpha* butterfly criss-crossed our

path as we waded. We'd seen this species before. Both Tom and I liked to imagine it was the same one, that it was watching over us. It was a bright metallic blue. We'd first seen it at Cloudy Base and it had become our lucky emblem. As long as we kept seeing it, we believed everything would turn out all right.

We were ordered to wash when we reached some rapids. This was an unusual order: we never stopped to bathe during a hike. Something must be up. Nena and Loosey guarded us. It started to rain heavily, and we became nervous. Were they going to split us up? They'd talked about each of us having his own sleeping place, though what that would involve was a mystery. We wanted to stay together, aware of how much we were absorbing strength from each other. When we finished washing they escorted us from the river up a steep bank to a ready-made camp.

There was a grand air to this site in comparison to the others. The advance party had built a large rectangular hut of thick palm walls and a steeply sloping roof for us. Smaller bivouacs for the guards surrounded the hut. Two narrow doorways at either end of the hut led into two rooms, created by a wooden partition in the middle of the floor. Along the back of the hut hung a military poncho, curtaining off the view. I was led to a room at the western end. It was about eight feet by eight feet, its only feature a raised wooden bed constructed from branches. A thin layer of palms scattered over the bed provided meagre comfort, and what little light penetrated the jungle canopy was lost here. A few dim rays fought their way in through the open gable, but that was all. There was an unsettling feeling of permanence about the place.

A new guerrilla — who looked like Che Guevara, so I named him Lost Cause — came to see if I liked my new home.

'*Bien, bien, señor,*' I said with an exaggerated grin, even though I hated the look of it.

I asked him for a cigarette. He grunted and muttered a few swear words, but gave me a fag anyway. I smoked it in the dry hut. It might have been dark and claustrophobic, but at least it was dry.

As soon as he was gone, I clambered up onto my bed and looked through the open gable to the rear of our hut. There was another hut, identical to ours, about thirty yards away.

'Have you seen this, Tom?' I whispered through the reed wall that separated us.

In the other room, Tom climbed onto his bed but he couldn't see it.

'There's a hut like ours. Who do you think's in there?'

'They might have captured someone else.'

We were confined to our rooms in the hut for most of the day, something we weren't used to. When Smithy was in charge we were often allowed to wander around, or to sit outside the tent at the very least, but the regime had changed. Guards watched us all the time, constantly interrupting our sleep during the night by shining their torches into our faces. To baffle them, Tom performed a sort of human slide show. Whenever they shined the torch on his body he struck a ludicrous pose, perhaps with his legs curled in the air, or his arms crossed in front of him, pointing in separate directions. When they came back half an hour later or so, he would contort his body into another bizarre position. '¡Qué mierda!' I would hear them say. When they left we would laugh, me stuffing a T-shirt into my mouth to muffle the noise. Tom would always find a new pose to flummox them with the next time.

The only times we were allowed out of our hut were to wash and for an hour or so each morning to stretch our legs in the light. It was so gloomy on my side of the hut that reading was impossible, but then I only had the guidebook and by now I was an expert on South America. I didn't feel the need to increase my knowledge of Spanish. Lost Cause then started to build doors to hang at either end of the hut, and once he'd attached them it was even darker, little difference between night and day. Again to frustrate them, when we got the chance we'd cut the vines used to attach the doors. Lost Cause was endlessly repairing his handiwork.

'How did this happen?' he would ask Tom, the door lurching on its hinges.

'I don't know, señor. The wind?'

Frustration spread through the camp like disease. The guerrillas whipped themselves into a frenzy, believing the money would be paid tomorrow, always tomorrow. They talked about it obsessively, and it worried me. Scarface, a chubby new recruit with a fresh scar on his cheek, would come into both our rooms and shake his rifle, then mime cocking it and point it at us, trying to scare us. One of the other new guerrillas, Beanstalk, because he was tall and gangly, wanted to kill us there and then. Jackanory also loved to wave his rifle around while telling us one of his stories as we bathed. I hated it, mainly because I could see that the safety catch was off.

'If no money arrives,' he would say, 'the boss will kill you.'

'No money will arrive, señor,' I would tell him. 'You can have the traveller's cheques, though.'

I always hoped that I sounded more robust than I felt, which was truly terrified.

One day I was sure I heard Trapper fiddling about with a gun, threatening to shoot us. The whole thing was confusing the hell out of them. 'Why hasn't the money come?' was the question that ricocheted around the camp daily. 'If it doesn't come, can we kill them?' I heard another voice ask.

One day Tom told me that he'd overheard Jackanory telling the others that he had seen the money.

'He reckons he saw thirty-five million dollars, in a helicopter or something,' Tom said.

'And they believed him?'

'They seemed to. He said, 'It comes soon.' '

'When the fuck are they going to realize there is no money?' I said.

'And what happens when they realize that?' Tom said pointedly.

I said nothing. We were both aware of what

might happen and it was too awful to contemplate.

The first week rolled by and the camp began to expand. An earth oven was built, the foliage cleared and raised wooden walkways constructed because, as had happened at every camp so far, the ground had become a quagmire due to the rain and the daily traffic of guerrillas. Tom nicknamed it the 'Lost City', after Ciudad Perdida, an ancient city in the mountains close to Santa Marta and one of the largest pre-Colombian towns discovered in the Americas.

At mealtimes we counted the number of bowls filled with food. There were always two extra ones taken out to the other hut at the back of the camp. Tom and I discussed the possibilities. Had the people there been kidnapped too, or were they ill and being treated? Could they be civilians? Maybe gringos! Might they be soldiers of the Colombian military? We were kept apart, but I imagined they were in the same predicament. I called them the 'Bedfellows'.

★　★　★

TOM: The camp had a different atmosphere to any of the others, far less tolerant and more restrictive. The mood was determined by Trapper's personality, which was harsh and aggressive. Even Loosey and Señor Dama, who had watched over us in friendlier times, became hostile and cold. Perty was like that already so it was less noticeable with him. It was as if each

223

guerrilla were an empty emotional vessel waiting to be filled. Under Will Smith — dear old Smithy, as I thought of him, current circumstances giving him a rose-tinted glow — everyone had been laid back and tolerant. Then Trapper came along and filled them with disdain, hatred even. There would be no card playing, no draughts; the partition dividing us meant I was unable to play against Paul.

I resorted to endless games of patience, or spent hours designing plans to glass over the herb garden at Lullingstone. I filled days dreaming about my ideal garden. Each day it became more vivid in my mind, more detailed and crammed with every plant I had ever loved. Firstly, having a specialist nursery that focused on woody plants from temperate climates around the world was the optimum set-up. I appreciate the need for diversification in this increasingly competitive age — gnomes, water features and bedding plants, for example — but I wanted as little as possible of these in my dream garden. What I wanted was a stock of horticulturally endowed plants with big leaves, pungent smells and colourful flowers that could be seen in their mature state at Lullingstone, so if an interested customer wished to know what a certain plant would look like when mature, he or she could tour around my garden and see. The desire to purchase would then be irresistible.

I became more ambitious, a man with a mission. I decided the garden should contain exotic plantings, too, including some seldom seen in cultivation in Britain: *Agave americana;*

Rafflesia, the world's largest flower; an avenue of jacarandas; *Puya raimondii*, the world's tallest inflorescence; the Amazonian lily, the largest lilypad in the world (you can stand on it!); the durian fruit, which is banned from hotels in Singapore because of its smell; *Amorphophallus titanum*, the largest inflorescence of any herbaceous plant on the planet (and the smelliest — the stench makes your eyes water); and finally, the prehistoric-looking monster *Welwitschia mirabilis* from Namibia and Angola. And that was just for starters.

Naturally, it would have to be opened by a member of the royal family, preferably Prince Charles. It must contain a good percentage of the 422,000 known species of flowering plants, and it must also be a living plant heritage, containing many NCCPG (National Council for the Conservation of Plants and Gardens) collections of significant botanical interest that were well representative of plant families. There must be jaw-dropping herbaceous borders and a diverse arboretum, including specimens especially grown from seeds collected in Tasmania for the RHS and Kent Gardens Scheme. A structural asset in this sensually diverse garden would be a large glasshouse of some kind, perhaps a decorative Victorian-style greenhouse. This would increase the range of plants displayed, especially in the orchid department, an area that in my garden had to be the envy of any nursery in the world.

I estimated it would cost millions of pounds to do it, but in my imagination money was no object. I planned every species of tree I would plant, and where each would go. I wanted the general public to flock to look at this garden, to gaze at it in wonder, for everyone who saw it to become filled with the horticultural passion that possessed me. In my mind it inspired awe across the world and made the Lost Gardens of Heligan look like a cabbage patch in comparison. I even thought about whether or not to accept credit cards from the punters. These thoughts and plans occupied me throughout most of June.

Gardening had to be done in my imagination: opportunities for plant husbandry at Lost City were nil. I did try to grow an avocado stone using tent pegs, and some eucalyptus seeds from Australia I found in my waterproof, but Perty sabotaged the avocado and the seeds failed to germinate.

Paul and I were allowed to communicate only by whisper. If our voices rose above that level then Trapper would yell for us to shut up. I got the longest straw at Lost City: my room got more sun than Paul's. At first I slept under the tent to protect myself from mosquitoes, and Paul had the net. Every three days we swapped. I eavesdropped on conversations around the camp, able to understand more as my Spanish improved. For entertainment, I relayed news from around the camp to Paul.

For the first week at Lost City the talk was always of the money arriving 'tomorrow'. This would be accompanied by ecstatic chatter, laughing, whoops of joy and riotous games of dominoes. The next morning the cash would still be elusive. 'Let's kill them now,' Beanstalk would say, his murderous thoughts halted by a voice, often Jackanory's, saying, 'It comes tomorrow,' and the cycle would begin once more. They were like goldfish in a bowl. While talk of killing us never sounded serious, it was hard to ignore. However, I found that my fear of death was subsiding. It seemed less terrifying than it had done in those raw first weeks of captivity. Far worse to contemplate was these idiots getting their cash, particularly if it meant my family losing the home that had been theirs for centuries. 'Don't pay, Dad,' I would say to myself.

Helpless and confined to our hut, we started to take small steps to inconvenience our kidnappers. We instigated a 'soap war'. It was all part of a plan: drain the guerrillas of as many resources as possible so that the burden of keeping us became too great. Soap was a valued commodity, given their commitment to cleanliness, so every time we went for a wash we would continually rub away at the soap. We washed so much that our skin was in danger of coming off. Paul would lather himself up with half a bar until he was completely white, like a ghost, covered head to foot in suds. When the bar became smaller we would pretend that it had slipped out of our hands. 'Whoops,' Paul would say as it floated downstream.

This did not go unnoticed. Every night the guerrillas sat around and aired their grievances in what I guessed was supposed to be a democratic forum.

'The soap is very low,' one voice would say.

'The tourists use it all,' another would reply.

Harrumphs all round. Growls of complaint. Forced to take notice, Trapper would promise to investigate.

'Where's the fucking soap gone?' Trapper would ask the next morning.

'¿Qué?' Paul would respond, his face as innocent as a child.

'The soap, Pablo. Where is it going?'

'Sí señor,' Paul would say, smiling and nodding.

A non sequitur always incensed Trapper. '¡Majorda!' he would shout before storming off.

Jackanory watched over us as we bathed. It was his job to ensure we stayed clean. Once he asked me what 'Let's have a shower' was in English.

'I am a cock,' I said slowly.

For a good ten minutes he tried to emulate what I had said until he got it just about right. The next morning he bounded into the hut, a huge smile across his face.

'I am a cock, Tomás,' he said, loudly and proudly.

'Sí, señor,' I replied, smiling and nodding my head. Through the partition I could hear Paul laughing hysterically.

Paul and I had long whispered conversations through our wall about life back home, future trips and being reunited with friends and family. Using my penknife, we even cut a small letterbox in the partition to pass cards to each other. To compensate for the lack of exercise I was getting,

I performed a Saturday-afternoon workout to disco music on *Apartado Estereo*. Given the lack of space, I was unable to throw my limbs around too much, but it was exercise nonetheless. The rest of the time I cut holes in the hut wall so I could watch what was happening around the camp and increase the light in my room.

I could see Trapper becoming increasingly unstable. He kept a number of *perricos* on whom he lavished attention. All four of them perched on the branch of a nearby tree. One night he tried to coax them down, offering them food and cooing soothingly. His patience snapped when they failed to respond. '*¡Majorda!*' he cried, and picked up a stick, hurling it into the tree. One of the *perricos* fell to the ground and Trapper kicked it like a football. In a perfect arc it sailed down the hill. He went to collect it and returned to his bivouac where he cut off its legs and head with his blunt machete, swearing all the time. I resolved there and then never to get on the wrong side of him. Whenever I got the chance, I spoke to him: I asked him how he was, praised the birds, commented on the weather, anything to draw him into conversation. Keeping on the right side of this lot was essential. I did not want to be kicked and cut apart like an insolent *perrico*.

Trapper's sexual proclivities were also a subject of concern. The dreaded worms appeared again, in my bum this time, and Trapper wasted no time in telling me to take down my trousers and lie on the bench. As I did, he parted my legs, and I suddenly feared the worst. It was only with slight relief that I realized he was pouring gasoline down the crack of my arse. It stung like hell, but it was preferable to what I thought he might do. A consequence of jungle life, living mostly among men and away from female company?

Trapper was not the only one whose intentions I started to doubt. While bathing at the stream in my shorts, I was joined by Beanstalk, who stripped off completely.

'Tomás,' he said.

I turned around. He was standing there proudly sporting a grin, and an erection.

'¿Señor?' I asked innocently, desperately trying to maintain eye contact.

Out of the corner of my eye I could see Stalky, fully clad, his mad, staring eyes fixed on Beanstalk's, er, stalk and rubbing his groin.

'I see yours,' Beanstalk said.

I didn't know what to say.

'¿Qué?'

'I see yours. But first you put on your *banador*,' he said.

He wanted to see my penis in a pair of Speedos. I feigned incomprehension and walked away.

Things were getting worrying.

★ ★ ★

PAUL: The jungle was beginning to take its toll on my body. For several days now I had been troubled by five or six small bleeding bites on my left leg. A closer inspection revealed an

230

infestation of worms like the ones that had beset Tom at Cloudy Base. At night, as I lay waiting for sleep to come, I could feel them growing and wriggling about, gently eating into my flesh. Knowing they were there, feasting on me, made sleep impossible. There was nothing to do other than let them grow a little. The trick was to let them reach a certain size and then squeeze them out vigorously, like bursting a spot. Lost Cause and Beanstalk squeezed painfully hard to remove them, and one or two came out easily, but several obviously liked their new home and refused to be evicted.

Then the camp ran out of tobacco. This was depressing on two counts: smoking was one of the few luxuries I enjoyed, and nicotine and the heat of a cigarette end was a favoured method of coaxing the worms to the surface of the skin so that they could be extracted. Without tobacco, I resorted to covering the wounds in an oily paste — another guerrilla trick. Maybe it deprived the worms of oxygen and forced them to the surface. Over the next few days, with a little help from the guerrillas, all but one was removed. Unfortunately it had entered through my shin and there was no soft flesh to squeeze. Due to the atrocious light in the hut it proved difficult to examine and care for the small entry wound the worm had made.

The worm burrowed deeper into my leg. It chewed its way down to my ankle. I was beginning to worry. I had enough problems without being eaten by a bloody worm. Until this point the guerrillas had paid attention to our health; now the frustration at not getting any money was increasing and their interest in our welfare was waning. Within forty-eight hours of noticing the worm in my shin, my foot had ballooned to twice its normal size. I could not take my eyes off it. It looked unreal, as if it were prosthetic, the product of a movie make-up department. Walking became difficult and I was forced to hop around my room.

The feeling of having another living creature inside me, albeit a tiny one, made me nauseous. A throbbing pain enveloped the whole area. If I was lucky, I slept for an hour or so on my right side, then the movement in my foot and the discomfort of being in one position on a bed of uneven branches woke me. I would twist onto my back and stare into the blackness, trying to get to sleep again. Rogue mosquitoes buzzed through holes in my net and bit me, but they were the least of my worries. For extra comfort, I made more bedding using a couple of spare T-shirts and a jumper, but the tossing and turning continued: I had continually to move back onto my right side because the pain in my left foot meant I had to place it gently on top of my right.

I started to have a recurring dream; it came to me with the clarity of a flawless diamond every night. I was trapped on the London Underground, travelling continuously yet never getting anywhere. Eventually, at some nameless platform, I would get off because I'd seen somebody I recognized, or a group of people I knew. We'd greet each other and exchange a few words.

'Goodbye, Paul,' the person would say next, always cheerily. Then they would leave. I never asked how to get out, and I could never follow them or reach the surface. The cast was ever-changing: close friends, family, past school friends I hadn't seen for years, teachers, former work colleagues, people I had met only briefly in life, travelling companions I had spent only a few days with, even people I'd never spoken to and knew only because I passed them every day on the commute to work. I never saw the same person twice. It was not the most difficult dream to interpret: I was saying goodbye to everyone, preparing myself for the end. The dream always ended the same way: me not wanting to say goodbye, desperately wanting them to stay and carry on talking yet unable to stop them leaving me. I was afraid of goodbye; I was afraid of the end; I was afraid of the unknown.

The pressure built in my foot. It pulsated, became tender and more swollen. The worm wasn't going to come out. One morning I felt the pressure pop and a warm spurt of blood and pus wash down my foot. It almost felt like a relief, but the wound trickled continually. Several small holes opened up, all of them seeping bloody poison the colour of mud.

With some effort, I rocked myself upright on the bed. As I did so my hand slipped into a puddle of pus and blood that had collected on the palm leaves. Beyond being squeamish, I wiped it off on my shorts. Gently, I lowered my legs over the edge of the bed to the ground. Pain swept through me, as though it were running

233

through my veins. I felt dizzy and sick, but I was determined to get out of my room to find help. This was serious.

I tugged on my right shoe and hobbled towards the door, grabbing at the sides of the hut, my head reeling. I stumbled out of the hut and into an empty camp. Where was everybody? I staggered across towards Tom's, door clutching at the sides of the hut. Then I saw a guerrilla we had named Stalky because of his bulging eyes.

'Get back,' he hissed.

I wanted to scream, 'Fuck you, you twat!' But I resisted. I told myself to stay calm.

He looked down at my foot, at the spider's web of pus and blood emanating from the three exit wounds. There was no reaction; he didn't seem to know how to respond. Several others arrived, attracted by the commotion. They stared at the swollen, gory mess that was once my foot with a disgusted fascination. That was good. It needed urgent attention, and I hoped that seeing it in all its gruesome glory would jolt them into action. After all, I was supposed to be worth five million dollars.

I slumped onto a bench built of branches. Trapper was called, and Lost Cause also came over to inspect me. A crowd huddled around, looking at the foot and babbling away in Spanish. I understood nothing, though I heard the word *malo* — Spanish for 'bad'. That much I already knew. I wanted them to do something about it. If they failed to act now then there was every chance a serious infection would set in.

Trapper ordered Lost Cause and Beanstalk to

examine the wound. There was nothing they could do; their medical knowledge only went as far as squeezing the foot and massaging it so that pus squirted out. They employed this tactic for an hour, kneading me like dough, their callused hands making me wince. I counted to ten, took deep breaths, thought of home — anything to block out the pain. Pus and blood flowed like water from a tap. Blobs occasionally blocked up the holes, then, after a few minutes of hard squeezing, out would pop a lump of stringy, mucus-type liquid. I felt sick from the pain and the sight of this disgusting mess. The foot throbbed incessantly and turned red raw as a result of the guerrillas' persistent massaging. Finally, they said that was it. They washed the foot clean with river water and put me back in the hut.

I spent the rest of the day on my bed. The wounds continued to suppurate, soaking the cloth I was lying on. 'That's it,' I thought. 'That's all they're going to do.' There seemed little hope my leg would improve if that was the only treatment they could give. Perhaps I would have to rely on luck. I didn't feel lucky.

Later that afternoon I was called outside for a further examination. I shuffled out to the bench. Nothing had changed, the foot was still weeping. Further discussions were held and more prodding of the foot resulted in more globules of pus and dead tissue oozing out. The pain of placing my foot below my waist was now unbearable. My temples pounded with the agony. Walking was virtually impossible.

I couldn't understand what they were saying. Tom was still confined to his room, so he couldn't translate. After an eternity, some Deep Heat was produced. It was Tom's. Somehow they seemed to think this would be the magical cure, the perfect medicine. I looked up in horror as they explained that they were going to massage this into my foot. I might as well have been tended to by a sixteenth-century quack.

Trapper opened the pot of Deep Heat and smelled it. He pulled a face.

'It will be good for his foot,' he said to the others.

A murmur of agreement went around the assembly, who stood there like medical students gathered around the bed of a hapless patient.

'Hold him down,' I heard a voice say.

'You,' Trapper said to Lost Cause. 'Rub it into his foot.'

This was no sick joke. Fear prevented me from doing anything initially, then I became angry.

'No, señor, es malo,' I pleaded. 'Muy malo para mi pierna.'

'No,' he replied, 'es bueno.'

'No, it's not fucking bueno!' I felt like screaming, but my Spanish did not extend that far. I have never known frustration like it in my life: wanting someone to understand but being unable to explain anything to them.

Tom, upset at sitting idly by while I howled in protest, stormed out of his hut only to be ordered straight back inside by Trapper, who picked up his gun to back up the threat.

I pointed to the blurb on the case where it

236

advises the user against rubbing the cream onto open wounds or sensitive skin. My ankle was a lurid combination of both. It would be absolute agony. I just couldn't believe they would contemplate it. My body began to stiffen in anticipation of the pain. I yelled at them that it was a crazy idea — keeping the peace could go to hell. I was not letting them near my leg with that stuff. Yet they were insistent, and I was weak. Also, they had guns. Several of them held me down as Lost Cause applied the cream over the foot and wound. The pain was so intense I could barely breathe.

For the rest of the day it felt as though my foot had been thrust into a furnace. I didn't sleep, such was the burning, blistering agony. I lay on my bed, almost delirious. The next day the ankle exploded again. Once small wounds were now holes the size of fifty-pence pieces. The foot was a raw, throbbing mass of red flesh coated with pus and blood. That was it: the damage was done. I couldn't walk. Looking at it made me sick and dizzy. My strength was ebbing away. It was all I could do to raise the upper part of my body off the bed.

Food was brought to me three times a day but soon I started to lose my appetite and lethargy set in. I drifted off into day-dreams. I spent the whole time rolling and moving, trying to get into a comfortable position, though any comfort I did find was fleeting. I tried to pad out my bed with every item of spare clothing I could find, yet within ten minutes I would be fidgeting again. I couldn't even get up to go to the toilet, though fortunately I had an empty milk tin I was able to piss in. The wound festered in the windless, stifling jungle air. Pus and blood oozed over my bedding. Soon, the sheet was filthy. A guerrilla was ordered to clean it in the river, and I was amazed to see it come back a brilliant white.

I watched aghast as maggots appeared and began feasting on my rotting flesh. I was physically and mentally exhausted, surrounded by enemies and far from home. I cursed myself for not doing more to get the worm out when it first appeared. On my back in my dark room, I had nothing to do but think while I waited for my body to heal itself. I tried to snatch moments of sleep between periods of intense pain, but most of my time was spent lost in thought, staring out into the pitch-black jungle.

Until this point, life as a hostage had been too busy for thinking; there were always tactics to discuss and debates over what might or might not happen. Now, immobile and weak, I wondered how I had got myself into such deep shit. Why hadn't I made more of an effort to settle down in the UK? I could have got a full-time job, bought a house and done all the things 'normal' people do, mundane though I thought they were at the time. I had become addicted to the thrill of temporary freedom. And where had that got me? Life seemed temporary now, all right. Oh for that boring job at the bank and all its reassuring bullshit. The 6.43 from Chelmsford seemed like heaven on earth.

Crossing the Darién would have proved nothing to anybody but myself. And all it would

238

have given me was a few tales of adventure to tell my mates in the pub. Most of them would have paid little attention. I had been looking for adventure, an experience that allowed me to escape from the daily routine and grind. That's what had urged me on. I hadn't known how to explain it to any of my family or friends back home. I wished I could get the chance now, though.

I made promises to myself which, in the event of my release, I knew I wouldn't be able to keep: buy a house, get a full-time job, that sort of thing. Deep down I knew that if I ever made it back home, after a period of adjustment and reflection I would be out looking for my next adventure. I would be searching for a mountain to scale, a rock to climb or another risky place in the world to go to. I even started to think of other trips I could make. In the Algerian Sahara I had met a German who had ridden an Enfield motorcycle back from India. It seemed a good idea. These thoughts girded me. There was also a lot more climbing and mountaineering I needed to do. I needed to get better.

★   ★   ★

TOM: 'Come look at this, Tom.'

Paul's withered voice contained a note of surprise. I was allowed into his cabin to clean his bedding because he was unable to do it himself. I got out of the tent, pulled on my boots and walked around to him as quickly as I could. As I opened the door I was almost knocked out by the appalling smell: a rank combination of rotting flesh, piss and shit. Paul was lying there, trying to prop himself up to see his engorged, discoloured ankle, his sallow face shocked at the bloody sight. The white towel beneath his leg was stained red.

'It went off like a bomb,' he added, shaking his head in disbelief. 'The pressure built up and it just popped.'

I started to clean up. I picked up his pisspot and his pus- and blood-stained bed mat and bandage to take to the river to clean.

'You'd make someone a good nurse, Tom,' he said, a weak smile on his face.

His condition was deteriorating. The guerrillas had no idea how to treat him. They'd smeared Deep Heat on his leg, poured boiling water on it and massaged it daily. He was often in agony, and it was heartrending to hear his cries of pain echo through the jungle as another ham-fisted guerrilla squeezed and pummelled the infected holes. Often I was allowed to sit outside on the 'operating bench' by our hut as they treated him, but other times I was confined to my room. To hear him scream and yell and not be there to help or comfort him in some way was upsetting. One time, Trapper and Señor Dama were going to work on his leg and seemed to be relishing Paul's agony, paying no heed to his begging for them to stop.

'All they want to do is kill me and cause me pain!' he screamed to me.

I felt so angry that I stormed outside, but Trapper went straight for his gun. Reluctantly I

240

retreated, almost in tears myself.

It became worse when the maggots appeared. I tried not to wince when I first saw them but the sight was so appalling it was impossible not to. I began to feel his leg would have to be amputated. It was a horrible thought, yet inescapable. Sat in my room I worried about him, wondering how he would cope with one leg, and how it would affect our situation. It seemed hopeless anyway, and I felt helpless. I kept these thoughts to myself, though. I presented to Paul every day a smiling face, and made jokes and comments to make him smile, trying desperately to give him hope.

'A friend of mine cut his leg when he was in the Canary Islands,' I said, 'and it got infested with maggots. Then it cleared up. The maggots cleaned the wound.'

'Really?' Paul said, his face brightening.

'Yes,' I said, nodding vigorously. 'In a few days he was fine.'

It was a lie, and when I left his hut I felt guilty for telling him it. Yet it seemed to help his mood, and that was my aim. I thought of telling him the truth but decided against it.

We talked for hours through the wall in the hut, about our homes, our families, our friends and our plans for the future. We discussed where we would go once we were released.

'We can go and get the boat to Turbo,' Paul said.

'Then tell the police about what's happened and get a bus to Medellín,' I said.

'No, let's not tell the police. They might think

we're civilians who've been recruited by FARC. They'll give us a real grilling. I've had enough of that.'

'I fancy going to Peru after that.'

'Or the Andes. I wouldn't mind skiing and doing a bit of climbing.'

'Not many orchids on ski slopes, Paul.'

'Well, we can discuss it when we're free.'

'Can you pass me the Lonely Planet? I wouldn't mind reading up on Peru.'

'Tom, you've read it twenty times.'

'You can't beat a bit of planning.'

He handed it to me through the slit we had cut in the wall separating us, which we jokingly referred to as the mailbox.

'Do you know if there are any guerrilla groups in Peru, Paul?'

'*Sendero Luminoso*. The Shining Path.'

'Come to think of it, I've always wanted to go skiing.'

Our other main topic was what would happen when we got back to England.

'We should hold a reunion every year, on the day we were captured,' I suggested.

'Good idea. We can eat some monkey.'

'And get our friends to lock us in a shed and stand outside holding guns.'

'Then play cards with us in the evening.'

'We can dig holes in my parents' garden and crap in them. Dad'll think we've got moles.'

The idea soon became a serious one, however.

'We'll put up a marquee on the lawn at Lullingstone and invite all our friends,' I said.

'I'll bring my mates from college,' he said.

'We'll need food and booze, Tom. Loads of it.'

'How about roast chicken? Or roast beef and Yorkshire pudding with gravy?'

'Bangers and mash.'

'Chips with ketchup.'

'Stop it, Tom, I'm drooling. Can you cook, then?'

'No, I'm hopeless.'

'We can buy a book.'

'Yeah, with a recipe for chocolate cake.'

'And lemon meringue pie.'

'And Victoria sponge.'

'With ice cream.'

'And chocolate sauce.'

'And ice-cold beer on the side. Crates of it.'

'And Coke, too.'

This sort of talk continued for days and days. By day we talked about travelling, by night, eating. Each night we planned increasingly elaborate menus, constructing each course in great detail. This might have had something to do with our diet, which was getting increasingly exotic. To add to the deer, gua-gua and monkey we had already eaten, at Lost City we ate armadillo, freshwater turtle and, the *pièce de résistance*, squirrel soup.

But as time passed, talk of England and what we'd do when free began to fade. So did any talk of travelling.

'Tom, when we get out of here, I'm going straight home,' Paul said.

Increasingly he felt less and less like talking and was spending more time in deep thought, barely responding to my attempts to cheer him up. I returned to designing my dream garden and eavesdropping on the comings and goings around the camp. The few conversations we did have were now less upbeat.

'I'm worried, Tom,' Paul said once, late at night.

'Why?'

'They're still so pumped up about this money. I don't know what they're going to do when they finally realize it's not coming.'

'Maybe they'll just let us go,' I said, as hopefully as I could.

'But who cares about two tourists lost in the jungle? No-one cares, no-one will be looking for us,' he said mournfully.

'I've still got a bit of faith in Trouble Ahead. Perhaps they're negotiating now.'

'We would have heard something, Tom. I'm sure of it. It's not happening, mate. They're just trying to keep everyone happy by saying it will come tomorrow. We've got to accept what might happen if they don't get the money.'

I knew what he meant. They would kill us.

'We're in their hands,' is all I could say.

'It's our own fault,' he continued. 'We should never have come. We'll just have to pay the price.'

I refused to let us become too depressed, though, and seized any opportunity for something to do, to occupy the time. I heard on the radio that Wimbledon had started, so I predicted results in my exercise book. I seeded the best players whose names I could remember, drew them against other players I'd heard of and worked out who would advance. I got Paul to help me to predict the winners. In the men's singles I forecast Pete Sampras to beat Tim Henman in the semi-final, before beating Goran Ivanisevic in the final, while Martina Hingis was predicted to overcome Lindsay Davenport in straight sets. I also heard mention on the guerrillas' radio of a Grand Prix, so I started to forecast who would win the season's drivers' championship. Paul knew nothing about Formula One racing, so I filled him in on some details. Mika Hakkinen was first with eighty-five points and Michael Schumacher second with seventy-three points, followed by Coulthard, Frentzen, Barrichello and 'a Williams driver' whose name I couldn't remember.

★ ★ ★

PAUL: Time passed slowly and painfully. My foot wasn't healing and infection was becoming a serious threat. The stifling jungle humidity was the perfect breeding ground for it. The guerrillas mocked me, suggesting that if necessary they could always cut the foot off. '*Sí, sí señor, bien, bien,*' I would reply, smiling. In my mind, however, I was preparing myself for the agony and horror of such an operation. Just thinking about it made me feel sick, though. After witnessing their medical skills during the Deep Heat episode, my confidence in their surgical abilities was hardly sky high. The image of Dr Trapper wielding a hacksaw was an appalling one. Did they have anaesthetic? In keeping with their quackery, they would probably try to knock me out. Without proper medical facilities the infection could easily run out of control.

The thought of losing my foot was unbearable. To them I was worth $5 million with one foot or two. At least that meant they would keep me alive, though it crossed my mind that if I became too much of a burden they might seek an easy way to get rid of me.

I became filthy, lying in my own waste and the putrescence created by my injury. But I was going beyond the point of caring. Dark thoughts swirled around my head, thoughts of death. My dream continued, every night the same, only the faces changed. Discontented mutterings spread around camp about the smell from my hut and my personal hygiene. Tom passed these worries on. The problem was, they wanted me to bathe but I was unable to move without suffering the most appalling pain. To be honest, the last thing I cared about at this point was my cleanliness. Tom, as bright as ever, had the solution.

'I can carry you to the river,' he offered.

'Are you sure?'

'It's not as if you're the heaviest bloke in the world,' he replied. 'And after a month stuck in here, I could do with the exercise.'

He came round to my side of the hut and I shuffled myself to the edge of my bed. The foot was very swollen and it hurt like hell when I swung my legs around and tipped them over the bed and below my waist. I was sweating from having to concentrate to block out the pain. I put all my weight on my right foot and hopped onto

246

Tom's back as he bent down. As we emerged from the room, the camp stopped and looked around to see what was going on. Lost Cause and Trapper were standing close by.

'Buenos días.'

I smiled to them both through the pain. Tom started to make his way towards the river, Jackanory following and babbling away. As Tom carried me I could hear laughter breaking out behind us. The sight was obviously causing them much amusement.

'Ow!' I heard Tom cry.

I looked over my shoulder and saw Lost Cause holding a sapling and braying like a donkey. He ran up to us again and whipped Tom on the arse with it while making his donkey noises. Tom ran even faster to evade Lost Cause. The camp fell into riotous laughter, bent double, mocking my affliction and what they viewed as Tom's servility.

We continued to make our way down to the river, to Jackanory's constant chatter. I just ignored him. Tom skilfully negotiated his way along the muddy path and down to the water, a journey of about a hundred yards. We stopped a few times so Tom could catch his breath, and occasionally I had to jump up higher on his back after slipping down. Every jolt was agony, so I was happy to reach the water. Precariously balancing on one foot or sitting down in the water, I washed myself. It was a relief finally to feel clean again. Tom waited nearby for the piggyback home, Jackanory jabbering on witlessly at him the whole time.

247

The ankle continued to suppurate and I was barely able to move anywhere without Tom's help. Yet there were positive signs. For one, the repulsive maggots disappeared. I also gained another caring nurse when Maria returned. I was happy to see her. There was something about her calm and gentle manner that reassured me. She was more mature than the others; they were like frustrated children. She examined my wound attentively.

'¿*Duele*?' she asked. It hurts?

'*Sí*,' I replied emphatically.

The expression on her face acknowledged that my leg was in a serious condition. She collected some warm salted water and started to clean the wound. Carefully, she dropped the tepid water over the opening, pushing away blood and other material with her fingertips. This removed the loose surface debris. Rather than feeling tense and terrified, as I did whenever Trapper and his cronies treated me, I relaxed. I was in the hands of someone with at least some idea of what she was doing. She saw that the wound needed even more thorough cleaning, so she took a twig and split it down the middle, removing the outer bark to reveal the clean inner core. It was basic, but about as clean an instrument as you could find in this forest. With it she gently scraped the wound free of all its gunk, washing it regularly. Before long it was clean, and my foot looked a damn sight better than it felt. Maria stayed for a couple of nights and each day she attended my foot carefully. I was disappointed when she went; she'd been kind to me. Weeks ago, when she'd guarded us under Smith's charge, she had taken a liking to my shirt and had asked for it as a present. I'd refused, saying I'd only give it to her when they let me return to England. She'd been disappointed. Now I felt guilty about my reluctance, even though she was part of the crime. Her kindness touched me.

I wondered if she really believed in the kidnapping or whether she was just following orders. Perhaps, like the others, she really thought that the untold riches we would bring them would improve her life. Though what they would do with all that money in this fetid jungle was beyond me. They simply didn't understand just how much they were asking for. They had no idea of the way things worked in the West, that most people, however wealthy, could never dream of getting hold of the amounts of money they were expecting. But then, who was I to judge? We understood neither the workings of Colombian politics nor the complexity of ordinary Colombians' lives, so there was no reason to expect them to understand ours.

The real turning point so far as my leg was concerned came when Trapper and his crew gave me antibiotics. An array of unused needles appeared, much to my delight. I could have done with these a week or so earlier, but I wasn't in a position to complain. Slowly, the wound started to seal and heal, though the swelling remained. A combination of the injections and Maria's intervention meant the ankle started to get better. Tom was fantastic, always keeping up my spirits and uncomplainingly doing what he could to keep me clean, and sane. With his help, I soon became less self-absorbed, and regained an interest in our environment and what was happening around camp. Before long I was able to walk the hundred yards to and from the stream on my own with the aid of a stick, though my progress was ponderous and the effort painful. The leg needed more time to recuperate.

Yet no sooner had I got back on my feet than the order came through to move again.

11

BEDLAM EXPRESS

PAUL: It was the middle of July; we'd spent exactly six weeks at Lost City. Leaving felt strange, sad almost. Despite the torrid time I'd suffered with my leg, it had felt like a home. The hut was dry and comfortable and I'd enjoyed having my own room, murky though it was. I feared leaving, even though I knew the sense of security the room gave me was false. Yet it had provided a cocoon of privacy where I could block out, deny even, all that was happening around me. It was a place where my foot could heal in peace. I needed time to convalesce and regain my strength. Now we would be walking again, though for how long and to where we had no idea. My main concern was whether my swollen foot could cope with the strain of walking. Would it even fit into my boot?

On the morning of our departure, I bound the wound with my last remaining bandage, which was flecked with dirt and pus. I looked at in disgust knowing that it virtually guaranteed infection, but some protection, however soiled, was preferable to none. I took care to use as little of the material as possible, knowing that the foot was already too swollen to fit easily into my boot. Over the top I slipped a thin, worn sock to hold it in place. Gingerly, I slipped my left foot into my boot. It slid in the first few inches, then stopped. I tugged gently at the back of the boot, pushing the foot down a little more, and was rewarded with a stab of pain. I pulled hard, fighting to squeeze the foot in further, but it only moved an agonizing extra inch. Still I yanked vigorously at the boot, but to no avail. Ten minutes of struggling and squeezing later my foot was finally in, though it pressed hard against all parts of the boot. I let it settle into this strange position for a quarter of an hour until the pain subsided to a throb.

Then I discovered, to my delight, that the boot acted like a splint, supporting my weakened ankle. I hobbled out of the hut and Trapper handed me a walking stick he'd fashioned from a branch of wood. I shouldered my pack and, with my guards Scarface and Señor Dama, stumbled down to the river. Tom went ahead with another set of guards. As we walked across it, the cool water poured into my right boot and trickled into my left, providing a soothing, anaesthetic effect. I waded downriver at my own pace, using the stick to balance and aid my walking. The lack of rain meant the river gurgled only gently around my knees and thighs, while the smooth, sandy riverbed provided a good walking surface. Scarface and Señor Dama wandered idly alongside me, chatting to each other. They seemed unfazed by my slow pace.

The day was a short one, maybe two or three hours. Camp was established at the junction in the river where we had stopped on our way up to

Lost City. The Bedfellows were still with us, though we had yet to see them and they camped on the opposite side of the bend in the river.

The next day we were woken, fed and ordered to take down our tent and pack up. They then moved us into dense undergrowth at the back of the camp and stationed a guard to watch over us. We spent the day baking in the heat, swatting away mosquitoes while the guerrillas appeared to hold a meeting to decide what to do with us. I didn't know what they had in store for us but it didn't worry me: my mood had become fatalistic. We would discover the outcome of their discussions over the next few days or so. Whatever it was, we would have to bear it. They were in control of all aspects of our existence.

Later, we were allowed back into camp. I collected my things together and limped slowly out from the undergrowth. Tom had already left, but I hadn't gone far when he came racing back, his long straggly hair billowing out behind the 'tea cosy' cap he'd taken to wearing, babbling in a voice that always indicated excitement.

'Paul, you have to see this new gorgeous woman. She has got *the* most amazing breasts,' he said.

My immediate thought was that Tom had finally cracked; this was not the sort of place you encountered beautiful women. I reached the clearing and was met by a black woman with long dark hair, wearing combat trousers and a bra. Obviously Tom had been in the jungle and away from women for too long. She certainly had an impressive chest, but there was something about her, an arrogant look in her eye, that spelled trouble and made her particularly unattractive. That and the fact that half her right thumb was missing. She handed me what she called a *bocho*, a maize cake. It tasted good, and I was grateful for it. After a little small talk she went to wash in the river, Tom following like a little lapdog, his tongue hanging from his maw.

I decided to cadge a cigarette off somebody. At Lost City they'd run out of tobacco, but I was sure they'd have some new supplies because a number of new guerrillas had surfaced from somewhere (and I was right). I counted four new people: the 'beautiful' woman (Baps); a well-built black guy with a long thin face and buck-teeth (Goofy); another young black guy, built like the proverbial, who had arrived on a horse (The Knight); and a *mestizo* male who was immediately noticeable for the amount of jewellery he wore around his neck (Chainy).

The next day we got up early and set off once more. Again, it took me a while to put on my boot. The evening before I had been able to remove it only with the aid of Tom. I'd held on to a tree while he almost removed my leg, much to the camp's amusement. Today Loosey and Baps were guarding me and they accepted my slow pace. I wondered if their patience would last.

It was a short but exhausting walking day, most of it spent travelling south. When I arrived in camp some time after Tom, he told me how Beanstalk had barracked him and bellowed at him to move faster. I found this alarming. Tom was fit and able to cope with the terrain, so it was only a matter of time before their anger was directed towards me.

I started to write a diary in the back of my South American guidebook — very short notes about our direction of travel, its duration, and anything of significance that we encountered. I was desperate to keep track of where we were in case we were forced to make an attempt to escape.

The next day we moved west, and then south into Los Katios National Park on the Colombian side of the Darién. I knew that because the terrain became hilly and our direction of travel meant we had to hit Colombia at some point. At first, Tom and I marched together with the two women and Trapper, though soon we became lost in the jungle maze. Trapper had been so intent on taking us around a felled area where local Indians had been spotted that he had lost his sense of direction, not to mention the rest of the group. He swore, and stalked around trying to find a path. The others bristled, and I felt angry eyes settle on me. 'If it wasn't for this bloody cripple,' the looks said, 'we wouldn't be lost.' Eventually, Goofy found us and directed us out.

We marched all day, and I limped along using my stick as best I could. They had a couple of mules, one of which was deputed to carry my rucksack. We climbed hills, clambered along ridges and waded across rivers without resting. Our mood was boosted by frequent sightings of our lucky butterfly. In the afternoon, torrential rain soaked us, and we slithered on over the jungle mud, finally making camp on a steep hillside above a small stream. I was exhausted and slumped down on my rucksack, not wanting to move an inch. Tom set up the tent, food was cooked and eaten, and I fell asleep within seconds.

The next day brought more of the same, across rough terrain. We received no lunch. Only once before had we missed lunch, but then so had everyone else. Not this time. This was malicious. Tom and I were forced to watch the whole group eat. From the smirk on her face, my feeling was that Baps lay behind it. Through exhaustion, that afternoon I was unable to keep up with the rest of the group. Chainy was assigned to walk with me. I limped alongside him ponderously, though he let me set the pace.

My foot throbbed and frustration welled inside me. Stopping was not an option because there was every chance the foot would relax, then seize up. Getting going in the morning was always difficult, though it warmed up after an hour's walking and I grew to accept the monotonous, dull ache. At times, however, I wanted to give up, but I knew I couldn't. Onwards I drove myself, desperate not to flinch or show weakness in front of the guerrillas. I have always prided myself on being a strong walker, having walked in mountains all over the world, easily strolling up peaks in a few hours. To be reduced to hobbling with a stick like an old man was exasperating, and at the snail's pace I was travelling at it was a question of when, not if, their frustration would boil over.

That night in camp Tom told me how Baps had kicked and harried him all day.

'She even tried to kick me in the bollocks. If I hadn't closed my legs quickly, she would have caught me unfairly and squarely,' he said angrily.

This infuriated us both, yet, as ever, it was essential we remained calm and peaceful. It was gentle stuff at the moment; they were merely venting a bit of frustration over the fact that none of their plans seemed to be working. Nevertheless, the name Baps was replaced by a more appropriate moniker: The Bitch.

After another full day of trekking we arrived at a large, fast-flowing river. The river headed south, and I suspected that we had now passed into Colombia. That night we became acquainted with virulent Colombian mosquitoes, which descended on us without mercy. All night I could hear Tom slapping at the invisible enemy in the dark, and I did the same. Sleep was impossible, and in the morning light I found myself littered with itching, swelling bites. Hundreds of bloated mosquitoes drunk on our blood bounced wearily on and off the tent fabric, desperately trying to find a way out. I took great delight in popping each one like bubble wrap between my fingers.

A routine took shape as we struggled on through the jungle, deep into Colombian territory. We rose at dawn, and I patched my leg up and tugged my boot on before we decamped and ate breakfast. Before setting off, we collected a lunch of boiled rice, *plátanos* and meat in a plastic bag, then walked until elevenish. Lunch would be half an hour, then we'd plough on until mid-afternoon, sometimes later. This allowed us time to wash, set up camp and eat before crashing when the sun went down, at about six. The camp was always split into two parts — one for Tom and myself, and the other for the Bedfellows, whom we'd still not seen — and we walked as two groups too. Every evening I collapsed into a deep sleep, spent from the constant trekking. The pain had become part of me.

Three days into the trek, Trapper, Lost Cause and a few others disappeared. We carried on through the deserted Los Katios National Park, frequently getting lost on the way, then down into the swampy lowlands where the heat and humidity were debilitating. The rains created boggy paths into which I would often sink to my knees. I'd take one step forward, plant my walking pole, then wrench the other leg from the mud and step forward, sinking back into the mud. This continued for hours and hours. We crossed river after river. Life became a constant fight against the elements and a battle to keep my leg moving. The wet permeated everything and I was always covered in dirt and exhausted. Thorns ripped at us, shredding our clothes and cutting into our bare arms, neck and face.

After a week of this we came to a dilapidated house surrounded by fields, where the jungle had been cut back. We rested for a day there, then continued. There were civilians nearby, and we bumped into the young guerrilla who had so memorably tried to disperse the wasp nest in Tom's rucksack. He directed us around the civilians through dense undergrowth. He greeted me with a friendly smile and we shook hands. One of his arms was horrendously burned and scalded. He explained that he had suffered an accident, though it didn't seem to bother him much. He was obviously accident-prone.

Onwards we walked, further into Colombian territory, passing through areas which looked to have been cultivated at some point. We passed abandoned villages and farmsteads, testimonies to the savagery of the Colombian civil war, places from which civilians had fled to the safety of the cities and major towns to escape the endless fighting. Further into the lowlands the region became more populated and we were often hidden in the undergrowth or guided around hamlets and villages. Whenever they hid me in the undergrowth I made sure that I always coughed or sneezed so that when the civilians passed they'd hear and look in my direction. Often the guerrillas didn't hide me well enough and the civilians could see me anyway. Some of them seemed to support the guerrillas — we suspected it was they who provided the food 'drops' — though whether that support was genuine or the result of fear I didn't know. I suppose that if one group or another walks into your village armed with guns then it's politic to do as they say. One benefit of travelling through this populated area was an abundance of supplies: delicious coconuts and bananas grew everywhere, new fruits were available and cigarettes plentiful. I even got my own lighter.

After ten days, Tom succumbed to a fever and we had to rest for one day to let him recover. I was glad of the rest, but the next day we were off again and the environment continued to take its toll. One day I discovered that my faeces had blood in it. I was told there was no medicine, so I continued to walk.

We crossed open fields for hours in the blazing Equatorial sun and I limped on while the tension mounted over my slow pace. Occasionally we came across rivers too wide to cross and they arranged boat trips. My spirits lagged and I found it difficult to keep up. The pack animals had disappeared so I was carrying my rucksack again. I worried about further infection in my foot; still the wound wept. While walking through the many bogs we came across, all sorts of debris would find its way into my boot. The guerrillas yelled at me to go faster, but it was impossible. For days I marched with the constant irritation of them wittering away in my ear. I knew I was going slowly, and I didn't need it explained to me again and again. I maintained my composure by just plodding on, head down, impervious to their shouted threats and exhortations.

Early one morning, about three weeks into the trek, I caught up with the group at a coconut tree where they were greedily gulping the sweet water from the shells. With a malicious smirk The Bitch ordered the others not to give me any. This irked me, though there was nothing I could do so I carried on walking. Then it began to rain.

A few hundred yards further on I stopped to put my cigarettes in my rucksack to protect them from the downpour. While I was doing this The Bitch came up behind me.

'Move!' she screamed.

I did not move quickly enough, so she pushed me hard. I fell sprawling on the muddy jungle floor. She stood over me, shouting abuse.

'Fuck off!' I shouted back, getting up.

I'd had enough. I wanted to show them that they could only go so far and that if they overstepped the line they could go to hell. I could accept the idea that we had been kidnapped — after all, we'd walked into the Darién of our own accord. I could even accept the possibility of being shot for our error. But I would not accept any unnecessary physical abuse. If I was to be executed, I wanted it done quickly.

The pushing and shoving continued, The Bitch loving every moment of it. Goofy and The Knight each put in their penny's worth. I fought to regain my composure, levelling a look of pure hatred at her. She hit me with all her might, using sticks to strike the backs of my legs as hard as she could. I was walking in shorts because I had only one pair of long trousers and I needed those to sleep in because they stopped the mosquitoes from eating me alive at night. She found thorny plants and whipped the backs of my legs.

'You are a bitch!' I screamed. 'You are an ugly fucking whore!'

My vehemence caught her by surprise. There

261

was fear in her eyes, and she raised her gun. Despite the volatility of the situation, part of me was very pleased to provoke this reaction. The AK-47 shook in her hands as I continued to spew out all my hatred and bile in her direction.

'Just what is the point of all this? Just what is the fucking point? You walk us this way, then that way, then we stop for weeks on end, then we move and you never get anything. What is the point? Tell me!'

Of course, to her it was no more than a torrent of incomprehensible sounds. I took a deep breath and tried to control my anger. If I pushed it too far then they would just shoot me. Sometimes that didn't seem a bad option, but really all I wanted was for this walk to be over so that I could rest and allow my foot to heal.

A few days later we came to a large village and made camp on a hillside on its fringes. We rested there for a few days while various people and commanders came to visit us. They brought gifts of sweets, cigarettes and bread. I salivated at the thought of bread and sweets but we got none, and I was happy to settle for the cigarettes. Then we set off again, for five days, almost continuously.

On one trek, I stumbled into a clearing and slumped down next to Tom. Everybody was there, waiting and resting. The guerrillas began to talk among themselves.

'Paul,' Tom said, 'can you understand what Goofy and The Bitch are talking about?'

'No.'

I listened intently. Tom explained that she was

saying she was tired of the hard life and all the killing. Goofy was explaining that they didn't have a choice, it was the way it had to be. In the absence of any money, Tom and I were liabilities.

'Paul, we have to get out of here,' Tom whispered. 'And soon.'

★ ★ ★

TOM: For weeks we descended the slopes into what Paul believed was Colombia. Any hope of being taken back to Payita and released swiftly evaporated with this realization.

We walked without stopping. The Bitch, who would swear at me, push me or even hit me with a stick whenever I so much as peered at a plant, curtailed any botanical forays. I suppose I was guilty of being cheeky sometimes. 'I'm walking as fast as I can,' I would answer back when they complained I was walking too slowly. I would get a beating then. Loose Teenager sometimes joined in, trying to please the new alpha female by copying her aggressive behaviour.

As we traversed one fecund slope we came across a grove of *Ceiba pentandra* — giant trees with fat, straight trunks. They were so wide that four of us joining hands would have failed to encircle any one of them. I let out a whoop of joy and went straight to the nearest tree. Tapping the grey, smooth bark, I could hear the sound of water sloshing around inside.

There was a slap on the back of my legs, and I turned to see a furious Bitch staring at me. I tried to tell her how rare it was to find so many of these extraordinary trees together in one place, but she was having none of it. She hit me again and I was forced on my way.

As we trekked further into Colombia the mosquitoes became ferocious. They had been a problem on a few occasions so far, but nothing compared to the swamps and lowlands of Colombia. At every opportunity they attacked. Even as you walked, they would amass behind the small of your back and feed their appetites. I took to stopping and turning around quickly, much to the annoyance of The Bitch, and was faced every time with a swarm of mosquitoes in the shape of a flying 'V', just waiting to feast on me. They bit every available piece of skin; even clothing proved no barrier to them. We marched to the regular beat of people slapping their heads, faces and arms.

The conditions were hellish: eight hours a day of walking, mosquitoes everywhere, intense heat and the camps temporary at best. At least I had the Wellington boots. My old boots were tied by their laces and attached to my rucksack. As well as containing the money, the other held the receipts for my traveller's cheques. One night we came into camp and I threw my rucksack down on the floor. I felt exhausted. It took me a while to notice, but only one boot was attached to the rucksack. It was the left boot, too. The right, with the money, was gone.

I looked around the campsite but there was no sign of it. There was also no chance of retracing our steps. I would have to accept it was gone.

The guerrillas had always wondered why I carried my battered old pair with me when I never wore them; now Goofy came over and picked up the remaining boot.

'Now you do not need this,' he said triumphantly, and hurled it into the bushes.

An hour or so later, Paul hobbled into camp.

'Paul, I've lost one of my boots.'

His face turned ashen.

'Not the right one?'

I nodded slowly.

'Shit!'

It was a real blow to our morale. Having that money on us had always given us hope. There had been many times in the tent, moments when we'd felt powerless and frustrated, when we pulled the money out from the sole of my boot just to stare at it. The sight had never failed to lift our spirits.

'This,' Paul would say, waving it like Loadsamoney, 'is our ticket out of this place. If we get out of here then this will pay for a boat, some food or a bribe.'

How we would get out of 'here' was undecided, but I think we both realized that escape was beginning to look like our best and our only option. Nothing appeared to be happening about the ransom, and therefore a release looked increasingly unlikely.

We therefore felt desperate after losing the money. Now we had nothing.

★　★　★

PAUL: They forced us to wait at this camp by the wide river for a few days, confined to our tent at the rear in dense undergrowth where the mosquitoes and humidity were unrelenting. New personnel dressed smartly in their clean and pressed army fatigues came to examine the merchandise. Motorized boats raced up and down the wide river carrying guerrillas and messages as the news of our arrival spread. Gifts of gua-gua, brandy and cigarettes arrived shortly; the camp was in an optimistic mood. I saw a seedy-looking man in a Panama hat speeding downriver in a motorized pirogue. He was a cross between a classic movie villain — ever-present cigar, narrow eyes, leathery, permanent tan — and the man from Del Monte. He spoke to the guerrillas and they afforded him respect. He was a civilian, but he appeared important. We were ordered to pack up our equipment and get ready to move that evening.

I went out to the riverbank looking for a cigarette, fully expecting to be shooed back into the sweltering tent. I found Goofy, Scarface and Perty lounging on the grass swigging brandy and smoking, all of them in a relaxed mood. They gave me a cigarette, chatted away cheerily, and even offered me a swig of brandy, which I took. It was bad, but I suppressed my wince. They laughed at the face I pulled, though.

'*¿Vamos hoy?*' I enquired. Are we leaving today?

'*Sí, en la lancha,*' Goofy replied, pointing to one of the boats.

It appeared we were going to travel downriver that night. I limped back to tell Tom, unconvinced it would actually happen.

A few hours later, as dusk fell, the command came through to prepare to move. Tom and I walked out to the riverbank with our packs.

'You are with the military. I don't want any noise or talking,' Goofy informed us sombrely. 'You understand?'

'*Sí*,' replied Tom.

'Explain it to Pablo,' Goofy added.

But I'd already understood what he'd said and I was trying to stop myself laughing. There are probably gangs of girl guides bearing more similarity to the military than these idiots.

Soon we were speeding downriver in the moonlight. Everyone was in the one vehicle, together with all the equipment. I tried to use the moon to gauge our direction, but I soon became lost in the many twists and turns of the river. Tom and I sat next to each other, forbidden to talk or to look around. I knew the Bedfellows were sitting behind us. At some stage during the journey I was determined to sneak a look at them.

The Bitch tried to wind me up by using her hand to splash water over me from the river. 'Stop doing that, you stupid cow,' I said to her, partly out of annoyance, partly to let the Bedfellows hear we were English. Goofy agreed with me and muttered something to her. She stopped splashing and pouted. A minor victory.

We stopped at a village; torches were turned off so no-one could see us. We were ordered to keep our heads down. We heard some conversation, then a squealing pig was thrown into the back of the boat. We set off again, then stopped to pick up another guerrilla before speeding off down the river.

There was a jolly mood in the boat, everyone delighted to be able to put up their feet and relax. The guerrillas switched on their radios to listen to their favourite music, poked fun at one another, splashed water on one another, laughed and shouted. I felt thirteen again, as if I were on a school outing. It felt just like the chaos of thirty children running rampant on a coach, waving or making rude signs at the cars behind them while the teachers sat at the front blissfully unaware. Except this time there were no teachers to control it. Everybody was infected by the party mood.

The river ended abruptly and we turned into a large swamp-like area of shallow water. Behemoth trees reached out over the water silhouetted by a yellow, gibbous moon, vines hanging down from their branches. A frog chorus rang out in the night air. We raced along narrow waterways linking swampy zones, the engine roaring, music blaring out, all the guerrillas dancing and cheering. Soon we had to slow down and weave our way through the trees. The Knight jumped up onto the bow of the canoe holding a long sturdy pole, which he used to push the front of the boat away from obstacles. He successfully kept the prow clear of any objects, but then the driver revved the engine, increasing the boat's speed and flooring

The Knight. He almost fell into the water.

'¡*Carajo!*' he exclaimed. Shit!

A roar went up; shrieks of laughter echoed through the swamp. We crashed head on into a tree and abruptly thudded to a stop, all of us lurching forward with the impact. The Knight unsteadily got back to his feet and pushed the pole against the tree. The driver reversed a short distance, then revved the engine. Crash! We hit the tree again. Water sprayed everywhere. Another roar of delight went up. It was like being on a log flume at a theme park.

'¡*Carajo!*'

The Knight was flat on his back in the boat once more.

'¡*Aguante, aguante, aguante pendejo!*' Stalky cried out to no-one in particular. 'Put up with it, you jerk!'

The pig in the back of the boat squealed maniacally. The women were in hysterics. We kept trying to set off, The Knight pushing with his pole, but whenever the engine revved and we started forward, he would fall down and swear and everyone would laugh and shout. It happened again and again and again. Each time the uproar was louder than the last. The pig's squeals got louder, too. So much for travelling furtively at night.

The journey resumed, we soon arrived at a set of rapids. Large logs and river debris barred our way. The driver revved his engine loudly, accelerating us forward rapidly. I held on tight, then there was a crunching sound and we came to a sudden halt. We were grounded. There was

269

too much weight in the boat. The guerrillas jumped out onto the tangle of driftwood, ordering us to remain seated. They heaved and pushed, edging the pirogue forward, shouting, yelling and cursing. From God knows where they produced a chainsaw. It was fired into action and used to cut logs underneath the boat, screaming away just a foot from my face. It was not the place to be: the chain was slack, and wood chips and water flew in all directions. More tugging and heaving followed but the boat shifted only slightly.

I felt a sudden urge to get out of the boat. I wanted to see the Bedfellows and, more importantly, to escape the chainsaw. So Tom and I got out, explaining that it would lessen the load for them to lift. In the torch beams I could make out two *mestizos* in T-shirts and Wellington boots. They sat patiently in the boat behind each other, their eyes covered with towels. It was only a fleeting glimpse but conclusive proof that others had been captured. I wondered what they were thinking with all this commotion going on around them. They could only hear the chaos and confusion. For some reason, we hadn't been blindfolded.

Eventually the boat was pulled over the logjam and we carried on through the swamp, arriving at more open waters a few hours later. The forest was now behind us, and we found ourselves cruising through a channel surrounded by tall reeds. Brandy and cigarettes were produced. I was allowed to finish off the brandy. Tom took a swig but it made him gag. I finished it off and threw the empty bottle into the water.

The boat was steered into a side bay and we got out to be greeted by Panama Hat. How he'd arrived ahead of us was anyone's guess. He led us to a sleeping village where we spent the night in a hut, before being woken and moved on an hour before first light.

12

STEALING FOR BRITAIN

TOM: 'We are staying here for ever.'

Goofy's jaw jutted out defiantly as he spoke, but then it always did. The new camp looked unpromising, but then they always did. At least, after a month on the move, the travelling was over.

'*Bueno, señor*,' I replied enthusiastically.

I think Goofy thought his comment would perturb us, and inwardly it did, but I was never going to show him that so I looked around at the damp mass of jungle like a pioneer gazing at a new frontier. Goofy grunted and went off to start building.

It was a blessed relief to rest. My legs were strained and layers of skin were peeling from the soles of my feet. But the relief was tempered by the fact that our new camp was bordered on one side by a creek with no flow. The murky water simply stood still, barely shimmering in what little breeze there was. Paul and I were expected to wash in this, where the guerrillas also scrubbed their utensils and clothes. They disappeared out of the camp, to another water source presumably, to bathe. Within only a few days of striking camp the water had become stagnant and soiled by waste washed from

272

cooking tins; oil and detergent filmed the surface. It worsened, if that was possible, at the end of that first week when a crocodile was caught and slaughtered for food. Slowly, inexorably, its intestines drifted downstream. The whole area stank of sulphur. Much as we hated it, bathing was strictly enforced, but it was impossible to get clean; we were even expected to drink from the stream. To avoid the very real danger of catching typhoid or dysentery, I built us a device for collecting rainwater — huge *Heliconia* leaves supported by V-shaped sticks — but any precipitation was erratic. Disillusioned by such a dank, dark camp and the ever-present and hungry mosquitoes, we named it Stagnant Creek.

The Bedfellows were on the opposite side of the camp, hidden behind a fringe of trees. The Knight camped alongside to keep a close eye on us, while the others bivouacked on the ground between our fellow hostages and us. Goofy and The Bitch took pride of place in the middle, a pet squirrel and tortoise tied to their shelter. The poor tortoise had had a hole drilled in its shell to which a piece of string had been attached as a kind of leash. Each day it would strain ponderously forward, trying to break the shackle. Why they kept it tethered was beyond me. Given half the chance I would have freed it, but I didn't fancy its chances of a quick getaway.

Paul was as depressed as he had been throughout the whole ordeal during that first week. He barely said a word to me or anyone else. I asked him what was wrong and he said he was missing home. He spent most of his time in the tent, either sleeping or thinking. The leg injury, the walk and the prevailing tension simply sucked the energy from him.

Meanwhile, I sat in silence, bored, doing little except smoking — I was having one cigarette every evening now, enjoying the dizzy head rush it gave me — while the guerrillas became farmers. Food was in short supply so a vast area was cleared and maize sown. A smaller separate area was felled and sacks of young rice plants were brought in and planted. The quick and efficient way they approached the task suggested that many of them came from a farming background. I attempted to develop a small patch of my own, cultivating maize, citrus fruits, squash and papaya, but transplanting and germination proved impossible in such a badly drained plot. They slaughtered a cow and I tried to use its intestinal tract, blood and stomach contents to persuade my crop to succeed, but to no avail. I could only look on with envy at a guerrilla we had named Smurf, because he bore an uncanny resemblance to one of the short, stumpy, bulbous-nosed cartoon characters. He successfully cultivated a cabbage patch in an open, well-drained site. The only horticultural uplift I received at Stagnant Creek came when I managed to slip away for a second to see an outstandingly beautiful and stately cannonball tree (*Couroupita guianensis*). The arching cannons were sensational but I could find no viable seed to slip into my pocket. Then there was a shout, and behind me, sure enough, stood

274

The Bitch, beady-eyed as ever, swearing and cursing at me.

She more than lived up to her name around camp. On Saturday mornings the radio would blare out some station that played Colombian folk music. The Bitch insisted I dance with her. 'Dance, Tomás!' she would bark. She'd grab my hand and we would do a Colombian dance called the *vallenato* for a while. Despite my having the proverbial two left feet, she became furious if I stopped.

'Why not dance?' she would scream.

'Because I'm tired.'

'Dance or die!' she would shout.

Put like that, I felt I didn't have much of a choice. I dreaded Saturday mornings.

The earth oven they'd constructed soon became flooded with rain, and frogs started to hop into camp. The whole place resounded with their croaks. In turn, they attracted the attention of predators. A yellow snake slithered into camp one day. It was in fact a regular visitor and I had watched it many times when it came looking for food in my failing vegetable patch. This time it made its way towards the frogs and I watched as it dislocated its jaw and went to swallow one of them. Then The Bitch came over and with a stick started to beat the snake ferociously. She did this for ten minutes until the snake was just a shredded bloody pulp on the ground. Scarface looked on with concern. When she'd finished massacring the snake, he spoke to her.

'It wasn't poisonous,' he said.

'I don't like snakes,' she snapped back.

I looked at a few of the other guerrillas. They were all shaking their heads.

★ ★ ★

PAUL: I'm sinking. It's more than five months since our capture and it feels like a careering juggernaut has crushed every ounce of energy out of me. The attrition of the situation is overwhelming. The guerrillas are so determined to get some money for us, or keep us for ever in this hole of a jungle. They're certain to kill us when the ignorant idiots realize we serve no purpose. I don't know what to think, or to say to Tom. For five days at Stagnant Creek I have been silent. This is unusual; we always talk, joke and laugh. We rely on each other to keep morale high, to stand defiantly and united against these people. Now I feel I'm fighting a lone mental battle. I'm fighting the demons in my head and I have no right to burden Tom with them. Could this really be the end? '*Siempre en la Selva.*' You will stay in the forest for ever. The words repeat in my head ceaselessly. I feel as if I am teetering on the edge of existence.

I lie in the tent doing little, feeling little. All my optimism is spent. I'm trapped, alone and frightened with only a vast expanse of nothingness stretching out in front of me. Just nothing, empty and void. I don't want to die. I am too young and inexperienced. I haven't lived enough and I have so many more things to do with my life, so many good times and laughter ahead. But I can't shake this feeling, this crushing emptiness. I cannot escape the depression and weariness. I hate the daylight hours, when I can see a reminder of my error: the decision to come here. I hate the guerrillas and their constant vigilance. I want to be alone so I can try to work things out in my mind. I am disappointed and angry that my life is destined to end in this pointless way. During the night, though, I'm safe and comfortable. Ensconced in the tent, I can curl up and feel secure, away from the maddening guerrillas, and when I sleep, I can escape. But I still have the dream. Trapped on the tube, buried alive.

When I can't sleep I stare into the night. My mind races with thoughts of home, thoughts of my youth, of carefree days, of memories good and bad, of regrets, of failures, of successes. Sometimes I switch track abruptly and spin off in another direction, making plans for the future. Then reality hits me like a bolt of lightning and with a force I cannot comprehend. The emptiness. Once again I am left reeling, confused and dazed. My fitful sleep continues all night, sometimes broken by my dreams, sometimes by the guards shining a torch in my face. The night passes in a gentle delirium. Towards dawn, when I am exhausted, I fall into a deep slumber.

When I wake I am in a daze, and it takes me ten minutes to collect my thoughts and realize where I am. Yes, I really have been kidnapped and I have been in the jungle for months. Yes, I walked freely into this hellhole. During the day, I'm silent. I desperately try to escape the nothingness by dropping into a routine. Keep

277

your mind busy, I repeat to myself. Get up and have a cigarette, eat breakfast, run through facts, figures, places and countries in the Lonely Planet. But I'm bored with my guidebook; I have read every page many times over. I eat lunch, smoke, wash, smoke, waste away the hours sleeping, eat dinner, smoke and return to the night and the dream. Cards, draughts, chess — everything bores me. The busy mind that has saved me so far is now empty. The plug has been pulled. Overwhelmed by lethargy, I start to accept my fate.

★　★　★

TOM: Among the Spanish and Latino pop, an occasional Western hit thundered out around the camp. It was always a delight to hear one. 'Sweet Dreams' by the Eurythmics was popular on *Apartado Estereo*. One day Bon Jovi's 'It's My Life' rang out around the camp and I ended up humming it for days afterwards. Until, that is, the irony of the words occurred to me. It may be my sodding life, Jon Bon, but who's in control of it now? Not bloody me.

Singing along to the radio was inadvisable whenever The Bitch was around. She had moved on from forcing me to dance the *vallenato* to making me dance for her whenever it took her fancy. Heaven forbid I ever hummed a song. '*Dance!*' she would exhort, and I would have to find suitable moves to accompany the Spice Girls song I'd been humming.

I was out in the camp one evening when a

ferocious thunderstorm broke, so I sought shelter in the food store until it passed. Next to me were stacks of food, and before I'd even stopped to think I'd picked up a pack of Mr Quaker's maize cake powder and tucked it under my shirt. Once the rain had subsided, I went back to the tent, clambered in and showed Paul the booty.

'Where did you get that?'

'I stole it.'

'You what!'

'I sheltered in the food store, saw it and thought, 'What the hell!' Screw these bastards. They're not giving us anything.'

It was true. They rarely shared the best food with us now; our diet was a monotonous parade of *plátanos*, cow and rice and little else. Some days they didn't feed us at all.

I opened the pack and we ate it uncooked.

'That is truly revolting,' Paul said, and I had to agree.

But I was hooked. Each time it rained at night, I would pull on my boots as gently as possible, unzip the tent tooth by tooth and tiptoe — a difficult thing to do in wellies — out, the noise of my clumsy gringo footsteps drowned out by the hammering rain. I'd creep to the store, past the sleeping Goofy and Bitch, and steal as much as I could in pitch darkness. Once I'd worked out the route it was fine. My shirts and shorts filled with goodies, I'd creep back.

The best was always *panela*. Paul and I loved this snack, made from the juices of crushed sugar cane, boiled until solid. When I first brought it back we licked it until we were almost sick. I was addicted now, and I would go out even in a brief shower, though not always successfully. One time it was so dark and the rain so light that I became paranoid. I grabbed the first thing I could find. Back at the tent, Paul inspected the swag.

'This feels a bit funny for *panela*, Tom.'

It turned out I'd stolen a pack of fifty chicken stock cubes.

'What are we going to do with these? If the guerrillas find them they'll go berserk.'

Good point. We tried to get rid of the evidence by licking them, but we suffered chronic bellyache. The only option was to take them back. With only darkness to cover me, I made my way to the stall and put back as many as I could before hurrying back to the tent. The Bitch stormed over.

'Who has been out?' she demanded.

We both shook our heads and shrugged our shoulders.

'There are mosquitoes in here,' she said. 'Someone has been out.'

'Oh, *señora*,' I said all of a sudden, 'I went to urinate.'

This placated her. It was only when Paul went for a piss first thing next morning that he noticed I had dropped stock cubes from the tent door to the store, leaving a perfect trail of guilt. The Bitch had not seen them in the muddy path and had trodden them into the dirt.

It was not only mosquitoes that had entered the tent during my raid. Unbeknown to Paul, a scorpion had scuttled in and curled up inside his warm, inviting armpit. He noticed it the next morning.

'There's a scorpion in my bed,' he said, a bit like someone might say, 'There's a fly in my soup.'

Without any histrionics or any betrayal of fear whatsoever, he calmly and carefully picked up the unwanted lodger and deposited it outside the tent.

'Watch out next time you go stealing,' he said matter-of-factly, lying back down on his bed.

Despite my narrow escape, the stealing continued. August Bank Holiday was the most successful: I conducted one raid in the early hours and one as dawn rose. It was not even raining during that second raid. I was in danger of becoming cocky, but neither Paul nor I complained as we munched our way through four blocks of *panela*. By the time we'd finished we both felt sick. Then they called us to collect our breakfast — an unappetizing plate of meat. If we refused to eat they would become suspicious, so we forced it down. I was unable to move or sleep that day because I felt so bloated.

To steal successfully from the guerrillas was one of the most rewarding, morale-boosting and adrenalin-packed experiences of my life. Every trip filled me with feelings of power. Both Paul and I grinned because we knew that although they were in control, we could find ways to fight back. Thankfully, this had a good effect on Paul. Secretly eating our haul in the tent, with the guerrillas oblivious only a few feet away, was immensely satisfying. I felt almost patriotic, as if I were stealing for Queen and Country. Britain expects its hostages to swipe sugar!

Yet one thing could not be ignored: *panela* stocks were getting low and suspicions were being aroused. Vague mutterings started to circulate around camp.

'You're going to have to chill out, Tom,' Paul reminded me, 'or they'll get really suspicious.'

I agreed and, to my disappointment, the raids ended.

★　★　★

PAUL: Tom boosted my spirits brilliantly. His forays for food gave me a real lift. Sitting in the tent licking blocks of sugar and giggling like schoolkids while the guerrillas wondered what the hell was going on did wonders for my mood. The dream became less frequent. I felt my strength returning and I began to shake off my bout of self-pity. There was no way I was going to let them beat me.

I emerged from the tent more and more. Tom tried to interest me in what was going on. One day he called to me from across the camp where he was standing behind a tree.

'Have a look at this!' He was wide-eyed, his voice a hoarse whisper.

I can't say I was too excited; I expected an orchid of some sort. Instead there was a spider the size of a dinner plate. Well, at first glance it looked that big. Closer inspection revealed it to be the size of an outstretched hand. Still, big enough. It had fat, hairy legs that moved slowly and deliberately as it crawled around. Its iridescent pink and purple body was covered with a form of fur that stood on end, sparkling in the dappled morning light.

'It's magnificent,' Tom exclaimed.

We stared at it for fully five minutes.

'Let's not make too much fuss,' I said eventually. 'We don't want The Bitch to come over here and smash it to pieces with a stick.'

We went back to the tent. Neither of us would ever flinch at the sight of a household spider again, that's for sure.

After breakfast each day I would go out and sit on a log in the cool morning air. Here the area was cleared of vegetation so few mosquitoes disturbed me. I would spark up and have a few words with God. I always smoked while praying.

'Sorry about the fag,' I would say. 'I'll stop once I'm out of here.'

It always felt odd to be talking to Him. Although I'd been raised a Catholic, I'd let this lapse many years ago. But I found solace during those times on the log. I didn't want to disturb God too much and felt a little hypocritical about it all; I'm not a very religious person and I knew full well that it was the moment of crisis that was provoking the need to pray. But it was usually just a simple prayer, asking him to protect us and to comfort everyone back home and the many others in worse circumstances than ours.

I don't think either of us ever enjoyed a full night's sleep when we were in a permanent camp; the exhaustion from a day's march was necessary to get decent rest. As we lay awake one night, we both heard a crashing sound. My first thought was that a large branch had fallen and landed on something. Deadfall in the jungle was an ever-present danger. Almost immediately the camp exploded into noisy activity.

'Bloody hell, what's going on out there? Did you hear that crashing sound?' I whispered to Tom.

'Yeah, it sounded nasty.'

A few minutes later, Scarface poked his chubby head through our tent door and hissed at us to wake up. Tom reacted first. I heard a garbled conversation in Spanish.

'What's going on?'

'I don't know for certain. Someone's been hurt. I think it could be one of the Bedfellows.'

There was more conversation.

'They're asking us for some cream,' Tom said.

More guerrillas joined Scarface and the conversation continued. Then they disappeared.

'Tom, they want the Deep bloody Heat. Jesus, they still think it's the miracle cure for everything.'

'What should we do?' Tom asked nervously.

'Don't give it to them. Look what it did to my foot. It's hardly going to help some poor bastard who's been hit on the head by a tree. Say you haven't got it.'

'But if I tell them I haven't got it and they find it, they'll know I was lying.'

'In the morning, when I go for a dump, I'll bury it in one of the shitholes. They won't find it there.'

Tom seemed happy with this though he was still very nervous. I was adamant, though, as one who had suffered from their quackery.

The next day, after interring the Deep Heat, I caught a glimpse of one of the guerrillas piggybacking one of the Bedfellows across to another shelter. He was dark-skinned and possessed a mass of curly dark hair. It looked as if he was badly hurt. The guerrillas came looking for the Deep Heat again but we said we no longer had it. They were upset, but accepted the explanation.

The next morning, Tom came back from a dump.

'Paul,' he said nervously, 'last night's rain flooded the shitholes. I could see the top of the Deep Heat bobbing around in there.'

'What did you do?'

'I pushed it back under the surface with my foot.'

'We're going to have to keep an eye on it. Make sure you take your boots off before you come into the tent.'

As time passed, we discovered that there was only one Bedfellow left. We never found out what happened to the other one.

The Bitch was still giving me problems. Nothing stopped her antagonizing me, and she never seemed to bore of the constant and unrelenting harassment. She always served the food with a smirk, dishing out as little as possible to us and keeping the best bits for herself and for everybody else. She never, ever cooked and did no other work around the camp. She did what she wanted, which was usually nothing, apart from trying to goad the gringos.

'Are you angry, Pablo?' she often asked as she gave me my bowl.

Angry? I'm furious with you. I hate everything about you. But I won't give you the satisfaction of seeing this.

'¿Qué? . . . Sí, mucha energía, muy sabroso, muchas gracias,' I replied, pointing at the 'tasty' food.

'No, are you angry?' she repeated harshly.

'Gracias, muchas gracias,' I said.

She looked at me in disgust, then looked around hoping to get a reaction from one of her cohorts, a comment or some attention. But they were more interested in eating. Frustrated at not being able to bait me, she gave up.

Throughout the kidnapping Tom and I always maintained our manners in true English style, though often we would ham this up. We'd never let a moment or comment pass without saying thank you or please or how lovely the camp is or how tasty the food is or how kind it is of you to provide a horse to carry my pack. At first this amused them; please and thank you rarely appeared in their vocabulary, and I think they thought us a little eccentric. Now they were bored with it, just as they were bored with the whole situation. When we complimented the food, the camp, their dress sense now they either stared angrily or swished an arm and cursed.

Every day, just after lunch, The Bitch ordered us to wash with her. By now the water was truly appalling. Soap and bits of food mingled with the dirt. You could cup a small amount of this water in your hand and not be able to see the skin beneath because of the filth suspended in it. I went to rinse my hair once and succeeded only in making it greasy. As I ran my hands through it, I could sense it was cooking oil. Bits of rice stuck to strands of my hair. Attempting to wash it out made it greasier and dirtier. The whole thing made me sick.

The banks of the creek were too muddy and strewn with thorns to make access easy, so the guerrillas built a bridge flush with the surface from which to wash. Typically, The Bitch ordered us to bathe away from the pontoon. We had to wash knee deep in mud and be careful where we trod. I cleaned my body and upper legs, though when she saw that I had done this she would come over and hurl mud at me, ordering me to wash again, cackling like a witch. This would be repeated several times. Every day we went through this tiresome ritual and there was nothing I could do but put up with it. Any reaction from me merely encouraged more mud slinging. Bathing became completely pointless and a wearisome task; I'd always finish dirtier than when I'd started out. I seethed with resentment.

★　★　★

TOM: Paul's mood continued to improve and his old defiance returned. We pestered them continually for access to a freshwater source because the creek was by now covered with an inch-thick layer of grease. Eventually they relented, and we were allowed to go and fill our bottles at another, far less grimy, stream at the other side of the camp.

As we set off one day for the stream, The Bitch asked us to fill her two plastic soda bottles for her. At the stream, Paul diligently began to fill them.

'Dare you to piss in it,' I said, half-joking.

I should have known Paul was not a man to dare. As he peed, the water turned a light yellow.

'Shit,' he said, 'I think she'll notice.'

'Hang on.' I shook the bottle and the colour dissolved. There was only the slightest tinge of yellow now. 'You're not going to give it to her, are you?'

Paul simply smiled and took the bottle back to camp. He handed it to The Bitch.

'*Gracias, Pablo,*' she said with a leer.

She unscrewed the bottle and took a deep, hearty swig from it. Paul and I went straight into our tent and stuffed clothes into our mouths to muffle the laughter.

A few days later, she fell ill.

Talk among the guerrillas about our being 'problems' continued. In a way, this was heartening. Go on lads, solve your problem: release us!

Then one day I overheard Scarface and Goofy arguing about Paul and me. I couldn't make all of it out, though I did hear someone say the words 'Paul does not serve'. They had mentioned this before: *Pablo no sirve*. The conclusion seemed to be that Paul was worthless and they

288

should get rid of him. How that would be expedited, they didn't say. Furthermore, I could swear I'd heard Scarface say that I had a 'pretty house'. This sent my mind reeling. Had they found out about Lullingstone? I was terrified, and ran straight to Paul to relay the conversation.

'They know about Lullingstone,' I said breathlessly.

'How?'

'I don't know. I've just heard Scarface say I've got a pretty house.'

'It's just bullshit, Tom. Don't worry about it.'

'I heard them, Paul.'

'How could they find that out? Neither Colombian newspapers nor radio stations would give out that sort of information.'

His conviction was reassuring. Paul always managed to put me at ease whenever I became scared or worried. He was a good person to have beside me in a situation like this.

13

LET'S ESCAPE

TOM: The foul, polluted stream eventually became too much even for the guerrillas to bear, and on 9 September we moved from Stagnant Creek. The next choice of camp was superb, by far the best yet. Free of the stifling jungle canopy and atop a hill, it was near a clear-flowing stream that led to a small waterfall. The trek there was a short one, too, and the first thing we and everyone else did was wash. Shedding the layer of grime accumulated at the last camp felt like putting on a new skin. Mosquitoes were few and far between and a fresh breeze blew around us, keeping us dry and acting as a palliative to the intense jungle heat. Small luxuries once taken for granted had become the biggest deals: wearing dry clothes, a stream with a current, feeling fresh not fetid air on our faces. Spectacular sunsets and pale moonlit nights gave us a sense of freedom, a sense of new beginnings. Paul in particular looked revitalized by the change, as if he had scrubbed away his doubts and despair during our dip in the stream.

The site, unlike the others, was already a cleared area. There was a wood hut there; a vegetable plot, too. Goofy and The Bitch took the rancho, as we called the hut; the rest of their bivouacs were built from scratch. Paul and I were also in a hut, open-ended at either side with a raised platform, on which we erected the tent. The camp was on the crest of the hill. Running eastwards down the slope was a maize field, which turned into another containing sugar cane. Beyond that, out of sight, some thirty minutes' walk away, was a village. Because of the proximity of the crops, food supplies looked more promising. The guerrillas bought a clutch of chickens, presumably from a trader in the village. The Bitch was fond of bragging how these chickens could lay up to fifty eggs a week. After a week, however, not a single egg had materialized. They were all mystified. The Bitch got angry.

'Where are the fucking eggs?' she shouted at the chickens, who in the face of this verbal onslaught understandably began to cluck in a disconcerted fashion.

It became the hot topic of conversation. Debates raged about the unproductive chickens and the reasons for it. Could it be the heat? The feed, perhaps? Or were they just rotten chickens? Voices were raised and, as usual when a number of the guerrillas joined in and became excited, translation became an inexact science. The next day, Scarface ended the debate. It seems he'd gone to the local village to investigate the mystery.

'They are all female,' he said.

There was a stunned silence. No-one laughed. Well, no-one apart from two gringos who giggled away furtively in their tent for a good hour.

As they busied themselves building camp, I constructed a bench on top of the slope out of wood from the trees they'd felled. When I'd first seen the camp my mind had turned to horticulture: a slope = good drainage; no canopy = excellent light source; fertile soil = ideal for cultivation. Immediately I decided to build the mother of all gardens. Not quite the ambitious multi-million-dollar glass-covered dome I'd been sketching in my diary for my return to Lullingstone, but one that would test my gardening abilities all the same. As yet there was not enough room to work in — the maize field hemmed us in somewhat — but the prospects were good.

One evening, Paul and I were sitting on the bench eating our evening *plátanos* and rice. We'd been at the site for about a week. As we ate we gazed at a glorious sunset, commingling with a rainbow caused by a tropical storm rumbling somewhere in the distance which painted the sky in a kaleidoscope of oranges, pinks and purples. The awesome sight silenced us.

'Let's escape,' he said, all of a sudden.

I nearly fell off the bench.

★　★　★

PAUL: 'We've no choice, Tom, we've got to escape.'

He recognized the seriousness in my voice, but he didn't react. Before this point all talk of escape had been in jest, nothing more than a fantasy. Or it was always planned for some indefinite point in the future. However, during these first few days in this new camp our first real opportunity arose.

Tom had been down to the cane field to collect dessert and had noticed a small path that ran out the back of it.

'I looked down it,' he told me. 'All I could think about was running down it and getting away from these idiots.'

Below us, the maize field was ready to be harvested. The plants were more than head high. Within seconds a person could be among them and out of sight, completely covered. In my mind, I'd formulated a plan.

'Tom, we've been held for six months now and they're still determined to get their money, which we know isn't coming. They probably haven't even made contact with anyone yet. The longer this goes on, the less likely it is that we'll get away with it.'

'Do you mean it?'

'Yes. They'll kill us, won't they?'

'No. Do you mean it about the escape?'

'Absolutely.'

'How're we going to do it?'

I pointed down the slope to the maize field.

'We'll make it into there when no-one's looking. We can't do it at night because of the guard, but you know how lax it can be during the day. Perhaps when we're having a wash.'

There was yet another long silence as Tom thought about it. Flashes of lightning scratched across the multicoloured cloud.

'By the time they realize something is up,' I

added, 'we'll have a decent start and be on our way.'

He put down his plate of food and turned to look at me, his eyes bright and dancing with excitement.

'Let's do it.'

That was all I wanted to hear.

'What about your leg?'

'It feels OK. Not sure how fast I can run but I'm sure I could keep going.'

I'd been hoarding painkillers, and I already had twenty of them — two a day for ten days.

After six months of guarding us it was true that the guerrillas were relaxed in our presence, to the point where it was obvious they expected us never to run, an attitude we had encouraged by never giving the impression that we would rebel or cause trouble. Should they believe we might escape, or that the money would never arrive, then it did not require a genius to work out that we had learned a lot about them and the region they controlled; therefore, if we escaped, we could lead the military or whoever directly to them. We could offer up all the assurances in the world about not telling people who they were and where they were, but the chances of their accepting that were nil. Dead men don't tell tales. Our only option was escape, but if we took it then it had to be planned to perfection and carried out with conviction. If we messed up, or were half-hearted and were caught making a run for it, the guerrillas were almost certain to kill us.

Other than finding a quick, direct route to safety over traversable terrain, the major obstacle was lack of food. Battling our way through the jungle might take some time, perhaps a week or more, so we needed to have at least a week's supply. Even that might not suffice, but it would do. The rest we might be able to scavenge from the land. No-one in the region could be relied upon or trusted to help us.

I decided to steal food whenever possible. Luckily, at this new camp, which we'd named Inspirational Site because of the resurgence of energy and will we experienced there, the guerrillas were careless: the food was piled up on a wooden dais under a spacious open-sided tin shelter. This shelter provided the only seating area for us all during the day when it was raining or when the sun's rays became too powerful, so I had an excuse to gain access to it. I could sit near the pile of dried food for as long as I wanted, just waiting for the chance to spirit away a bag of rice or a block of *panela*. Tom's face screamed concern whenever I sat there biding my time. His raids at Stagnant Creek had been opportunistic hit-and-run affairs. My strategy was stealthier.

The first strike came the morning after we reached the decision to escape. I sauntered across to the food hut with my Spanish phrasebook and sat down on a stool, sheltered from the burning sun by the corrugated iron roof.

'Get lost, son of a whore,' hissed Scarface, shoving me from the stool.

This was something I'd expected and planned for. The stools were for guerrillas only, so I was forced to make a seat for myself on bags of rice. If anyone asked why I was sat there, I could reply that I was obeying Scarface's orders. For a few hours I sat there reading my book, practising my Spanish and swatting away the odd mosquito with my towel, waiting patiently for a moment, the briefest opportunity, when their attention was diverted. As the morning progressed, one by one they left to clear the maize field.

My breathing was shallow with nerves and my palms were wringing wet, but I tried to look as composed as I could. The Bitch was the only one left in camp now, swinging lazily in a hammock in front of me. Then a voice called out from the field and she got up to investigate. As she did so, I swatted an imaginary mosquito with my towel then brought my hand down onto a bag of rice, carefully picked it up and rolled it into the towel. Casually, I stood up and walked back to our tent, rooted around pretending to search for my guidebook, deposited the rice under my pillow and returned to the pile of food to continue reading. No-one suspected a thing. I flashed Tom a triumphant smile and he gave me a discreet thumbs-up. Our escape bid was under way.

I became addicted to stealing from right under their noses and thought nothing of spending two or three hours under the shelter waiting for the right moment. Far from being bored, I enjoyed it. It was a nine-to-five job, staving off thoughts of death and fantasies of home. Every bag of rice, every item I stole, was a small revenge on our captors. As I sat there, the adrenalin careering through my body, thrilled by my own

296

audacity, I felt delight in the knowledge that the guerrillas were oblivious to what I was doing.

The next day I woke with renewed vigour and optimism. This was short-lived. Shortly after breakfast, I noticed that the men had moved to the bottom of the field and had started to clear the maize from there.

'They're going to clear the whole field,' I told Tom.

'That means we'll have to cross open ground before we can hide.'

'I'd better get the food together before they clear it completely,' I said.

The race was on.

That day I stole two items, and the next day, three. The competition hotted up: the guerrillas busily cutting back the field, singing and shouting while they worked, me busily relieving them of food at every opportunity. Days that had once crawled by painfully now passed in a flash. My audacity increased: even when the men stopped work and came back into camp, I continued to steal. They played dominoes close to me, even sat next to me and talked to me, but my larceny continued unhindered. The risk had to be taken. One afternoon a tree fell onto the roof of the food store during a storm, knocking down a panel of corrugated iron. In the mayhem and confusion that followed I stole two bags of rice.

Within two weeks each of us had what I estimated to be eight days of food. In total there were six half-kilo bags of rice, two bags of beans, twelve chicken flavourings, primarily for their salt content, and a few other items. We chose not to steal *panela*; it would rot quickly, was too sticky to carry and if it rained it would turn into an inedible mass. Tom chipped in after his initial reluctance with a bottle of cooking oil, part of a broken machete blade and a kilo of dried maize from the crop right next to us.

Yet not everything was going to plan. We'd lost the race against the field. The guerrillas had worked phenomenally quickly and there was now two hundred yards of open ground between our tent and the jungle. That was a heck of a long way to have to go without being seen.

Luck was with us, though. The day after I decided we'd collected enough, the food was moved from the wooden dais and stored more securely. Thankfully we already had everything we needed. I cannibalized other items we might need to survive on the run in dense jungle and made small survival 'pods'; Tom used his small rucksack, while I detached the top part of mine. They were hidden in our tent ready to be used at a moment's notice.

While I was stealing I had managed to avoid thinking about it, but now I had to face a major dilemma: I didn't know the best way to safety and civilization. I figured we were deep in Colombian territory, though exactly where I was unsure; my instincts told me we were probably further south than Río Sucio. Escaping eastwards or southwards would lead us nowhere but deeper into Colombia and more trouble. Trekking north-west towards Panama was impractical: the border was probably a month's hike away and the jungle between us was impenetrable in places, hence the need for us to travel by boat on the way here. Therefore we had two choices, both daunting. One was to head in a northerly direction for Turbo on the Caribbean coast, which, from what I could see on the map and had gleaned from the Lonely Planet, meant crossing interminable swamps. The distance covered in a day would be measured in metres not kilometres and we would have to rely on finding a river and floating down it for a hundred miles or more on debris. On the plus side, this route was more populated, so stealing food from plantations would keep us going. The more dynamic alternative was to rush west to the Pacific coast and then try to make our way north. The mountains in our path would be easier to traverse than the swamps, but it would take a long time — a month, maybe more — and it would be difficult to supplement our meagre supply of food. Furthermore, we didn't know if any of the coastal towns were guerrilla-controlled. Even if we made it that far, we would have to make our way up the coast to Panama. Either way I didn't rate our chances highly, but they were the only choices we had.

Tom and I discussed this problem at length.

'What do you think our chances are of making it from Robert to Tiny Tim?' Tom would ask.

'It looks almost impossible,' I would reply, looking at the map. 'We'd have to float down the Big River. It's a long way from the Mad City.'

At Inspirational Site we often coded our conversations. This had started months ago as a

299

means of disguising mention of the paramilitaries and FARC. But we needed to extend our vocabulary so that we could talk freely about the towns and villages in the region. We gave them Christian names: Colombian towns were male; Panamanian ones female. Río Sucio became Robert, Turbo was Tiny Tim, Púcuro and Paya were known as Patricia and Patsy, while Medellín was the Mad City. Tom and I were so absorbed in this newly found language that we even started to code innocent items. The humble *plátano*, the mainstay of our diet, became affectionately known as a 'stubby'.

The first stage of our escape plan was working out how to get cleanly away from the camp. Outrunning the guerrillas from a standing start wouldn't work: over the past six months we'd seen how they could cross the jungle ground far quicker than us. It was essential to get a head start through confusion and deception. If we left an obvious trail they would soon track us down. Due to their industry, escaping under the cover of the maize field was no longer an option. At night we were too closely guarded, and the coal-black jungle night made travel virtually impossible. Getting away during the day was impossible, too: we were constantly watched, though they didn't seem to insist on seeing both of us all the time. Often, if one of us was about, the other was able to wander freely and out of sight for a short while.

My lucky one-dollar watch was just about clinging on to life. The moisture in the jungle had ruined it; the hour digit was broken, but the minutes still showed. I used it to time how long I could bathe at the stream out of sight and unchecked. Once I managed forty-five minutes. I reported back to Tom. Then I persuaded him to join me to see how long we could both bathe before someone came to check on us.

'No-one else washes in the mid-afternoon, Tom. If we both go down there at that time we might get a head start.'

We managed thirty minutes before a stone-faced Perty came to see if everything was as it should be. That confirmed it as our best option.

There were other problems to solve, namely how to get our survival packs out of the camp unseen. They were too bulky and obvious to carry down for a bath. We could hardly strap them on our backs and say, 'Hi, boys, we're off now, thanks for the food and guiding us around the jungle and all that, but we need to go home.' Somehow I didn't think it would wash.

★ ★ ★

TOM: We watched the camp carefully, getting to know exactly who was where when and which guard was on duty, studying their movements as intensely as possible to see if there was some routine to it. But it was hopeless. In World War Two films German guards work like clockwork, with established shifts that allow Major General Tufton-Bufton and his escape committee to calculate the exact time to send Smiffy over the wall. This lot were anything but Germanic. I've yet to come across a single war movie where

301

'Jerry' disappears to have a shit by the river or spends all day dozing in a hammock.

Chinks and glimmers of hope appeared, though. One day the entire male population of the camp disappeared for a few hours, leaving just The Bitch and Loosey. (Nena had gone.) The idea came to us to knock these two out, and run away with the Bedfellow.

'But what happens if we fail to knock them out?' Paul asked. 'They'd scream the place down and then we'd be completely screwed.'

'Perhaps we could seduce them. I'll take Loosey; you take The Bitch. Then, when they're vulnerable, we can knock them out.'

'I think I'd rather just top myself now,' Paul said.

'What about if we grabbed one of their guns and blew The Bitch's brains out?'

There was a silence.

'Not sure if I fancy that.'

'Me neither.'

These plans, and others like them, came to naught and we settled on making a dash for it while the guerrillas believed we were bathing.

'We've got to go now,' Paul said to me one morning.

'All right,' I said, taking a deep breath.

This was it. No more planning, no more worrying; we were going to try to make a break for freedom or die in the attempt. The plan was to transport all the food and equipment down to the river bit by bit. When it was all stored down there, we would say we were going for a bath, collect our stuff and leg it. We estimated we'd have around twenty minutes before they became suspicious — enough for a reasonable head start.

I stuffed my Wellington boots with as much of our stolen supplies as possible and made my way to the river. There were a couple of guerrillas in camp but I gave them a jaunty wave and they assumed I was going for a dump or a pee, failing to notice that my ankles had mysteriously swollen overnight. I emptied out all the food, together with a machete I'd procured from the guerrillas in order to build a garden, and hid everything in the undergrowth before returning to the tent.

'What's going on?' Paul asked nervously.

'Nothing much. Just The Bitch and Loosey moping about. Chainy was a bit suspicious about things. He gave me a funny look, but I don't think he knew what I was up to.'

Outside, I could hear Chainy's voice. I got out of the tent. He was holding the machete.

Shit.

I tried to understand what he was saying. I didn't hear my name being mentioned, only that he'd found this — he waggled the machete in his hand — by the river. He looked over at me but there were no accusations. Perhaps he didn't know whose machete it was. Without it, escape was unthinkable. The prospect of fighting through thick jungle without a cutting instrument was preposterous. I could hardly go and ask for it back. I told Paul.

'Shit,' he said. 'We'll have to rethink. He probably hasn't seen the food. Yet.'

So, after a reasonable pause, I made my way

back down to the river for about the fifth time that morning. It didn't go unnoticed by The Bitch.

'*Majorda*, Tomás. Are you ill?'

I shook my head and carried on down to the river, refilled my boots with our supplies and trudged disappointedly back to our tent. Escape would have to wait for another time.

The guerrillas continued to raze the maize field until within a matter of days there was even more open ground stretching out in front of us. The chances of reaching cover before someone became aware of what we were doing were practically nil. Almost a month had passed at Inspirational Site, a month during which we had obsessed over escaping without ever really grasping the chance. It was just too daunting a prospect. We continued to hope for a more propitious moment.

A few days later, annoyed at having our escape foiled, I ran down the now decimated field and disappeared into the regrowth at the bottom where a tangerine tree grew. I picked a fruit and sprinted back into camp, fully expecting to be abused and shouted at by the guerrillas for disappearing so suddenly. But as I sauntered back into camp, no-one said a word. No-one had seen me go. Apart from Paul, who sat on the bench shaking his head in disbelief.

'I can't believe you got so far,' he said. 'It must have been two hundred metres. That could have been it. We could have escaped.'

'Let's do it, then,' I said.

'No, Tom. They might not have seen you just

now but what if they do next time? We can't risk it like that.'

Paul was being sensible, and I deferred to him. Part of me was willing to go whatever the risks, while another part of me knew it could be suicide unless it was carefully thought through and well executed.

★　★　★

PAUL: The plan faded. Being on constant alert meant we were always in a state of tension. Delaying the escape meant we could relax. I was disheartened, but I felt sure another chance would arise. It seemed clear that the guerrillas intended to keep us for a long time. Two years had been mentioned on a few occasions. We had the food, but we needed to be patient, to wait for them to make a mistake. Anyway, escaping from that camp promised to be a Herculean task. Deep inside Colombian territory, surrounded by enemies who were much faster than us and, worst of all, fenced in by impregnable swamplands, a successful flight was unlikely. We were not the SAS. Ideally, we would make the escape through Panama and go out the way we came in. It was imperative that when we made the break everything was loaded in our favour. We'd only get one chance.

Life slipped back into its old languid routine. One evening my interest was pricked when Goofy gathered the camp around him and delivered what appeared to be some form of lecture. He was no orator, but between us Tom and I managed to pick up snippets, not all of which made sense.

'We fight . . . England. The United States have everything . . . they take from the poor . . . they take from our country . . . politicians are corrupt . . . big companies give nothing to people.'

It seemed to be a pep talk justifying their actions. At one point, he held up a manual.

'We are here to protect the villagers . . . we are military . . . we must treat civilians with respect,' he continued.

Later, after the meeting broke up, I could see the guerrillas reading the manual, passing it around. I caught a glimpse of FARC on the front. They also had a copy of Sun Tzu's book *The Art of War*.

Unfortunately, it was easy to see that, for Goofy in particular, Tom and I represented the West; we had walked straight into Colombia's political chaos. Goofy was angry with us, angry with the West, and kidnapping us was justified. It was that simple. Part of me empathized, but I still wanted to make clear to them our lack of worth and our innocence.

Loose Teenager managed to provide us with some entertainment one morning when I caught her emerging from the bushes with The Knight, buttoning up her shirt, her hair dishevelled. The Knight, who must have been no more than nineteen but was built like a heavyweight boxer, only ever gave me fierce looks, but the look this time was coy, and Loosey tried to veil her embarrassment by giving me a playful slap when I smiled at her.

'Morning, Pablo,' The Knight said.

Odd. He never said 'Good morning'.

He shuffled back to camp. I decided against telling him this, but he was not her only suitor. Both Chainy and Smurf had tried in vain to woo her, offering gifts as a token of their admiration. Neither stood a chance compared to The Knight. Both of them were short, stubby characters. He towered over them.

14

LANDSCAPE GARDENING UNDER PRESSURE

TOM: Many times during our captivity I had dreamed about building my garden. At Inspirational Site I was able to put some of my ideas into practice. If I was not able physically to escape, then I could seek solace in plant husbandry and landscape gardening. I had to do something.

I'd taken the first steps when we'd arrived at Inspirational Site: using skinned poles and two V-shaped sticks, I'd constructed a bench outside our palm hut. During daylight hours my colourful Guatemalan rug was placed on top. This bench was used for socializing with Paul, practising Spanish, constructing materials, planning thieving raids, eating, reading and smoking. It was a place for thought, and it was here, watching the macaws, toucans and other brightly coloured tropical birds that circled the site at dusk, that I planned my real-life garden.

Inspiration came when the guerrillas cleared that maize field, revealing an orange-coloured substrate that felt like clay and cracked in the baking sun. Unlike previous sites, which were waterlogged and cast in deep shade, this site (approximately thirty feet by twenty-five feet) was open and free-draining. In other words, a perfect place to experiment with some original designs and tropical planting schemes.

First I created the framework of the garden. Using the guerrillas' spade and my homemade digging sticks, I cut a series of paths, and steps on the steepest parts, into the slope. I then used the excavated rusty-coloured soil to construct a small, attractive mud wall to form the garden's perimeter, creating a 'drunken square' with steps off to the right where we could urinate. The main planting region was the centre of the square.

Using a machete, I cleared unwanted scrub and herbaceous 'weeds' and pollarded and coppiced selected woody plants. Pollarding and coppicing as a form of management ensure that any regrowth is vigorous and produces large, decorative foliage, especially in the case of woody subjects from the pea family (Leguminosae) and *Cecropia palmata* (Cecropiaceae). This latter species is a fast-growing ornamental tree I decided to plant for its well-endowed palmate leaves. It's a pioneer species with pith like timber, attractively stilted roots and hollow stems in which ants make their home. These ants (*Azteca* spp.) have a carnivorous lifestyle, feeding on food bodies (glycogens) at the petiole bases on the *Cecropia* and attacking other grazers, especially leaf-cutter ants, but also the green fingers of a certain English hostage. I also pruned some cocaine bushes (*Erythroxylum coca*), which quickly sprouted producing a

309

lush, lime-green foliage.

No-one ever harvested it though. One day Chainy took a package wrapped in newspaper to Goofy's shelter. He came out to inspect what it was, while a few of the others gathered round. I was working on the garden when I heard Goofy hiss my name and gesture for me to join them. I walked over. Goofy was holding the package, now unwrapped.

'Do you know what this is, Tomás?' he said.

I bent over to take a closer look. I saw a large mount of greyish-white powder. I knew it was cocaine; it was similar to the stuff I had seen the Kiwi girls snorting in Panama City and I'd heard one of the guerrillas whisper '*cocaina*' as they'd come over to look.

But I thought it unwise to reveal my knowledge. I decided to remain the innocent abroad.

'Milk powder?'

There were a few sniggers. Goofy shook his head slowly. Chainy looked at me, then leaned forward and pretended to snort something up his nose. Then he opened his eyes and nodded vigorously at me.

'Are you OK, *señor*?' I asked, feigning concern.

His face darkened. He told me to fuck off so I went back to my garden. I have no idea what happened to the drugs, but I never saw anyone take it, or any signs of anyone having taken it, so I assume it was sold.

All this growth provided shade for the plot and gave a structure to it.

Using a pointed stick, I then removed a circle of weeds around each plant to reduce competition and increase its aesthetics. This method of cultivation was applied to all plants in the garden. Areas for planting (central square and perimeter borders) were dug over, and stones collected from the riverbed enhanced drainage. I sowed maize seeds (*Zea mays*, three to six per hole) on the lower perimeter and left-hand-side border as a screen against our captors. I tried to transplant young maize plants, but generally this proved unsuccessful because of the root damage and disturbance caused during the move, coupled with the underwatering of newly transplanted specimens.

Yuca (*Manihot esculenta*; Euphorbiaceae) stems were literally cut into sections by the guerrillas and plunged at an angle into disturbed ground in the maize field. I stole some for my plot for the central square region and they sprouted a treat. This provoked the occasional confrontation with Goofy, who was none too happy with my poaching. He would check his plot and then storm towards mine.

'Where are my yucas?' he would demand.

'Here,' I would say, pointing at the flourishing species.

'But it *was* over there.'

'But it's here now. Look, *señor*, it grows so well.'

'*¡Majorda!*' he would spit before storming off, shaking his head.

The yuca's lush, purple, deeply palmate tropical foliage proved to be a fertile backdrop for other plantings. A felled mature *plátano* (*Musa* × *paradisiaca*; Musaceae) was transplanted using a spade and heeled in — mature leaves were cut to reduce transpiration and thus stress — to form the central piece of the garden. Chainy offered me snippets of useful advice about dividing and transplanting suckering growths from other adult *Musa* plants into other areas of the garden. The broad leaves of taro (*Colocasia esculenta*), the tuber of which is used as a starch substitute, combined well with *Cymbopogon citratus*, commonly known as lemongrass, and the 'grassy' foliage of *Saccharum officinarum* (sugar cane). I collected short sticks from the nearby sugar cane field, which rooted easily when placed in disturbed ground.

My next creation, an utterly essential one for any decent garden, was a compost heap. Here I was helped by the guerrillas' slaughter of the local wildlife. A live cow appeared and was tortured while tied to a tree, strangling itself slowly as it tried to break its tether. First it was stabbed in the neck, then the heart, and then anywhere else it pleased both Chainy and Stalky. The glee and excitement with which they carried this out was unsavoury — both Paul and I felt ashamed to witness it — and deeply, deeply worrying. I wondered if they would treat humans in the same barbaric way if their financial requirements weren't met. Still, needs must. Once the cow was dead, and as vultures circled overhead, I popped open the cow's stomach with a machete and emptied out the green, warm, moist manure, moving the sludge to the garden area for the heap. Paul's look while I did this was not approving. Undeterred, I applied some of the cow's partly-digested foods 'neat' to the 'feet' of my cultivated plants in my ever-diversifying garden. This green manure served as mulch to reduce weed competition, it looked decorative, was almost odourless and fed the garden plants. At least the cow's horrific death contributed to the continuance of some form of life, I told myself.

With everything growing nicely, my attention turned to non-horticultural additions to the garden. I positioned a pull-up bar between a limb of a large tree, located at the bottom of the garden, and a seven-foot V-shaped pole. This structure formed a straight arch over the width of a portion of the lower path. A raised push-up bar was also placed in the far left-hand corner of the plot, among the cocaine bushes. For press-ups, going right down to the floor rather than just to the bar, as in a push-up, I sculpted 'pads' from split miniature logs to avoid the problem of muddy palms. Every day, in the late afternoon, before my wash, I performed a 'garden circuit'. This comprised fifteen press-ups, ten pull-ups and thirty push-ups, then some star jumps and running up and down the steps, mixed in with sprints to the river and the odd jump over a barrel. Soon the Bedfellow caught the fitness bug and decided to improvise, jogging and star-jumping in his basket-like hat in his restricted space. The guerrillas became competitive about the pull-up bar, seeing who could do the most, and the press-ups sparked the odd

313

challenge too. Loose Teenager, whose sugar consumption meant she was piling on the pounds, could never manage a single press-up, and The Knight would have to haul her up from the floor by her bra strap.

The garden was a beautiful place to sit, particularly by a full moon, when the banana tree, the main feature of the garden, was lit up and threw wonderful silhouettes across the whole space. I sat there looking at it bathed in its spectral light and thought longingly of home. By day, however, the sun was devastatingly hot, burning our skin so that it peeled. To lessen its effect — the only shade in my mini-Eden could be found under the large 'pull-up bar' tree at the bottom of the garden — two more benches were developed. The original bench outside our hut was shaded only until 10.30 in the morning, so I built a bench at the bottom of the garden that caught the shade between 10.30 and 12.15. The final seat was situated beyond the bottom of the garden, affording cool, dappled shade from 12.15 until 1.30. The baking heat didn't calm down until about four in the afternoon, so I fashioned a 'Hawkshead sunhat' from my old Hawkshead shirt and a few pieces of wood. It looked more like a kite! Unfortunately, these seated, shaded areas also provided respite for our captors who went there to clean their guns, sew, make gun belts or listen to their transistors, which at the time were transmitting results from the Sydney Olympics. Paul became increasingly territorial, sitting on the benches whenever possible to ward them off.

'It's our bloody garden,' he would say to me, 'not theirs.'

Over time I made ornamental additions to beef it up: a papaya (*Carica papaya*) seedling developed without my interference near our palm hut; a naranjilla or *Solanum* from the potato family was grown for its edible, though sour, orange fruits. The thorny, furry leaves and purple flowers were extremely decorative. Pepper (*Piper nigrum*) proved a useful gap filler. Both the pepper and naranjilla cultivars had regenerated freely in the garden, presumably from parent plants used as a crop by a previous farmer. The land had probably been cultivated for many years. *Annona squamosa*, or the custard apple, was transplanted from near the guerrillas' rancho to the garden. It would take many years before it fruited, but, hey, I thought to myself, I probably will see this small fruit tree in full bloom if these idiots keep this farce up. *Manilkara zapota* (Sapotaceae), although small when transplanted from the nearby river course (one foot high), filled me with enthusiasm. The latex of this tall tree supplies chicle, the most important base for chewing gum. The tree also produces the edible sapodilla fruit.

The most exciting addition, however, to the lower part of the garden was the yellow oleander, or *Thevetia peruviana*. Young seedlings germinated upon the disturbance of the soil, from the seed of a mature plant once grown there, or so I assumed. *Thevetia peruviana* is widely cultivated for its ornamental, mystically scented, large yellow flowers. The hard seeds are considered a

315

good luck charm. If Paul Winder wasn't to be my lucky charm, and the evidence thus far had been less than encouraging, these seeds would have to do. They never produced any fruit.

The garden became my outdoor 'room', a place in which to reflect, socialize with Paul and exercise in my wellies. I constructed a hardwood cricket bat and balls made from balsa wood (*Ochroma lagopus*; Bombacaceae) and we played some evening cricket on the specially levelled, bouncy pitch on the lower path. The paradise garden relaxed both of us. As a well-tended garden should.

Watching it fill out so quickly in the tropical, hot and humid climate pumped me full of joy. The maize plants were flowering, the vigorous stump regrowths were lush and the banana plants were throwing up their characteristically gigantic leaves. Taros, yucas and sugar cane planted in the 'central block' also thrived. The cane's grassy-looking leaves quivered mesmerically in the slightest of breezes. The Panama hat palm (*Carludovica palmata* — only six young leaves are required to make the famous hat), which I'd collected from the surrounding hills, however, was struggling under the beating rays of the hot sun. This wasn't my only mounting problem: my horticultural activities were causing conflict with the guerrillas. Goofy enforced strict yuca planting guidelines, his patience exhausted by my moving of plants to fit my design. He counted the yuca (*cassava*) plants within the garden's boundaries, noting their location. Worse, I was banned from using the spade and machete.

Keen to defuse these escalating problems, I put a stop to any new developments and concentrated on preservation and maintenance. Simple fences were constructed on the upper perimeter of the central square in order to prevent guerrillas taking a short cut across it — much like school children cutting the corners on a lawn. Aside from the obvious damage to plants, it also caused soil compaction. In flat areas, where compaction became a serious problem, water would remain on the soil surface for days on end and I had to dig out drainage gullies and place logs over the soggy clay. The compaction reduced healthy growth, especially in the maize plants, which then became weak and susceptible to pests and diseases.

The fence proved unpopular and was kicked to pieces. I tried to rebuild it but they always kicked it down, Perty the worst culprit. So I turned my attention to the steps, which had become cracked through overuse. I swept both them and the pathways with a broom I had made from *Cecropia* bark, freeing them of sugar cane peels, loose mud and leaves. Other chores included bench maintenance; weeding pathways; weeding near cultivated specimens and trimming their edges using the broken tip of a machete scavenged from the guerrillas; thinning the regrowth of pollarded and coppiced plants; realigning the push-up bar; regularly pinching out new cocaine growths to produce thicker, bushier specimens; and cricket bat and ball replacements after another orgy of destruction by the vandal Perty and his shady accomplice, The Knight.

Some pests were easier to repel than others. Paul and I banned the guerrillas' irritating *perricos* from the garden by muttering verbal abuse, throwing stones at them and kicking them if necessary. Naturally, when our captors weren't looking. The *perricos*, together with the resident crows and chickens, liked to nibble the young maize shoots and to steal the seeds. Further niggling issues were larvae root damage, wind damage to the banana tree and the wilting of my yuca plants, caused by unidentified burrowing mammals that wreaked havoc on the roots. Despite these obstacles, the garden looked outstanding, an English country garden transported to the jungle of Central America. Not that your average English garden includes an array of cocaine plants, of course.

★ ★ ★

PAUL: The guerrillas were becoming increasingly frustrated and bored with us. Open talk of our execution was becoming commonplace.

On his way back from washing one morning, Tom came over wearing a look of bemusement.

'What's wrong?' I asked.

'They keep on repeating a verb I haven't come across before.'

'What is it?'

'*Degollar.*'

It meant nothing to me either.

Tom buried his nose in his dictionary,

318

desperate to solve the conundrum.

'Here it is,' he shouted a minute later.

There was a pause.

'Come on, then. What is it?'

'It means to slit the throat.'

'Oh. Wonderful news.'

'Look, Paul, this is how to conjugate it.'

He started to explain. I stopped him.

'Tom, I don't know much Spanish, but of one thing I'm certain: I don't want to know how to conjugate the verb to decapitate.'

'Slit the throat, Paul.'

'Whatever.'

Personally, it was a part of my Spanish vocab I could happily live without.

Yet the guerrillas, despite their threats, were still insistent that they would get what they wanted out of us. Once, while sitting on the pile of food, Perty and The Bitch threatened me directly.

'Where is the money?'

'*No hay*,' I replied. There isn't any.

'If no money comes then you will be killed,' she told me with a relish that indicated she would lose little sleep over it. Perty followed this up by taking a machete and slicing it across his throat to illustrate how it would be done.

Later, when I'd calmed down a little, I dismissed it on the grounds that it had been said with no authority. I decided not to tell Tom, knowing he was nervous enough as it was. On another occasion, Chainy pointed a pistol at my head, though by now I was used to them waving guns about and I hardly noticed it. I noted it

319

wasn't directly aimed at me anyway, just slightly off to one side. The threat wasn't serious.

Another morning, as I bathed, The Knight passed by with Chainy and Perty on their way into the forest. They said something in Spanish I couldn't understand. The Knight wandered over to me waving his machete, a smile on his face. I decided to join in the joke. I guessed it was about killing me, so I went down on my knee and bowed my head forward, as if putting it on a chopping block. The Knight, giggling like a child, brought the machete very slowly down onto the back of my neck. The others laughed so I played up to it further, clutching my throat as if in pain. We laughed some more, then they disappeared into the forest.

They wanted to chop our heads off, or they would shoot us, or the money was coming soon: what to do with us was forever the topic of heated debate. They often discussed what had happened in other kidnappings. As far as we could make out, they'd either ended with money changing hands or in death. Understandably, Tom took this badly. Unlike me, who could pick up one word in a hundred, he could understand a lot more. Their morbid chats therefore affected him more.

They reverted to the original plan of splitting us up and sending one of us home, emphasizing this time that they'd prefer it if I was the one to go. I tried to persuade Tom this wouldn't happen.

'We stay together, whatever happens.'

★ ★ ★

TOM: The atmosphere around camp was agitated, even among the guerrillas. Machismo oozed from so many of them: Goofy, The Knight, The Bitch. Whether out of boredom or sheer competitiveness, they continually challenged one another to a series of bizarre games.

One was 'I can hold more dominoes in one hand than you'. In this, a guerrilla would try to grab as many dominoes as possible. The person with the biggest stack in their paw was declared the winner. The Knight, who had hands the size of satellite dishes, always won.

'I can jump over more people lying down than you' was another. This was hampered slightly by there being an insufficient number of people willing to offer themselves as obstacles. Thankfully, Paul and I were never asked. There were games to see who could do the most press-ups, and who could kick flowers the furthest — that one always broke my heart. The rivalry between Goofy and The Knight became increasingly intense because Goofy kept losing, which he found infuriating. The Knight could do more press-ups one-handed than the others could manage with two.

It all culminated in one of the strangest sights I've ever witnessed. From what I could make out, the aim of the game was to see who could headbutt the roof of the rancho the hardest. Goofy went first and narrowly missed. He tried again, straining and groaning with the effort.

'¡*Majorda!*' he screamed as his head at last connected.

Then came Smurf. He was terrible, but then he was no more than five feet in height. He bounced up and down like a child but it was a pathetic attempt. Perty was equally unsuccessful; Chainy was weighed down by his jewellery and also failed. The Bitch and Loosey declined to join in the fun.

Then came The Knight.

'My money's on him,' I told Paul.

He steadied himself, hands by his side, then crouched down before launching himself athletically into the air. With an almighty thud his head smacked into the wooden beam, the impact echoing around the jungle. The whole rancho shook. He betrayed no pain. Loosey gave him an adoring look, but Goofy shook his head, thwarted again.

The garden aside, life was boring; cards had lost their appeal, ditto draughts and chess. But I managed to borrow a children's copy of the Bible from The Knight (he said he would kill me if I failed to return it) and I idled away the time in the early evening translating it for Paul while we smoked a cigarette. Paul loved it.

With the tension still mounting, the excitement from the proposed escape still with me and sheer boredom still taking its toll, one morning I went down to the river, ostensibly to wash my pots and pans. To help relieve some of the strain, and with no-one around, I started to masturbate. I must stress at this point that this was not something I was in the habit of doing. But when you're bored, tense and harming no-one, why not? In my mind I fixed a picture of one of my more attractive female friends and buckled down to it. A few seconds later, when I'd finished and was pulling up my trousers, I heard a twig snap behind me. I turned round and spotted Stalky walking away.

'Did he see me?' was my first thought. 'Oh please, God, no!' was the second.

I took my time getting back to camp. As I approached I could hear nothing: no radio, no pointless chatter, nothing: 'That's strange,' I thought, and I knew something was amiss. I wondered what they would do if Stalky had indeed seen me and had told them all. It could be a complete no-no in Colombia, the ultimate taboo or something, the sign of a depraved, sick mind. It may be nowhere near as bad as being caught by your mum, but armed guerrillas must rank high alongside those people you'd rather not have happen upon you when you're masturbating. It even occurred to me they might be so offended as to shoot me on the spot.

I strolled back into camp as nonchalantly as I could, even whistling to show I was a man without a care. The guerrillas were sitting around the fire, all of them looking at me. They were completely silent. This, too, was very unusual. Something was definitely up.

'Tomás,' Goofy said, gesturing me over. 'Come here.'

I walked over.

'¿Señor?'

His tombstone teeth twisted into a seedy grin.

323

'*¿Tirando la paja?*'

Eh?

'*¿Tirando la paja?*' he repeated.

He was saying, 'Pulling the straw?'

Giggling broke out, though Stalky skulked about at the back, half embarrassed, obviously slightly concerned about his cohorts knowing he had watched me. I wondered what to do next. I decided to do what I always did — play the fool.

'Aaah, you mean pulling my penis, *señor.*'

'*Sí,*' he said, '*pene.*'

'Oh, I do that every day. It's good exercise and I enjoy it loads!'

The Knight looked at me, then lost it, breaking into laughter. The rest of them fell about, apart from a slightly bewildered Loosey, who seemed to want further explanation, and Perty, whose face was a picture of righteous indignation. A bit rich, I thought, from a man who spent most of his day playing with his bollocks.

I went to tell Paul, leaving a mess of hysterical guerrillas behind me.

'What's so funny, Tom?'

'Stalky caught me having a wank.'

There was silence.

'You are joking of course?'

I shook my head slowly.

Paul dropped his head into his hands. 'Oh. My. God,' he said.

The camp laughed about this for a whole week. Whenever I was having a bath, they would come up to me and say, '*¿Tirando la paja?*' It opened up a whole new topic for discussion: the

324

way to achieve the best orgasm. It lasted for a whole week and diverted them from talking about the money, our lack of compliance and ways of disposing of us.

'How do you do it in England?' Goofy enquired in all seriousness.

I turned it into a whole joke, making things up.

'If you put your left arm under your right leg and hold your nose, then when you shoot your load it's unbelievable. If you can sneeze, it's even better.'

Scarface watched me demonstrate, mesmerized, then tried out the position. For the rest of the day I could see him thinking about what I'd said, then he'd slip his left arm under his right leg, bow his head and try to reach his nose. When he finally managed it after almost breaking his back in the attempt, his face was a picture of delight.

It was by far the most serious they had ever been with me outside an interrogation and the longest we had spoken for for some time. They asked about the Korean girlfriend I had, what positions we tried, that sort of thing.

'How are your English women in bed?' Goofy said salaciously.

'*Muy sabroso*,' I said with a knowing nod. Very tasty. I did not want to explain that I had never slept with an English woman.

Goofy's eyes opened wide and he grinned like Albert Steptoe, all teeth and leer. I turned the question around.

'How are Colombian women, *señor?*'

He refused to answer. Typical. They always wanted information about you but when you asked for something in return they shut up.

All the men loved these chats, Perty aside. He just continued to stare in horror. Stalky loved it, though.

'Have you ever tried two hands?' he asked once, miming to me.

'No, but next time, eh?'

He nodded his head vigorously.

*   *   *

PAUL: We celebrated 5 November with a small bonfire and Tom constructed a guy using tissue and cloth on a wooden frame. From a distance, the whole thing looked a bit like a cross. I tried to explain what this celebration meant to the English, but the guerrillas remained uncomprehending. We stood it on the fire, much to their dismay — a state of confusion heightened by our dancing around the fire as dusk fell, howling like dogs into the night.

They were also perplexed because they thought we were burning an effigy of Christ.

'You burn Jesus,' said Loosey in an awed whisper.

'No,' said Tom. 'Guy Fawkes. He tried to blow up Parl — '

He stopped when he realized that this lot might have sympathy for Guido's cause.

Their confusion, almost anger, worried me a bit, but not much. They had arrived, so it seemed, at the conclusion that we were mad.

Often they referred to Tom as 'Bobo'. The clown. It was true he gave them much amusement, deliberately so. I only hoped they did not decide to keep him forever as camp jester.

Almost two months had passed since our arrival at Inspirational Site. In that time the small valley of scrub had been cleared, so much so that we could clearly see to the other side of the camp where the solitary Bedfellow lived. Every morning I would get up and sneak a wave to him. His cheery smile never waned as he waved back. The guerrillas got to know we did this but never made too much of a deal out of it. When we were given a pile of sugar cane we threw pieces to him, always being careful that the guerrillas didn't catch us.

Boredom was still a major problem, though I was excited when Tom borrowed that children's Bible from The Knight and began to translate the stories for me in the evening as we smoked. It was my first experience of the Old Testament, having studied only the New in religious education classes at school. I was hoping to find solace in the readings, but found none. Instead, all I heard were fables brimming with blood and gore, smiting and begetting. I didn't enjoy it that much, but I decided not to tell Tom because he seemed to love it.

★ ★ ★

TOM: The sixteenth of November came and went. It was exactly three years since I'd left England and a host of memories flooded back. I

327

was tearful, scared, increasingly so because the atmosphere around camp was becoming more fraught and threatening. They mentioned splitting us up. 'Paul goes home and Tom stays here' was a common view. Stalky kept saying, 'Is that what's going to happen?' 'Yes, that's what's going to happen,' was always the reply. Talk swirled around about killing us, and I was convinced they wanted to do it. For some reason they had got it into their heads that I was a liar. At first, there were random comments — 'Let's kill Tom,' that sort of thing. But then they got progressively more frequent and they became like children: once they heard something they would start repeating it. It seemed that every minute I overheard them talking about how they were going to murder me. It had become their sole topic of conversation. 'Just bury him,' I heard one of them say, and the voice was excited. It was awful. I was a bag of nerves.

Then they announced we were about to move; horses turned up, along with some new faces. I was convinced I was about to die. 'Paul goes home,' they had said, 'but Tom is a liar and must die.' I tried to prepare myself for the end, praying to God that he would allow me into heaven. I decided to write a will on a page of my diary to give to Paul because I felt sure they wouldn't kill him. As I sat there writing, for the first time in the whole of our ordeal I began to cry, tears spilling onto the page, memories of home filling my mind. I felt this would be the last communication I would ever have with my family.

Dear Mum, Dad, Gran and all those I care about.

It is the 17th November today and we are moving site. Spirits are extremely high and Paul provides endless amusement. It is very hot here. Eight months in. Love you all loads and so much more than is imaginable, something I've realized since I made the error of coming here. All very friendly and we are fed exceedingly well. I love you all and you will read this if Paul returns before me.

Lots of love and hugs, Tom.

P.S. Bristles [my sister Anya], the stamp collection and all the money I have is yours and for all your various trips and interests. Love you, Ann.

Crac [my gran], you have been my lifelong inspiration and you are the best gardener and grandparent anyone could possibly want. The gum trees must be growing strong together with an updated and superb Queen's piece. Love you Crac, Tom.

Paul attempted to give me hope. 'Screw them,' he would tell me, 'they're full of bullshit.' But the sheer frequency of their threats overwhelmed me. Ignorance was bliss for Paul: he didn't speak Spanish and couldn't understand what they were saying. Yet I could, almost every word, and it's a terrible thing to hear people discussing ending your life in such a casual, matter-of-fact manner.

329

You don't want to listen, but you can't stop yourself. Throughout our whole time in captivity I'd listened in on the guerrillas' conversations to provide entertainment. Eavesdropping was one of the few diversions we had. It was a blessing, but now it was a curse. It became impossible simply to switch off. My death, I felt convinced, was imminent.

★　★　★

PAUL: Things started to change. We'd got used to regarding the camp as permanent, but now a move seemed to be in the offing. Tom and I discussed all the possibilities. Maybe a new command was taking over; maybe we would go back to Panama for another grilling at the hands of Trouble Ahead. The possibilities seemed endless. This sitting around in the jungle couldn't keep on for ever. The uncertainty sharpened us, bringing escape to the forefront of our minds again. It might be our only option. The atmosphere was strained. There was little communication between our captors and us. When Tom spoke they often ignored him, fuelling his paranoia. The future was uncertain, impossible to predict. Tom handed his will to me and I decided to write one too. We exchanged them in case only one of us got home.

Dear Mum, Dad, Bill and Kev,

Here's wishing you a Happy Birthday Mum from this magical and inspirational hilltop

330

site. We have been here for two months with rainbows, tropical birds and beautiful sunsets. Tom will fill you in on the adventures we have been having, make sure you invite him round for a Sunday roast. I can't say the rest of our company have been as good companions.

Well I've really landed myself in it here, some friends will say it was bound to happen.

Tom and I have stuck it out together but now we are on the move again with the possibility of a split, thus this letter if only one of us makes it out. I'd just like to tidy up a few things. I've got a bit of money, give half to Amnesty International or an African charity, split the other half between Kev and Bill on the condition they use it for something useful like a deposit on a house. Something I really should have done but couldn't bring myself to do. I never liked the idea of owning things or being stationary.

Give my regards and friendship to my mates. Tell them to have a beer for me.

Don't be sad about anything, spirits are high here and I really look forward to seeing you. You're great parents and Bill and Kev are great brothers. Live life to the full.

Paul.

TOM: Everything was prepared for the move. The chickens were executed, and Perty took great relish in destroying my garden, smashing the cricket bats, uprooting the stumps, throwing away my carefully carved balls and jumping up and down on the cultivated area like a child throwing a tantrum. I looked on silently, but wistfully. I knew I would miss the Inspirational Garden but my foremost thought was for my own safety. I was filled with foreboding. Why were we moving? If they were going to keep us for two years, then why not keep us at Inspirational Site? The location was perfect. The only explanation I could muster, gleaned from their constant threats, was they intended either to kill me or split us up. Paul said they were talking bollocks, that they had no authority to carry out what they'd threatened to do, but he didn't convince me. The sheer avalanche of death threats and the talk of us being parted was too much to ignore; I saw it as inevitable as the coming night.

As we packed our rucksacks and started out, I was certain during those first few hours of walking that we would be parted. Paul would suddenly disappear, bundled off into the bushes while I remained with the main body of guerrillas. As we descended the hill away from the camp, Paul started to get further away from me. I hurried along trying to keep as close to him as possible in case either of us was snatched away without the other being aware of it. I didn't take my eyes off him, whatever the diversion, in case they tried to distract me and Paul disappeared. I felt that as long as I could see him things would be all right, that the moment he

332

was out of my sight, that would be it, I would never see him again.

But we just carried on walking to another camp beside the village.

15

TO FLEE OR NOT TO FLEE . . .

TOM: My relief at not being separated from Paul was soon replaced by a burning determination to escape. Unlike the long walk from Panama, we were now on constant alert for a chance to bolt. It did not matter where we were, whether we were in camp or on an eight-hour hike, eating our lunch or asleep in our beds, every situation would be assessed. If the chances for escape were more compelling than the reasons against, we decided we'd go for it.

An opportunity arose immediately. Within a few hours of walking we'd stopped near a local village and were ordered to pitch our tent behind a thick layer of shrubs, presumably to hide us from the villagers. Yet it also meant that we were out of sight of the guerrillas, even though they could hear us. As we put up the tent I looked around at the jungle and saw that crashing a path through it was possible. Paul sensed my excitement and I could see he was working out the pros and cons. At one point, he sneaked up to a vantage point a hundred feet or so above us to see the surrounding area.

As far as I was concerned, the ayes had it. Firstly, we were hidden; within seconds we could be in the jungle and away. Surely this was the critical moment? We waited in the tent to see if anyone would come and check on us, but they didn't. Three hours passed. I knew this was it. In the tent I rooted out my survival pod and placed Paul's cooking pot and my mosquito net and spoon inside. I was ready to go. I turned to Paul. He was not moving with the same urgency.

'I'm surprised they can't hear my heart beating, it's thumping so hard,' I whispered. 'This is it, Paul. We've got to go.'

'I'm not sure, Tom.'

'Why? They can't see us; they won't know we've gone. Before they realize we'll be in the jungle and away.'

'What happens if they come and check on us immediately after we've gone?'

'What if they don't? Paul, we won't get a better chance than this.'

'They'll know something's up if the tent goes quiet and they can't hear our voices,' he maintained.

'This is our chance, Paul,' I insisted. 'Come on, let's go!'

My confidence was affecting him, I could see. He paused for what seemed an age, then he shook his head.

'No,' he said sternly. 'We'll only have one chance at this, so it has to work. I don't want to fuck up our chances. They haven't a clue we have the compass or the food and I don't want to risk losing them if we do mess it up.'

'But what if we don't get another chance better than this?'

'We will. Look, when I went up to the hilltop

335

earlier all I could see was swamp. We'd just end up thrashing around in that for days getting nowhere. Then what?'

'I'm willing to give it a try. Anything but waiting to die here.'

But the more insistent I became on leaving, the more determined he was to stay.

'The next opportunity may be even greater,' he said. 'I think we're going back to Panama. We'll have a better chance there.'

'But Paul — '

'We can't screw this up, Tom. Not now.'

I backed down, throwing my pod on the floor in frustration. I wanted to go. I couldn't bear this waiting around. For five minutes we sat there in silence. Then the bulging eyes of Stalky popped through the door of our tent; he checked everything was all right and disappeared. If we'd gone, our head start would have been all of five minutes — perhaps a hundred metres, given the terrain. Paul had been right. I felt spent.

★ ★ ★

PAUL: For the first time the guerrillas left us unwatched for three long hours. I desperately tried to calm Tom down. I could feel his nerves seeping into me, putting me on edge, but I didn't want to be panicked into doing something stupid. I managed to persuade him that it was not the right time. It was definitely our best chance yet, though. Tom's disappointment was palpable, and I felt guilty. We were still too far from safety, I was certain of that. Holding our nerve a bit longer might provide a better opening. My mind turned to Christmas, a little more than a month away, and the chance that celebrations might distract the guerrillas. I hoped fervently that I hadn't wasted our final chance to escape.

Soon we were moving north and I recognized the land as the same we'd journeyed across three months before. My excitement and optimism grew with every step. The journey was tough: unrelenting bogs and swamps and endless hacking through dense jungle, which made me feel that I'd been right to delay any escape attempt. For the first week of walking my foot coped adequately with the terrain. Then the pain returned. Thankfully, rather than let me slow down their progress, the guerrillas provided a horse for me to ride and I was able to continue the journey in comparative comfort.

Escape remained the sole subject of our thoughts and conversations. We briefly considered a violent breakout. Often the guerrillas left their AK-47s lying around. I had fired one in the past. I'd been travelling in the third world for a lot of my adult life and come across a few; any serious traveller knows how an AK-47 works. The gun is more common than Coca-cola in many parts of the world. Once I'd even fired a grenade launcher. I went as far as to explain to Tom how the gun worked. But the idea was swiftly dismissed; I had no wish to kill anybody, even if they were holding us against our will. It also raised the ridiculous prospect of our fighting our way out of the jungle Rambo-style, up against a group with experience of tracking and jungle combat. In a game of hunter versus hunted, I didn't fancy our chances. We even joked about the plan when we realized how ludicrous it was.

'Knowing us, Tom, we'd probably press a lever on the rifle and the whole thing would fall apart, then we'd be blown to bits.'

On the way north we ran into other groups and civilians on the paths. I took every opportunity to make my presence known. We wanted everyone to know we'd been kidnapped and were being held against our will. Given the chance, I wanted to chat with the locals. During one arduous day of walking, we were hidden in undergrowth just outside yet another village, out of sight. No-one was guarding us. Escape was mentioned again, but my leg was feeling particularly lame so it wasn't a realistic option. I was desperate to go to the toilet so I worked my way further into the undergrowth, discovering a pathway in the process. I pulled down my pants and squatted in the middle of the path. Eight months of jungle life had eroded any self-consciousness or worries over privacy. All of a sudden, an old man rounded the corner and stopped right in front of me. Our eyes met. Understandably he was startled to see a semi-naked gringo taking a crap on his path. A few seconds of uncomfortable silence ensued.

'*Buenos días, señor. ¿Cómo está?*' I asked innocently, trying to ignore what I had been caught doing.

'*Días,*' he replied nervously, looking like a startled rabbit.

'*Soy de Inglaterra,*' I offered, stumped for anything else to say in the circumstances.

He just stood there, paralysed.

'*Me llamo Pablo,*' I continued, standing and pulling up my trousers.

Still no reply. First impressions counted, and they hadn't been good, so I tried to start a polite conversation.

'We are walking,' I continued.

Again, no response. Just a blank stare. My first meeting with the locals wasn't going too well. I got the impression he couldn't get away from this gringo soon enough. Sure enough, with a baffled stare we parted company; I didn't offer him my hand to shake. But as he walked away down the path, I gave it one last try.

'We've been kidnapped,' I said, painfully aware that my faltering Spanish did me few favours.

He turned around and gave me a stare that suggested I might have come from another planet. 'That's no excuse for taking a dump on the path,' his look said. I must have disabused him of every view he ever held about English gentlemen. 'The English are filthy pigs,' he would tell his mates over a cup of tinto that evening.

I returned to a giggling Tom who'd heard the entire episode through the bushes.

'That's a sight he won't forget for the rest of his life,' he said.

The trek continued. Slowly, we started to lose

people; already the last Bedfellow had disappeared. The Knight and Loosey were the next to go. She'd found her man at last, and she'd certainly played the field to achieve it. Everyone had been in the running; once I even caught her in the bushes with Perty. Scarface was another who disappeared shortly afterwards.

Soon we reached Los Katios National Park, where we waited a day before using a boat to move upstream. Our progress on the way back was much quicker and there were now two boats, which the guerrillas raced against each other. Trees washed down the river during the rainy season blocked our way, and we cut through them with the chainsaw.

Back on land, I was significantly slower than the rest because of the park's hilly terrain. The horse hadn't made the boat trip so I was back on foot, but apart from an isolated instance or two my lack of speed no longer seemed to bother the guerrillas. I was assigned one guard who'd let me walk ahead while he rested, then catch me up an hour later. They often left me to walk alone. I was sorely tempted to slip off into the jungle and escape, but with no means to communicate with Tom and co-ordinate our escape, I couldn't. I recognized all the jungle paths; we were getting close to Payita. Our best chance for escape. On the walk, for the first time, I saw two of our lucky butterflies together. I took this as a sign that Tom and I were going to make it out of this side by side.

★ ★ ★

TOM: The walk back to Panama was not as arduous as our journey into Colombia had been. We wondered why we were going back and decided that another interrogation with Trouble Ahead was the most likely reason. Still the talk of my killing continued, particularly from an increasingly irate and blood-thirsty Goofy. While making a bench at one of the camps, I broke the machete and he became furious, shouting and swearing at me. I could pick up little from this verbal onslaught other than his determination to see me dead.

'People from Colombia do as they are told,' he told the rest of the guerrillas, 'but Pablo and Tomás walk slowly and complain. If the money does not turn up then we have to kill them.'

If the likes of Goofy held sway, we were dead men walking. Once again, the need to escape was uppermost in my mind. I allowed myself to dream of making the phone call home from a Panamanian army barracks, of hearing the delighted voices on the other end of the line; I thought about the prospect of Christmas with my family, presents under the tree, carol-singing in the church. But I had to stop because it was too wonderful and therefore too painful to contemplate.

As the march went on, relations between our captors and us continued to deteriorate. After the return journey by boat through the swamps we were forced to put up our tent in the pitch darkness, rain battering down around us. Someone had spilled a can of diesel in the boat where it had mingled with the river water and irritated our skin. Paul looked at the proposed site and the sticks the guerrillas had collected for us to use as tent supports. They were all different sizes and some were broken or split.

'We can't use these tent supports here,' he said dismissively. 'This is pointless.'

The Knight — who thankfully was very soon to leave us — saw Paul's disdain and lost it. He ran across yelling, towering over Paul, waving his machete in his hand. He pulled back behind his head as if to strike a blow. I closed my eyes. I felt sure he was going to attack Paul. When I opened them again, to my relief he was holding the weapon less menacingly, but he continued to yell and scream abuse at Paul.

We put up the tent.

Paul's leg was becoming a problem once more and I began to fear for our chances of a successful escape. The guerrillas' frustration soon boiled over. Stalky started to beat him with a stick on one occasion. Paul dropped his rucksack, turned around and shouted at him at the top of his voice.

'For fuck's sake, stop it!'

A visibly shaken Stalky went for his gun, which he waved at Paul.

'Come on then, you fucker! Come on!' Paul screamed.

I'd never seen him this angry. I looked at Stalky to gauge his reaction. He was scared, uncertain of what to do.

'Idiot,' said Paul, and he hoisted his rucksack on his back and carried on.

Paul's reaction shocked me, but I understood.

On another occasion while walking I'd lost my temper. Unsurprisingly, it was with The Bitch. She threw a coconut at me; it slammed into my ribs and hurt like hell. Instinctively, I picked up the coconut, ran over to her and pulled it back behind my head as if to throw it at her. She recoiled and swore quietly. I badly wanted to bring it crashing down on her skull but I knew that would mean certain death for me. Out of the corner of my eye I could see Paul looking at me intently, shaking his head, a gesture for me to drop it. I let the coconut fall to the floor with a thud and turned away from her. I noticed that Stalky was laughing, obviously finding The Bitch's discomfort funny. It was the last time she ever threw a coconut at me.

We were not the only ones unhappy with the current regime and way of life. One night during our hike the whole camp was woken when Smurf and Goofy came back drunk, presumably from a nearby village, singing songs at the tops of their voices and falling over. Goofy went to bed but Smurf stayed up, shouting and cursing, before becoming maudlin.

'I am poor,' he wailed. 'I have no money.'

'Shut up!' someone shouted.

'¡Majorda!' he screamed in reply. 'I deserve a better life. Not this. I want to see my family, my friends. But no, I spend all my time in the jungle. I deserve better!'

Eventually he tired, and the camp was able to get some sleep.

Paul told me that he thought we were back in Panama, and we spent every waking hour

343

looking for escape routes. None materialized; we were guarded too closely. As we trekked, at regular intervals we ran into other patrols. We saw Tooth Bird, Mr and Mrs Comb and a few others from our earlier days. It seemed as if guerrillas lurked around every corner.

'How the hell did those Americans get through here, Paul? I don't understand. There's more guerrillas than bloody trees!'

He smiled. 'They must have got lucky.'

On 9 December we camped in a small valley. There were other guerrillas here, some familiar, some not, but that didn't bother me. What did bother me was the murderous mood Goofy was in. He'd learned about the incident where I'd threatened The Bitch with a coconut, and it made his antipathy towards me even more pronounced. He sought consensus for his policy of slaughtering the gringos. He was in the hut in front of us and I could hear every word of his conversation with the other guerrillas.

'The tourists must die,' he said. 'We must kill them now.'

There was not a single murmur of disagreement.

'If there is no money, there must be death. Tomás must die. We must kill him,' he said.

Again he'd switched from both of us to me in particular. At one stage I thought I heard him say that even $3 million would not be enough to prevent my execution. My body started to shake uncontrollably.

'They're going to kill me any day now. We have to escape,' I told Paul.

344

'We're near Payita, Tom.' There was a pause. 'We'll go tonight.'

★ ★ ★

PAUL: Our tent was at the far end of the camp. Chainy's was ten feet in front of us with the others spread out around a reed shelter. It was one of the rare times when they did not surround us. From the rear of our tent a small path ran out to the edge of a cane field and down to the river.

This was our chance.

'We're going tonight, Tom. We can sneak out the back of the camp unseen,' I said.

He was as ready as I was.

'How will we get out of the tent?' he asked.

'Well, there's no way we can go out the front of the tent; the guard will see us. But we can cut a hole in the back of the tent and sneak out that way.'

On our walk back to Panama, Tom had found a piece of sharp glass from a broken mirror. I used it gently to cut into the fabric, but it made a rasping sound, too noisy by far. I tried a machete blade Tom had appropriated a few months earlier, but it was no quieter. Trying it during the day was out of the question because leaving the camp unseen would be impossible. The only option was to hope that it rained during the night, forcing the guard to keep his head down and drowning out the noise of our leaving the tent and running to the field. For the rest of the day I practised opening and closing

345

the zip as quietly as possible.

That night we were both on edge. I felt as though I could hear everything much more keenly than usual, as if the fear had sharpened my senses. Night fell and the moon rose, basking the camp in a soft glow. I heard the guard change and could see him stoking the fire. Tom shifted uneasily next to me. His breathing was shallow.

We both lay there silently, praying for rain. The guard changed again. We gave each other an excited look when thunder rumbled in the distance. A storm would be perfect; the guard would be too busy trying to protect himself from the rain to pay much attention to our tent. I checked my pack for the umpteenth time and made sure I knew where my boots were. Then a flash of lightning lit up the sky. Tom shifted on his bed. We both waited, saying nothing but feeding on each other's nerves, psyching ourselves up.

'This is it,' I kept thinking. 'We're going. Keep sharp, keep focused.'

I heard a gentle tap of rain on the tent roof. Tom sat up.

'Get ready,' I said. 'When it gets heavy, we go.'

More thunder rumbled; lightning flashed in the distance. Was it coming closer? I tried to count the seconds between each clap and flash but it was impossible to concentrate. Then the drizzle stopped.

'Shit,' I hissed. 'Come on, rain, you bastard.'

The waiting continued. The storm growled on in the adjoining valley without getting closer. The guards changed regularly. Soon the first notes of dawn could be heard. It got lighter and the jungle came to life. Our chance had vanished.

'That's it, Tom,' I said. 'We can't go now.'

I could see his disappointment. I tried to reassure him.

'It'll rain tonight.'

★ ★ ★

TOM: I was completely crestfallen. Once again an escape had been thwarted. Surely that was our last chance? No-one was speaking to us; the atmosphere was hostile. It seemed few of them would mourn our deaths, and Goofy was so passionate about it I could think of nothing to assuage him.

In the morning I got out of the tent and looked around, convinced it would be the last day of my life. I sat outside the tent, drugged by a mixture of exhaustion and disappointment, bled of all hope.

Stalky and Smurf shouldered their rucksacks at about eight and left camp with their guns. Two hours later, they returned and spoke to Goofy, who kicked the ground angrily and swore. I heard my name and the words 'death' and 'kill'. His eyes were wide and white with fury. Again he launched into a tirade of abuse and kicked the fire. The embers stuck to his boots, and smoke started to billow from the bottom of his trousers.

'¡Majorda!' he shouted, brushing the ashes off.

The rest of the guerrillas gathered around him. I couldn't hear what was being said, but

Goofy continued to rant and gesticulate wildly. '¡No!' Smurf said to him at one point. It was the only word I heard and the first time I'd witnessed Smurf being so emphatic. I could feel the blood pounding in my head, in my ears. Something important was taking place. I had no idea what, but it was infuriating Goofy and that could only be positive news for us.

Then Chainy walked over and gave me all our documents: our passports, receipts, driving licences, even our bloody traveller's cheques. I looked at Paul and he shrugged his shoulders at me.

'Can I give Paul his documents?' I asked him.

He nodded, then told us to pack our bags, which didn't take long: we'd barely unpacked since arriving. Goofy ordered us to follow him, Chainy, Perty, and another guerrilla, and without further ado we left the camp.

'He didn't even say goodbye,' I heard The Bitch say.

We walked down a stream at quick pace for twenty minutes. None of them had their packs, only their guns. Were they the execution party? I didn't know what to think. Were they going to hand us over to another group of guerrillas?

We came to a stop. My throat was tight, dry. I felt faint. Goofy turned to me. He was much calmer now.

'You can leave and walk solo,' he said. 'Go that way.' He pointed in an easterly direction. 'Never come back here again. If you do, we will kill you.'

Then he turned on his heels and walked off. I could hear him swearing to himself. But Perty,

Chainy and the other guerrilla were still with us. What the hell was going on? I couldn't bring myself to believe they were just letting us go.

'What did he say, Tom?' asked Paul, who looked as nervous as the day we were captured.

'He said we could go. At least, I think he did.'

'To a new camp?'

'I don't know.'

'Guides will be arranged for you,' Chainy interrupted.

'¿Qué?'

'You will be able to see your house and family soon, Tomás.'

I nearly collapsed then and there, yet still I was unable to fully comprehend. They were just letting us go like that? Why?

'Who are we?' Chainy said.

Was this a trick question?

'Friendly people living in the jungle,' I replied.

'Who are we?'

The question was said more forcefully this time, but I repeated my answer. He said something to Perty that I didn't understand, and smirked.

'What's going on, Tom?' Paul asked, anxiety etched all over his face.

'Paul, I think we're going home,' I said weakly.

Chainy and the two others then gestured for us to follow them. At breakneck speed we marched further down the river then relentlessly up a hill. It was the fastest we had ever walked. Paul looked exhausted but he managed to keep up. Reality was beginning to sink in for me. 'We're going home,' I thought. 'We're going home for Christmas!' The tune to 'O Come all ye Faithful' entered my mind, though I tried to forget it and concentrate solely on getting out of there. We weren't free yet.

After more than an hour at running pace, which Paul managed to maintain despite his knackered leg, we reached the top of the hill and stopped. Chainy pointed to a trail.

'Follow that. In two hours you will reach a village where you can get a boat. Tell people you are lost.'

I nodded vigorously.

'Do not tell anyone you saw any women in our commands,' he said. 'We are bad people. Don't ever come back here or we will kill you.'

We had no questions. We just wanted to get away from them before they changed their minds.

'Good luck,' Chainy said, and thrust out his hand.

I shook it gingerly. I did the same with Perty. He even smiled. Unbelievable. It was the first time I'd ever seen the grumpy bastard do that.

'*Feliz Navidad*,' I said. Merry Christmas.

'*Feliz Navidad*,' they all said in reply.

Then we left them.

★ ★ ★

PAUL: We ran down the hill, sliding down on our backsides, on our knees, not caring how we did it so long as we kept moving.

'Jesus, those idiots have let us go,' I muttered out loud.

350

Nothing else was said. We were both in a state of shock and we were still in a very dangerous place, close to the border. A war was going on, paramilitaries were in these parts, it was imperative we got out as quickly as possible. I forgot my injured leg and we ran down the hill, adrenalin driving us on and on. Whenever we thought we heard someone nearby, the snap of a twig or a movement in the bushes, we tried to hide. This carried on without pause for several hours. We passed the concrete border marker and an abandoned Inrenare station. Still no sign of the village, though. We walked on, reached open grassland and saw an astonishing view: the sun was starting to set behind us; to our left lay Lago Unguía, the Atrato Delta was in front of us and the wide Río Atrato twisted and curled away to our right. More than two thousand feet below us we could see sunlight glinting off the corrugated iron roofs of abandoned farmsteads. The evening shadows raced towards the Caribbean as the sun fell closer to the horizon.

'We're free,' I said to Tom.

He grinned at me in delight.

We debated whether or not to make camp but decided to head on to Arquía; we were still near paramilitary-controlled areas and the thought of a new group bumping into us now was too hideous to contemplate. I also wanted to put as much distance as possible between our former captors and us in case anyone changed his mind.

On we went, until we reached a T-junction. I checked with my compass and chose the left turn.

'Head for that dead tree,' I said, hoping we might find a dry, secluded place to camp.

As we walked towards it, Tom spotted Will Smith.

'Hide!' he hissed.

We ducked into the long grass.

'What are you doing here?' Smith shouted.

Fuck!

We stood up slowly.

'What do we do now?' asked Tom.

'Tell them the truth, I think,' I replied hesitantly.

The warmth of his greeting quickly dispelled any fear. He treated us like old friends. Maria was with Smith, I was glad to see. She was one of the better ones. We shook hands and they gave us sweet tangerines and cheese to eat. Tom spoke to them and explained our predicament. Smith nodded sagely.

'We want to go to Unguía or Arquía,' Tom told him.

'It is too far,' he said, shaking his head.

I was adamant it was our best route from here.

'No,' he maintained. 'We will give you guides tomorrow. We have friends operating boats on the Río Atrato. You will get a free ride to Turbo and to freedom.'

Though it was friendly in tone, Smith's offer was a demand, not an invite. We could spend the night with them. The light was fast fading so we went back to their camp where we were met with surprised looks from Jackanory, Trapper, Beanstalk and Nena. Their reception was friendly, though when we returned from having a wash we could see that someone had rifled through our rucksacks. My first thought was that they had seen the stolen food! No mention was made of it, though. Only the broken piece of mirror was missing.

We went to sleep in our tent, sharing it with a few hundred mosquitoes bent on taking their last opportunity — or so I hoped — to dine on gringo blood. I was convinced the offer from Smith was genuine and in the morning we would be on our way. Tom, however, was less certain.

'What if they don't let us go?'

'They will, don't worry.'

'What makes you believe that? They might keep us for God knows how long.'

'I think Smith was telling the truth, that's all. Why would they keep us when the others let us go?'

Tom didn't have an answer, though I could see he was far from reassured.

16

LEAVING LA SELVA

TOM: On the morning of 11 December Will Smith and his gang served us with a generous breakfast of *plátanos*. Smithy also gave us some food to eat for our lunch, fresh water and, to our amazement, five thousand pesos (about £1.75) — 'To buy a soda,' he explained. We thanked him profusely. He introduced us to two guides he said would lead us in the right direction. One of them, ominously, had only one eye, though I was certain it wasn't Trouble Ahead. The rest of the camp came over and we said our goodbyes, once again shaking hands and wishing one another Merry Christmas. Then we left them for the last time.

The guides possessed no machetes so crossing the grasslands, with their tall razor-blade grasses, was tough going. The prospect of getting out of the jungle, however, gave us added impetus and energy; nothing was going to stop us leaving. We descended into the lowlands and after an hour of walking came across a path. Rain began to fall heavily. One-Eye pointed down the steep path and said we should follow it for three or four hours to reach *la paz*. Peace.

'Civilians without guns, like you, live there,' he explained. 'Tell the civilians you are lost and never say you have seen us or any women.'

They appeared very jumpy about anyone discovering women in their ranks.

'There is a hut over there,' he added, 'where you can shelter from the rain.'

After a quick handshake he and his mate were off. We were on our own.

We took shelter on the veranda of the abandoned hut and ate the lunch Smithy had given us, while outside the tropical downpour raged. We sifted through our documents in delight, unable to believe they had returned absolutely everything, bar the camera film Trouble Ahead had taken. Thoughts of Christmas, carols, family, friends, trees, freedom and my greenhouses pulsated through my head, and this time I was not forced to stash them away to protect myself. All these precious things would be experienced in a few days' time.

'I still can't believe they released us like that,' Paul said, shaking his head. 'Nine months, and for what? Nothing.'

'A ransom might have been paid,' I pointed out, but Paul disagreed.

'Surely there would have been some sort of rendezvous point,' he said. 'They wouldn't have got the money without handing us over.'

'In fact, they paid us to go free!' I said, pulling the five thousand pesos out of my pocket.

We laughed long and hard about this — the hostages who were given money by their captors to get lost.

'What's the first thing we should do when we get to Turbo?' I asked.

'Phone our parents,' Paul said.

The thought of it made us both smile and shake our heads, our minds bombarded with so many emotions: relief at our release, joy at the prospect of going home, disbelief at the way it had ended and still a niggling fear that there was some sort of catch, that it couldn't be so easy as a simple stroll to freedom. I could see Paul felt the same. He couldn't believe that it was all ending like this, no conditions attached.

'Then we can go to Bogotà and party,' I said.

We laughed again. I can't remember ever feeling happier than I did at that moment.

'We'd better phone the British Embassy, too,' Paul added. 'They've probably got us registered as missing. Then we can get a flight home.'

A British Airways flight home for Christmas! That had been something beyond my wildest dreams during the last few days of our capture. Now it was going to happen.

The storm subsided so we gathered our belongings and set off. Picking up a faint trail, we progressed slowly through the undergrowth. Flooded streams caused by the rain hampered our movement while the deafening noise of rushing water muffled any attempts at conversation. As I fought my way forward through the foliage, I turned around to Paul to comment on what a nightmare it was, but he was nowhere to be seen.

'Paul!' I shouted.

The only sound was rushing water and the sibilant hum of mosquitoes. I screamed his name again. No reply. I searched for footprints but the floor was a muddy, watery morass. I carried on shouting, feeling increasingly worried. 'Oh God, no,' I thought. 'Where is he? Have they taken him? Did he fall?' I'd heard nothing. I'd been concentrating on making headway through the undergrowth. I tried to remember how long it had been since I last saw him. I decided to turn back to retrace my steps.

As I did so, I heard a voice shout my name. It was Paul. I shouted his name back, and we carried on shouting and moving until we found each other again. The jungle was so thick that Paul had been concentrating solely on where his feet were landing. When he looked up I was no longer in front of him. Unable to follow me, he'd veered in a different direction. He'd been no more than ten or fifteen yards away from me at any point, but the sound of rushing water was so loud we couldn't hear each other's voice until we were within a few feet.

'Bloody hell, Paul, you scared the hell out of me there,' I said.

'I think we'd better go back to the hut and rest for the night,' he suggested. 'It might be easier going in the morning.'

★ ★ ★

PAUL: We left the hut the next day in high spirits, and in better weather. The area was uninhabited so the threat of meeting another hostile group was remote. The path was ill defined, not having been used for some time, and the going was often slow, yet my compass bearings indicated we were heading in the right direction. We twisted and turned, skirting between a swamp and the hills; the path gradually became more difficult to follow, crossing as it did a number of small intertwined channels. Soon we found ourselves in dense jungle with only old machete cuts to follow, and a few hours later we found a fresh cut in a tree with a slice of branch still attached to it. I consulted my map and compass and guessed that from here we needed to head south into the swamp making a beeline for the Río Atrato. From there we could flag down a boat and get to Turbo.

'South is that way,' I called to Tom, and we charged towards the swamp, kicking down the undergrowth, reeds, grasses and palms. It was a constant battle and we moved slowly, maybe only a few hundred metres in an hour. The land was relatively dry to start with as we kicked our way through a field of tall grass, Tom leading the way. Then I took over and we found ourselves in jungle again, crossing a few streams, bashing our way through a *Heliconia* field and into the swamp.

We took a southerly bearing, wading straight into the marshy, boggy water. Still, I figured, any moment now we'll hit the Río Atrato and come to the village where our boat ride is waiting for us. Soon we were up to our waists in stinking black swamp water, while the mud on the bottom reached our calves, almost tearing our knees from their sockets as we tried to lift our feet to walk. It took every last ounce of energy to extricate one foot before you planted it in front of you and concentrated on lifting the other. To progress, we also had to hack through thorns and thick undergrowth with only a broken machete blade as a tool.

'Three hours, my arse,' I said to Tom as we squelched along, as if through treacle. 'Bloody guerrillas.'

They'd mentioned nothing about a swamp. They'd made it seem so straightforward. But follow the path and reach freedom had been the gist of it. It was exhausting work, and the mosquitoes ate us alive. Soon it became obvious that night was drawing in. It developed into a race simply to try to find a patch of land dry and large enough for us to pitch our tent on. We charged on, beating back and slashing away the vines that attempted to hold us up, swearing and cursing the guerrillas for making the journey sound so bloody easy.

As we were about to be plunged into darkness we found a mass of roots belonging to two trees just about wide enough to pitch the tent on, though the corners dipped into the water.

'This place isn't fit for humans,' Tom observed miserably.

The adrenalin of our release had all but disappeared; we felt drained by the muscle-numbing efforts of wading through this stinking swamp. We were cold, knackered, soaked and smothered in bites. It was by far the worst camp I have ever slept in. The trees, the jungle, the swamp, everything made it look like the home of the Ewoks in the *Star Wars* films. For food we had only the leftovers of the previous night's rice and beans, but they were starting to rot in the putrid, dank air of the swamp. Tom opened the plastic bag we carried them in and almost passed out at the smell. It was inedible.

The next morning at dawn, hungry and shattered after a sleepless night, we ploughed on, hacking away at the creeping vines and bushes with the machete piece. Suddenly, the blade slipped from Tom's grasp and with a plop fell into the swamp. He rummaged around beneath the black, stinking water with his hands.

'Shit,' he said. 'It's gone. Sorry, Paul.'

I silently cursed him. It was a vital bit of equipment; without it we couldn't get through this stuff. Tom tried to look for it but it was no use. We were lost, the machete blade was gone and we knew that if we headed back north we would reach dry land. Obviously we had taken a wrong turn somewhere and we needed to go back and retrace our steps. I brought out the compass and took a bearing.

'Let's head north,' I said.

Unfortunately, as we made our way back we became lost. When your view is limited to barely a few feet then all sense of direction eludes you. Walking was immensely tiring and I feared another night in a hellhole. The damp jeans that the guerrillas had given me cut into my groin and thighs. Tom's legs were torn to shreds after wading through the thorns and regrowth. It was a bad idea to wear shorts.

★ ★ ★

TOM: Panic set in. The forest, not the guerrillas, would kill us. We tried to blast our way through the growth, pushing through bushes with our hands, launching our bodies into barricades of branches, but it felt as if we were going round in circles. Our limbs were torn and bleeding. On the way into the swamp I had tried to make marks on trees so that we could find our way back, except I had done it irregularly and the trail was soon lost. I despaired at ever getting out of the wretched swamp. We moaned about the guerrillas and their pathetic directions.

'I'm going to tell the world they have women guerrillas,' I vowed.

'Let's write a book, call it *All Their Guerrillas Are Women* and drop copies on the jungle from a plane,' Paul added.

'Then we can drop a nuclear bomb on this shithole as a follow-up.'

The day before I was dreaming of home; now I thought we were never going to get there. I desperately tried to keep myself together but I could feel the will to carry on draining from me. Eventually we emerged from the swamp but the jungle was denser, impenetrable almost, and thorns jabbed into our hands, arms and legs. It was no easier than the swamp. There was no sign of any sort of path either. We carried on travelling upwards, towards higher ground, swearing and shouting to overcome the pain and to drive ourselves on.

'Look!' Paul exclaimed.

I had no idea what he was pointing at.

'It's a footprint,' he said. 'The path must be close by.'

I wasn't convinced, but he was right: barely twenty yards away was a faint path. I offered up a quick prayer, and my gloom lifted. We camped next to a clear, cascading stream and scrubbed away the effects of the swamp, drying out our clothes on a nearby rock. There was a *plátano* tree nearby so we picked and ate some fruit, frying some rank rice to go with it. We pitched the tent, and while it was hardly comfortable, it was better than Ewok Site. As I tried to sleep that night one frustrating thought kept niggling away at me: Paul and I had been released by our captors and were free to go home for Christmas, but we just couldn't bloody get out of here.

The next day we returned to rest at the hut. We searched it thoroughly and to our whooping delight found a rusty, long-handled machete. Sitting in chairs on the veranda gave us a chance to let our weary limbs recuperate. The efforts of the previous days had caused us to suffer cramp so we decided to spend the night there and get some much-needed sleep before heading out once more the next day. I felled a custard apple tree and ate the biggest fruit I had ever seen, enjoying the bright, breezy conditions.

The bed was comfortable, but I was unable to sleep. Being this close to freedom yet not being able to achieve it meant it was impossible to relax. The path we followed the next morning was well trampled, but then we had already travelled along it twice. We followed our previous route but once again became unstuck when we hit the swamp. Despite several mini-excursions in search of another path we could not find one. Loath to go too deep into the swamp, we camped by the stream. The rain came thundering down and soaked us to the bone, and putting up the tent was an ordeal. We couldn't cook and there was little point having a wash given that we were so drenched.

'We're not going to make it back by Christmas, are we?' I said to Paul.

'I doubt it. By the time we get to Bogotà, all the flights will be booked up.'

After another sleepless night we decided to go back to the hut and take stock. Paul was lost in thought all the way. I felt low, perhaps as low as I'd been since our capture nine months earlier. Nine months exactly, too: it was 16 December. Things tended to happen around the 16th. It was the date I left England; the date we were caught; the date we moved camp at Lost City and Inspirational Site. I longed for something to happen now.

I looked at my feet. They were purple, studded with patches of raw flesh where the skin had rubbed off. The constant moisture had ruined them. It was the first sign of jungle rot. As they dried, deep cracks appeared and the skin flaked.

'There's no way I'm going back in that swamp,' I told Paul.

'I've got an idea.'

I looked up from my peeling, painful feet. 'What is it?'

'We've got to go back to the guerrillas and get some more directions.'

My first reaction was shock, swiftly followed by disbelief. Then horror. They'd vowed to kill us if we ever returned.

★ ★ ★

PAUL: 'If we don't do it, we'll die here,' I told Tom.

I could see he was horrified by my proposal but it was honestly the only way I could see out of our predicament. I'd thought about everything carefully. Our food supplies were low and we were lost. The directions were either wrong or we'd misunderstood them. Going back was a big risk, but to my mind it was a certainty that if we did not go back then we would die in this fucking jungle.

'The camp where Smithy and Maria were at looked pretty permanent. They're quite friendly. Chainy said they would kill us if we came back; well, technically, we haven't left.'

'But what if they think we've come back with 'others' to get them?'

'We explain what's happened: we got lost. We misunderstood the directions. They can see from the state we're in that we've hardly been living in luxury for the past six days.'

Tom was reluctant, understandably, but he agreed it was our only option. My only worry, and one I did not share with Tom, was that we would bump into a patrol containing Goofy. He was angry and would have no qualms about killing us there and then. It would be a question of luck.

The next morning, at about eight, we set off back to our point of release. We'd reached the bottom of the hill and were about to make our way up it when we spotted another path leading off to the left. Was that the one? It seemed to go in the wrong direction, away into the hills. We wandered up it for a couple of hundred yards but it seemed to be going back into Panama. I dismissed it. I didn't want to be thrashing around the jungle, lost again, with only half a kilo of rotting rice and a few mouldy beans for sustenance.

We climbed the hill slowly and warily — going up was a damn sight more difficult than coming down — keeping our eyes peeled for patrols all the time. We came across a camp; the fire was still warm and a set of beds suggested a group of around four people. We pressed on up the hill towards the place where Smithy was camped. Reaching the high ground gave us a view across the whole area. Tom spotted Lake Unguía off in the distance.

'Look at the view, Paul,' he shouted. 'There's the lake!'

I could not believe he was being so stupid.

'Shut the fuck up, Tom! There could be anyone around here. Do you want to get us killed?'

It was the first time either of us had lost his temper with the other throughout the whole ordeal. He looked shocked, but both our lives were at stake and it was vital that we kept as low a profile as possible. He apologized. I said it was OK. The stress we were under was immense. We pressed on.

'I don't like this, Paul,' Tom said after a while.

'Neither do I.'

'Let's do it on our own, then,' he implored.

'Going back's our only option, Tom.'

'What about that path back down the hill? Let's try that.'

'We have no idea where it goes. It could lead us anywhere.'

He looked around, took a deep breath and nodded his head slowly. He was scared. So was I. Neither of us knew what the reception would be.

Then I saw the small tower that was in the centre of the camp, some sort of radio mast that the guerrillas seemed to be guarding.

'This is it, Tom.'

'Paul?'

'Yes?'

'I'm absolutely crapping myself.'

★ ★ ★

TOM: Jackanory saw us first. This time there was no smile. No-one smiled, in fact. No-one waved. No-one said anything.

'*Hola*,' I said. '*¿Cómo está?*'

No response. It felt bad. Really bad.

A guerrilla who'd been with us briefly at Lost City, a dim-looking man whom we'd called Dense-as-you-like, was the first to approach us.

'Take your rucksacks to the bushes and drop them,' he barked.

No greeting, no handshake. I could not see Smithy or Maria anywhere. That was also bad.

Out of sight, we sat on our rucksacks and tried to explain. Jackanory, Beanstalk, Nena and a few others gathered round us in a semi-circle.

'Where have you been?' Dense asked.

'*Estamos perdidos*,' I said. We're lost.

The situation demanded some humour.

'We saw pigs, *señor*.' They had been grazing at the bottom of the hill. I performed a pig impersonation. It raised a few smiles.

'The commander will decide what to do,' Dense said.

We wondered who that might be. It was Trapper. A guerrilla fetched him and he strode over purposefully. He looked troubled, angry. My mind wandered back to the way he had dealt with his insolent *perricos*. I greeted him warmly.

'What are you doing here?' he said.

'We're lost.'

'Who did you speak to?'

'Nobody, *señor*.'

'What food did you eat?'

'Fruits, *plátanos*, rice and beans, *señor*.'

'Where did you get the rice and beans?'

'Er . . . ' I did not know how to answer. 'We stole it from you, *señor*.'

He didn't seem too surprised.

I was concentrating like hell in order to understand him and to keep my Spanish as clear and concise as possible.

'Which path did you take?'

I explained what we had done as best I could.

'That path is for the summer only,' he said. The right path was the one we'd passed on our

367

way up to their camp, the one Paul had dismissed.

'Would you like to go now or later?'

Relief spread through my body. 'Now,' I said, and I forced myself to listen to the directions.

From his jacket pocket he pulled a packet. He handed a cigarette to Paul and one to me, then lit one for himself. Beside me I could hear Paul inhale deeply. I nodded to him to indicate that everything was all right.

'How long will it take to reach England?' Trapper asked.

'Many months on foot, señor,' I replied. I didn't want to give the impression that we could afford a plane journey.

'It will only take a month to reach Bogotà,' he said. 'You could take a bus.'

I thanked him for his advice.

'We go now, señor,' I said.

He nodded that it was OK, so we stood up and shouldered our rucksacks.

'You can stay for dinner,' piped up Jackanory. 'We are having roasted pig.' He performed his own pig impression.

'Thank you, señor, but we must go.'

The choice between heading home for a juicy turkey or eating stringy pork with the guerrillas was not a difficult one.

Then, for the third time, we shook hands with everyone, wished them a Happy Christmas and walked out of the camp. I half expected to hear the sound of a shot, and a slug slamming into my back.

It didn't.

★ ★ ★

PAUL: Operating solely on adrenalin, we bounded back down the hill for yet another night at our hut. It was three hours to safety, so we were told — again — and night would fall before we reached the village, so it was best to rest and start out again early the next day.

While cooking up a meal of *plátanos*, all talk was of what had just happened.

'I can't believe we just did that and got away with it,' Tom said.

I agreed. It was incredibly risky, but it had worked. We now knew the right direction in which to walk and by lunchtime, God willing, we'd be on a boat to freedom.

After four hours of walking the next day we reached the Río Tilupo and I waded across it while Tom searched for some coconuts on the other side. I slumped down on the stony river-bank. A man appeared behind me. We exchanged pleasantries, neither of us looking surprised at each other's presence, though a little curious. He had a large paunch and dark spreading stains from his armpits. He swatted the mosquitoes from his body. Tom then waded across the river to ask me where he had come from.

'I don't know. It's always the bloody case in this jungle. Things just appear and take you by surprise,' I replied.

Another man turned up and we chatted. He was wearing a shirt with a badge on it. The words 'Los Katios' were emblazoned on it

— some sort of ranger's uniform perhaps. Most importantly, they weren't armed. He started to ask questions.

'What are you doing here?'

'We are tourists,' Tom told him.

'Are you Americans?'

Tom shook his head and said we were English.

'How long have you been here?'

'Nine months.'

'Where have you come from?'

Tom pointed out the route for him. He spoke some more, then Tom turned to me.

'He says we must go back to Panama. It is prohibited for tourists to be in this park.'

'Go back? Is he having a laugh?'

The ranger spoke again.

'He wants to know if we realize that there are dangerous armed groups in the area,' Tom told me.

'Do we realize? Tell him we've been with one for nine fucking months! Tell him what's happened to us!'

Tom explained our kidnapping. They took it in their stride, nodding casually.

'We are going to have a look at a waterfall,' he told Tom. 'You can wait here if you want and then we will take you to Sautata.'

They left.

'There is no way I'm waiting here,' I told Tom. 'We have no idea who these guys are. Let's follow the path.'

Tom agreed, so as soon as the rangers were out of sight we shouldered our packs and continued. The path was clearly marked and

370

along the way we found signs pointing out various places of interest in the park. For the first time in his life, Tom resisted any urge to observe the flora and fauna.

By late afternoon we had stumbled into the camp head-quarters of the Los Katios National Park in Sautatá. We slumped down and lay resting in a grass field in the gentle evening sun. I was impressed by the size of the camp. There were stables, houses, a show room and dormitories. It was all carefully attended to, though most of it was locked and there was no sign of life. I even found a real toilet with a sink.

'Check out the porcelain, Tom,' I said.

I gently sat on it and savoured the moment. The flush worked, too. I chuckled loudly to myself, then washed my hands thoroughly in the sink, delighting in turning the tap on and off.

'I bet they have beds and mattresses here as well,' I continued, gradually waking up to the delights of modern conveniences after the best part of a year living rough.

The thought of not having to spend another night in that cramped tent was wonderful. For the majority of those nine months Tom and I had lain cheek by jowl in the tight constraints of our Chinese tent, sleeping on a bed of sticks or on the jungle floor, constantly tossing and turning with the discomfort. To sink into the soft down of a mattress, to have it yield and fit itself around the shape of my body; the touch and smell of clean, crisp white sheets; a fluffy pillow on which I could lay down my head — these thoughts rushed back to me and I longed to savour them.

An hour later the two men we'd met earlier returned, and a gaggle of other men appeared out of nowhere. People were good at doing that in the Darién. The man who had asked the questions, who had made the bizarre suggestion that we turn back into the lawless jungle, came to take down our details, unperturbed that we'd run away rather than wait for him. He pronounced my name perfectly, which was heartening after months of being called Pablo. They showed us to a dormitory with beds replete with mattresses, sheets and pillows, and told us dinner would be ready in an hour and that he would use his radio to call the authorities.

'Radio, my arse. I bet they haven't got one,' I scoffed to Tom.

I'd lost all faith in anything anyone told me in this part of the world, but it didn't matter now. We'd made contact with civilians and from here it would be easy to get a boat out once we found the river.

An hour later, the ranger ushered us into a room. Despite my doubts, they did have a radio. He said they'd made contact with the authorities in Turbo, who in turn had established contact with the British Embassy in Bogotà. A man was waiting on the line.

'You speak to him, Paul. I don't know what to say.'

Tom lost for words — a rarity. I picked up the handset.

'Hello?'

'Hi, Paul, this is Chris Wigginton from the British Embassy. How are you?'

His voice was calm and reassuring. I felt the hairs on the back of my neck rise up and I almost choked on my words. This is what I had been longing for. I was about to go home.

'I'm fine.' I didn't know what else to say. There was so much *to* say. 'Er, how are you?' I added.

'Good,' he said.

'We've been in the jungle for nine months,' I continued.

'Yes, I know. We know all about you. A lot of people have expressed concern over your safety. We'd given you up for dead. Where are you?'

'Sautatá, in the Los Katios National Park. We're with a group of friendly rangers.'

'Can I confirm that you are with Tom?'

'Yes, we're both safe,' I replied.

'We need to arrange to get you out of the region tomorrow and get you to Bogotà. You're still in some danger there. I'll call again to arrange things.'

'No problem. I look forward to meeting you tomorrow. Bye, Chris.'

I walked outside to where Tom was waiting.

'Hey, mate,' I said, 'we're going home.' I gave the air a little punch.

That evening we ate and chatted happily with the rangers. We had plates and knives and forks, and we laughed and smiled. An electric light lit the dinner table. For once, we didn't go to bed when the sun set. When we did, I slept reasonably well, even though I knew we were still in a dangerous area and anybody who wanted us could easily take us.

★ ★ ★

TOM: That night, in a room shared with Paul, I barely slept despite my exhaustion. It was my first night in a bed for more than nine months and my body was not used to it. It felt strange, awkward. The realization that the guerrillas were only a three-hour walk away, at our pace at least terrified me. I kept expecting to see Goofy climb through the window. I got up to close it, despite the heat. The hour or so I managed to sleep was filled with terrifying dreams. Mercifully, the sun rose at last and I could see Paul was awake, too.

'Did you sleep?' I said.

'Wasn't too bad,' he replied.

Neither of us felt safe, nor were we yet convinced the whole ordeal was over. The events of the past day, past week even, seemed unreal to me now.

The rangers made us a wonderful breakfast of coffee, toast and eggs. Afterwards I showed them some of the seeds I had picked up during the past nine months. These were park rangers after all, and the likelihood of anyone back in England knowing what species they were was remote. They gave me all the common names of the palm seeds I'd collected, which lifted my spirits. I felt safer now. Both Paul and I realized the guerrillas were not going to get us again.

The boat to transport us was to arrive that morning, but it was delayed, so we ended up staying for a lunch of cold meats. By now I sensed the rangers wanted to get rid of us. We were in danger of eating all their supplies. To waste time, we looked around the deserted education centre where the maps fascinated Paul, his finger sketching out a trail of where we might have been. Eventually, in the early afternoon, we were taken by boat to a hut by the Río Atrato, a river about a quarter of a mile across. We sat there waiting, watching life on the busy river pass us by.

In the distance I could hear the whirr of an outboard motor, more powerful than the motorized boats that had chugged past. This was a speedboat, and a powerful one too. From the other side of the river we could see it skimming and bouncing across the wake, a Red Cross flag flying from it. It pulled up and we climbed in, shaking hands with a Swiss chap, who introduced himself as Rudy, and a black Colombian driver. There was a slight hold-up while the rangers signed documents, then Rudy pulled out a satellite phone and set it up.

'We've picked them up,' he said into it.

Paul and I looked at each other, wondering who was on the other end.

The boat started and at high speed we whizzed away from the shore. Rudy gave us tuna and bread and Coca-cola. The sweetness of the soft drink set my enzymes dancing with celebration. It tasted wonderful. Within seconds I felt light-headed, the sugar rushing around my body. 'Panela may be nice,' I thought, 'but it has nothing on this.'

As we ate and drank, Rudy pulled out a missing poster with our mugshots on it, our names underneath them. I'd been photographed buying orchids at the market in El Valle in Panama; Paul was sat in front of a waterfall in Mexico. The Spanish text said: 'Have you seen these two men? British tourists aged 24 and 29, travelling between Púcuro, Paya and Payita in Panama, through the national park to Cristales, Arquía and Unguía in Colombia, between March 10 and June 1 2000. If you have useful information relevant to these missing people, please contact the British Embassy in Bogotà or whichever organization is able to help their parents find them.'

We looked at it in disbelief. I felt a sense of detachment, as if the young, smiling face I saw on the picture was a different person, a stranger.

'A lot of people have been looking for you. These have been put up in Central and South America,' Rudy said.

We were speechless. It was only at that point it hit us that people might have gone to great lengths to find us.

'We heard about you guys going missing in July. Everyone thought you were dead.'

'Really,' I said.

He fixed me with a grave look. 'No-one comes out of the Darién alive after nine months.'

I'd no idea how to respond to that. Paul and I simply looked at each other.

'Fuck,' he mouthed silently.

'Which one of you is the orchid hunter?' Rudy then asked.

I put up my hand meekly.

'A member of your family came to Colombia looking for you,' he said to me. I asked who it was but Rudy said he didn't know.

'Was any ransom paid for us?' Paul asked.

Rudy shook his head. 'Nope. There hasn't even been a demand.'

The rest of the journey sped by, Paul and I lost in our own thoughts, watching the villages blur past. About forty-five minutes later we arrived in Turbo where we picked up a four-wheel-drive which Rudy drove to his house in Apartado. We showered and he gave us some clothes to wear, though none of them fitted me that well. Then he and his girlfriend took us to the airport through downtown Apartado. I knew more about that city than any other in Colombia because the guerrillas' favourite radio station had been *Apartado Estereo*. As we drove through the city I recognized many place and street names.

'There's a chicken restaurant down there,' I said. '*El lugar mejor en Apartado para pollo muy sabroso.*' The best place in Apartado for very tasty chicken!

Rudy nearly lost control of the car.

'And there are a couple of churches in the main plaza, and at the swimming pool you can have a cracking swim in the evenings after eight for thirty pesos.'

★ ★ ★

PAUL: 'Is there anything you want?' Rudy asked.

I was slightly baffled by the question. For the first time in ages I was being given a choice. I looked around the small kiosk at the airport and

377

spotted a can of beer in a fridge.

'A beer, please.'

He bought one for me. Like John Mills in *Ice Cold in Alex*, I licked my lips, cracked it open, let the froth well over my hands and took a deep gulp; I savoured the fizz in the back of my throat, let out a rasping 'Aaaah', wiped my mouth with my sleeve, and necked the rest in one. Even Tom had one.

Within a few minutes of arriving at the airport a twin prop plane had landed and parked with its engines running.

'Blimey, Paul,' Tom whispered, 'they've hired a plane for us.'

'Who's paying for it?' was my first reaction. Then I felt the tiniest bit daunted. Someone wanted us back and was prepared to go to any lengths to ensure we got home safely. Whoever it might be was certain to demand answers to a few questions, first among them, what the hell were we doing in the Darién in the first place? Still, a bollocking was a small price to pay for freedom.

Two Colombian Red Cross medics sprinted across the tarmac and greeted us in a babble of cheery hellos. Rudy said goodbye to his girlfriend and joined us in the small plane. The pilot taxied, yelling into his radio, and then we were off, motoring down the runway while the medics tried to stick needles into our arms, get us on drips and check our blood pressure. Immediately after getting airborne, Rudy put Bob Marley on the stereo and the party continued. They couldn't get a drip into Tom; they couldn't find a vein. In contrast, I drained two bags of saline. The cockpit babbled with excitement and talk which I hardly understood. All I knew was that everybody was excited and happy. I was among friends again, even though we had only just met. These were the good guys.

We flew high over the Colombian mountains and saw lots of little city lights twinkling in the valleys below. Soon we were descending steeply into Bogotà airport, where we were transferred to a minibus. I felt as though I was in a spy movie. The night was cold, and drizzle gently raked the airport. Our minibus came to a halt at a gate far from any buildings. I could see a couple of Land Rover Discoverys waiting in the gloom, two men standing beside them, huddled against the rain. They greeted the Red Cross medics and we were exchanged. The two men were Chris Wigginton and another embassy official by the name of Johnny Welsh. I shook them firmly by the hands. I'd never been so happy to see friendly faces. I said goodbye to Rudy, wishing him Merry Christmas and good luck. This time I really meant it.

In the Land Rover I didn't know what to say. Luckily, Tom perked up and talked excitedly to everyone. I leaned my head against the window and looked out, letting the knowledge I was safe seep into my mind.

They took us to the British ambassador's residence where Stella, the ambassador's wife, greeted us. She gave us beer, fed us and showed us to luxurious beds. I shaved and looked at myself in the mirror. I'd barely changed. In fact, I looked healthier than I'd ever done working and living in London. We watched the BBC news and saw that the weather in England had been awful; apparently storms had bombarded the country and it had rained endlessly.

As we sat watching the television, content and warm, Stella came in with an after-dinner snack: a box of Ferrero Rocher.

The ambassador's wife was spoiling us.

Stella said we could call our parents. I can remember little of the conversation other than how good it was to hear Mum's and Dad's voice after all this time. The only bit I can recall was Dad asking, 'How was it?'

'Hilarious. Mad,' I said.

I'm not sure if those were the adjectives he was expecting.

After getting up from a fantastic, restful night's sleep, I had another shave and a long, restorative warm shower. I felt vaguely nervous about my surroundings, as if it were all some dream, and that I would wake up and find myself back in the jungle. Instead, maids brought us whatever we wanted. Breakfast was laid out in the residence's opulent dining room. I sat down on a cushioned chair, marvelling at its softness. I felt as though I had woken up in paradise. Stella marked the occasion with a photograph of Tom, Chris, Johnny and me.

Then it was a case of tying up the loose ends so we could get home in time for Christmas. Chris and Johnny had prepared a busy day for us. The plan was to get us on a flight back that evening, yet there were a number of procedures to undergo. Under guard, we were chauffeured to a private clinic for a full check-up. Doctors and nurses examined us from head to toe, taking so many blood samples that I wasn't sure I'd have any more to give. Chris filled us in on the debacle of the American presidential election and the latest football results — I wondered if my friends had included me in their fantasy league for the season — and told us about a new television programme called *Big Brother*. It had gripped the country, so he said, though from his explanation I failed to see why.

'What? They just sit there doing nothing?'

It sounded a bit like our experience over the past nine months.

'Just watch it,' he told me.

Then we saw a psychiatrist. I told her I wasn't having nightmares, but that I'd had problems before I was kidnapped. Her puzzled look suggested it was a theory she might take seriously. After a quick chat to ensure I really was in good spirits, and not in a state of shock, she asked to see Tom. Good luck to you, I thought.

Once cleared, we moved on to the British Embassy to say hello to some of the staff. They'd built up a rather fat file on our case. Johnny and Chris showed us all the newspaper cuttings from when we'd first been reported missing in the summer. Then it was back to the residence to have lunch with Jeremy Thorpe, the ambassador, and Bob, his military liaison officer. They gave us a quick and informal debrief.

Officially we hadn't entered Colombia yet, so we had to report to DAS (*Departamento*

Administrativo de Seguridad) to get stamped into the country. By now the story had leaked and the media had somehow found out that we were alive. There was a *Times* journalist hanging around the DAS offices. A DAS woman started to ask me questions. I explained our story. She looked at me with a baffled stare.

'Are your parents rich?'

'No.'

'Why did they take you?'

'No idea.'

'When did you enter Colombia?'

'I'm not sure, maybe in July.'

We'd probably crossed the border three, perhaps four times. She stamped a random date into my passport and added a slip of paper.

'Colombia, it is a crazy place, yes? Locombia?'

Locombia, the mad country.

I agreed, and we laughed. I could also hear a torrent of laughter coming from the room where Tom was being interviewed.

As we left, Chris informed us that it would be best if we spoke to the press. They'd arranged a press conference for later that afternoon at the residence, and Johnny was kind enough to prepare a statement for me to read out. Facing the press was not something I was looking forward to; all I wanted to do was go home. Jeremy led us down the grand staircase to a barrage of camera flashes and into the drawing room where a gaggle of reporters and camera crews was waiting. I read out my prepared statement and fortunately Jeremy answered their questions.

When asked whether our expedition to find rare orchids had been unwise, Jeremy smiled, raised an eyebrow and said, 'No comment.'

We wished all the staff Merry Christmas and bid them farewell. A convoy, complete with bodyguards, was waiting to take us to the airport. I was glad the grilling was over, though we were warned to watch out on the flight back because it was rumoured some reporters had managed to obtain seats.

At the airport, over a coffee with Chris and Bob the military liaison officer, we were quizzed in more detail about the guerrillas and how they operated.

'The thing is, Paul, didn't you know the area was dangerous?' Chris said.

'Yes,' I replied.

He raised an eyebrow and shrugged.

★ ★ ★

TOM: Much telephoning went on in the car as we drove from place to place in Bogotà. That evening's BA flight home was fully booked, but twenty minutes later we had seats. We were told we would have to pay for them. As we travelled through the city, it occurred to me that it was Christmas and I had no presents for anyone. After the press conference we were whisked straight to the airport.

'Any chance of doing some shopping?' I said.

'Airport,' said a voice from the passenger seat.

'Not even one shop?'

'Airport,' said the voice again, more adamant this time.

'I only — '

'Airport!'

I gave up. They wanted to make sure we made that flight.

EPILOGUE

Paul: Flight BA 2048 from Bogotà to Gatwick touched down at 11.10 GMT. Among the passengers arriving home for Christmas were two very tired but very happy tourists, though one of them — me — was very worried that he would be getting a bollocking from someone very soon.

As the plane was preparing to land, and Tom was finishing his eighth bar of Toblerone, the captain strode down the aircraft towards us.

'Shouldn't he be flying the plane?' Tom whispered.

Before I could answer, he was above us, smiling and telling us that we would be met when we landed and could we move up to business class because we would be getting off first.

We were let off first. The doors opened and two Gatwick liaison officers greeted us.

'Apparently, you've caused quite a stir,' one of them said.

They whisked us off to a private suite where our families were waiting for us. There was time for hugs, hellos and laughter, but not much; the press was waiting. Dozens of photographers, journalists and cameramen filed in. 'Oh no, get me back to the jungle!' was my immediate thought, but it went OK. We made brief statements and they were very friendly, although the culture shock was too much to take in. The constant camera flashes left me dazzled. I was bemused and confused by everything that was going on around me.

When I got home I was too exhausted to do anything. All I wanted to do was sleep. I left my parents to be as diplomatic as they could with the press. The answer machine was clogged with calls from all the nationals and television channels. My parents answered a few questions and talked to a local BBC crew while I slept upstairs.

I dozed gently, sometimes sleeping, other times waking and thinking back over the last nine months. Everything seemed vaguely unreal. A surreal calm ebbed and flowed through me and I knew that I could relax for the first time in 278 days. I was alive, and I was safe. I went through everything that had happened to me, pinching myself to make sure that it really had taken place. The guerrillas really had let us go, we had got away with it; I didn't know how we had done it, but we had. I thought about all the times they had threatened us; they had been so real, but then everything was resolved peacefully. We had ground the bastards down, made them laugh and given them something to talk about for the rest of their lives.

Later, I wandered around the house, peering into the fridge at all the goodies and treats, though I didn't feel hungry. Then I made a cup of tea, watched a bit of television, read a newspaper and played on the computer. I had to be careful with them, I told myself. I didn't want them to disappear. I'd spent nine months fantasizing about doing things like this. I didn't want to get bored with them too quickly.

★ ★ ★

TOM: To see my parents and my sister was overwhelming. Little was said, but there was a lot of hugging. Anya had knitted me a scarf.

'How's Gran?' I asked eagerly.

Mum said she was fine and looking forward to seeing me.

'And my greenhouses?'

Mum said they were looking good too. She'd looked after them while I was away.

Dad showed me all the papers and the stories they carried. One of them said we'd gone back to the guerrillas to ask for a map! Then the press were brought in. There were cameras everywhere. I can remember little about it. Paul handled it mostly. One question I do recall: 'Was it worth it for the sake of a flower?' Having scanned only a few headlines, I was totally unaware that the press had portrayed us, erroneously, as orchid fanatics who had disappeared while searching for a rare specimen. I thought it was an odd question, faintly ridiculous to be honest, so I decided to humour the journalist.

'Yeah, flowers are great,' I said.

Luckily, it was edited from the evening news, though a lot of the papers got carried away by the comment the following day.

Then we left. Paul and I were separated for the

first time in ages. It was not a dramatic farewell; he merely went with his family and I with mine. I knew we would keep in touch, that, clichéd as it might sound, we would be friends for life. I'd spent nine months with him, sharing everything. I'd got strength, reassurance and resolve from his calm, determined manner and had revelled in his dry sense of humour. I hope I helped him at times, too. We'd swapped numbers and addresses earlier, knowing we would meet up again. Perhaps we would have that reunion at Lullingstone.

Dad drove us back home. At the village near the house, Eynsford, someone had hung a welcome-home banner on the Baptist church wall next to Unwins. At St Martin's Church there was a flag flying. 'In honour of the safe arrival of Paul and Tom' a sign said. It was remarkable. As we neared the house we could see journalists and photographers waiting at the gatehouse, so we drove round the back. Out of the car window I could see two eucalyptus trees which were three times the size of the ones I'd left.

'Look at the gum trees!' I shouted.

I leapt out of the car and ran across the lawn to hug them. The air was cold, drizzly, but most importantly, I was free. Our next-door neighbour, Caz, jumped out of her orangery window to surprise me and I hugged her too. Then with my sister I walked across to the gatehouse. Gran was waiting for me. Seeing her after all this time was overwhelming. I was home, in time for Christmas, too. It was slowly sinking in. I was safe. We had won, the guerrillas had lost. All the effort we'd put into mollifying them, annoying them, playing dumb, had been vindicated.

I remembered Chainy's face when they let us go, when he asked if I knew who they were. When I'd repeated 'friendly people who live in the jungle' for the second time, he'd smirked at Perty and said something. From the smug look on his face I'd known he was saying something like, 'These idiots don't even know who they are, never mind who we are.' Well, sod you, Chainy, all jewellery and no personality. And you, Goofy, you bad-tempered, ugly idiot, and your foul-looking, foul-mouthed, evil girlfriend, The Bitch. Up yours, Perty, you tit, and The Knight, too, more biceps than brains. I've still got your Bible. Kill me now, eh? Sod you all: Trapper, Stalky, Jackanory, Space Cadet, Señor Dama, Lost Cause, Mr and Mrs Comb, The Nutter, and the rest of you. Loose Teenager too, who got so fat eating *panela* that she was the size of a house. Even Smithy and Maria, the best of a rotten bunch. You picked the wrong people, and you lost. Big time. You got what you deserved: nothing. Nothing whatsoever.

We went back to the house and we chatted about the whole thing. I'd been through an extraordinary experience, and it bothered me whether or not people would believe us. It was impossible to convey the true flavour of it in one conversation. I needed time and distance to digest it all. I settled for a cliché and described it to them as 'a rollercoaster of emotions'. It was the most appropriate phrase I could find. There had been moments of genuine terror, and times of farce and hilarity. I had been paralysed by both fear and laughter. I'd been shocked, depressed, angry, determined, amused, anxious and bewildered. And that was in the course of just one day.

I was amazed to learn how much my parents had done to try to find us. I listened in guilty silence as Mum told me that she'd felt something was wrong as far back as April.

'I'd remembered that June the first was a time when you said you might be back so I converted the tea-rooms in the gatehouse to a living area so that you would have somewhere to live, so you would have your independence. But June the first came and went and there was no sign. Then came June the sixth; it was a Tuesday. I'd been out for the day with Anya. I came back and found your father very upset. A message had been left on the answering machine from Brian Winder. It was a strange message. We responded and found out you were with Paul through his emails.'

'Didn't you try to hack into my email account?'

'Yes, but we couldn't guess your password. We thought it might be a species of eucalyptus, so your friend Tom tried every one he could think of.'

I laughed.

'What's so funny?'

'Mum, my password *is* eucalyptus.'

Of course, the news had come as an awful blow to my family. My parents announced me missing to the local police and then made enquiries with the Foreign Office. With nothing encouraging emanating from official avenues — it is British policy not to pay ransom under any circumstances — they combined forces with the Winders to try 'unofficial' ways to find out where we were. To this end, Paul's dad had ventured out to Panama in the middle of June to make enquiries. Mum gave him a picture of me sitting in a eucalyptus tree to take with him.

'But the man from the Red Cross said to me that a member of my family came to look for us,' I said.

'That was me,' Mum said. 'I went to Colombia when Brian got back. We formed a sort of pincer movement. I spent six weeks in Colombia, staying with some very kind people. I spent a lot of time phoning, meeting people, writing to people, making contacts — my email became 'hot' — trying as hard as I could to find someone who might be able to help. I made some missing posters and we made sure they went to the relevant agencies and people of influence in Colombia and other Latin American countries via the backpacker network. We spoke to people who we thought could help us. I did all I could, but you'd just vanished.'

'Sorry, Mum.'

'A page three article in the *Sunday Telegraph* in the middle of July really let the cat out of the bag,' Dad added. 'By the end of that day there were thirty-eight messages cluttering the answer-phone, mostly media enquiries but some messages of consolation. I could handle my private grief, but public sympathy and loving condolences seemed tougher to absorb. You really started something when you tried to cross a bridge too far, Tom!'

The trouble, emotional upheaval and expense I had caused my family was dawning on me. A vigil for both of us had been held at the church of St Botolph's at Lullingstone — ironically the patron saint of travellers. Mum came back in August. Together with the Winders, they retained a pair of private investigators to find out what had happened to us, whether we were dead or alive.

'I never, ever gave up hope,' Mum said. 'Not even for a second. Even when we got intelligence that said, quite wrongly, that you were dead, I still believed you were alive. I prayed all the time.

'One night, when your father was away and I was in the house alone, I tried to reach you. I asked two questions. Are you alive, Tom? And if you are, are we looking in the right place? Later, a door opened, I walked through into the hallway and there was a definite smell of jungle. I knew then that was a sign that you were still alive.'

They'd received varying intelligence reports from the detectives hired: some said we were alive, others said we were dead. One in early November had offered renewed hope, and later tentative plans had been made by Mum and Paul's dad to fly out to Central America in the hope of negotiating our release.

'When did you hear I'd been released?'

'The embassy rang on the eighteenth of December. They said you and Paul had turned up, though it wasn't formally confirmed. However, they said it was definitely you.'

'What did you say?'

'I refused to believe them. It was wonderful news, but I wanted proof. I asked them to fax me on headed notepaper so I knew it wasn't a hoax.'

'And you never got my letter?'

'What letter?' Mum asked, a puzzled look on her face.

'We were told to write a letter that they said they'd send to you, asking for money.'

Mum shook her head. 'That's the first I've heard about any letter.'

God knows what happened to them. This established, at least, once and for all, that no money ever changed hands for our release. Which begs the question: why did they release us? Paul and I have speculated long and hard about this and are still nowhere near an answer. Was it because it was Christmas? No, Trouble Ahead didn't seem the sort to be troubled by thoughts of peace on earth and good will to men. It is possible that word had reached them about people looking for us, that they felt a force might enter the jungle and try to release the hostages, and that prospect scared them. But surely the idea of someone searching for us was what they wanted? Only then would they get their ransom. Perhaps they simply became bored with us; tired of having to feed and watch over two gringos, or listen to my endless talk on botany — perhaps my endless talk, full stop. Maybe we'd convinced them we were penniless backpackers; dumb innocents who'd stumbled unwittingly into trouble. Yet even if they did come to that conclusion, if they did believe we were worthless, then surely the safest and neatest way to get rid of us was to put a bullet in our heads? I'd like to think that was something they didn't want to do, that we'd managed to befriend them, form a bond and appeal to their better natures. But then I recall the hatred of Goofy and The Bitch; neither of them would have had a qualm about murdering us.

The only conclusion Paul and I can reach is this: when they realized no money would be forthcoming, Trouble Ahead, or whoever was in charge, was faced with two choices — kill us or release us. He chose the latter because he trusted that we wouldn't be too keen to lead any interested parties back into the Darién, and that by releasing us he would earn a modicum of good will from the outside world, whereas the discovery of our deaths might have severe consequences. Unfortunately, we will never know the answer.

The fact they didn't kill us indicated that the group who'd taken us hostage were affiliates of FARC and not, perhaps, the real deal. Given the lawlessness of the area, there is nothing to stop anyone picking up a gun, declaring fealty to a group such as FARC and then proceeding to act as a sort of freelance rebel group. Apart from the odd comment from Goofy, we got no sense of any real political imperative to our captors' actions, or any other motivation. Just a sense of a group of farmers or peasants, young men and women, who have been sucked into Colombia's civil war by forces out of their control, or for want of anything better to do. You get a gun, a wage, regular food and a sense of purpose. Most of them are certain to meet an early death. Paul and I have often spoken of this. Newspapers still carry almost daily reports of shootouts between government forces and the FARC rebels, death tolls often in double figures. There's a very good chance that the likes of Loosey, The Nutter, Maria and The Knight are dead, victims of an endless, suppurating war that has claimed thousands and thousands of lives.

That night at home I watched the news with my family and we all laughed when we saw Dad saying to reporters, 'It's the best Christmas ever.'

He was right, though.

★   ★   ★

PAUL: A few days after I returned, I drove to Chelmsford train station to greet James. In all the excitement of my return from the dead, he'd flown in from San Diego.

'You must be James.' I shook him firmly by the hand.

'Pleased to meet you. I believe we know a lot about each other,' he replied.

James was the author of the Darién memo, the one who'd crossed the Darién with a friend one month before us.

It had taken him eight days.

At home, we chatted over a cup of tea in the kitchen with Mum, Dad and my brothers, Bill and Kevin, who'd bought me a book called

Through the Jungle of Death for Christmas.

'We got your last postcard from Yaviza in April. I didn't worry until a few months later. I remembered that you went missing in the Sahara once,' Mum gently chided.

'I wasn't lost,' I said indignantly, 'there just aren't many phones or post offices in the desert.'

Mum raised an eyebrow, a bit like Chris Wigginton had done at Bogotá airport.

They explained that they'd tried the Foreign Office, then the Panamanian and Colombian embassies in London. They didn't know anything. Impatient with the lack of progress, Bill had tried a little lateral thinking.

'I tried legitimate ways to get into your hotmail account, but Microsoft demanded the authority of a post-mortem,' he told me.

'Typical bloody Microsoft,' I replied.

'So I just hacked into it. There was no outgoing mail after March the seventh, only lots of unanswered stuff. Though I did find one from a Thomas Hartdyke about attempting the Darién.'

They'd used this information, and with the help of 192.com had started a search for relatives. It yielded nothing.

'Then I tried Hart space Dyke,' piped up Kevin.

Bingo. Sarah and Guy, Tom's parents, were contacted.

They'd also looked through my other emails and found several useful names, including Patricia Upton. She'd given them two contacts,

James Spring and Eric Nicholas, a former US marine who helped my dad out in Panama.

'In June I flew out to Panama to meet Eric,' my father said. 'He introduced me to an Indian called Margarito. I hired the Indian to go into the Darién to try to find some clues.'

Margarito brought back information that confirmed I'd left Paya for the Colombian border with two guides, despite warnings from the village chief. I read the report my father had written up, confirming it all.

'After that we had nothing. You'd disappeared.'

Dad explained that they had tried to contact FARC, suspecting they might be involved. He wrote them an email:

Sir, my son Paul Winder, an English citizen, is thin and blond, aged 29, and had the intention to travel from Yaviza to Colombia through the jungle in March, three months ago. They went on foot with rucksacks. He has disappeared. We do not know where he is. Perhaps the route they took was Yaviza, Boca de Cupe, Púcuro, Paya, Palo de las Letras, Cristales, Bijao, Travesia, but I am not sure. Somebody in FARC may have seen a person who responds to these details? I respect your cause. I am a member of Amnesty International and have asked frequently for the Colombian government to show mercy to prisoners. Forgive me, my Spanish is bad.

397

There was no response. Undeterred, he sent another.

Please, please, can you tell me if you know anything of Paul Winder and his friend Tom Hart Dyke. They left Yaviza in March to go to Colombia through the jungle. They are not American; they are English. Paul is my first-born son. I cry for him. They had rucksacks and were very, very idiotic. Do you have any knowledge of them? I respect your cause. I am a partner of Amnesty International and frequently ask the Colombian government to show mercy to prisoners. Forgive me, my Spanish is not good. Please respond to this email.

Again there was no response, so he tried once more. This time, there was a brief reply: 'I have sent your message to our national command. I wait for an answer. As soon as we have something I will send it to you. Best regards from FARC-EP International Commission.'

The story broke in the *Daily Mail* and a few other papers around July. Few of them showed interest until one of Tom's sponsors let slip that he had been looking for orchids, which gave them the angle they always crave. Our parents also employed a detective agency, though my father had little confidence in them. Official routes such as the Panamanian police and the embassies revealed little, so our parents kept on using various means and contacts, trying to find first-hand information from Darién veterans.

'That's where I came in,' said James.

James had felt guilty because his memo describing his Darién adventure had been passed on to me. He had worried that despite its warnings it might have made us believe a crossing was possible.

'Don't worry, James,' I assured him. 'Even without the memo we would have gone. In fact, I was disappointed that you'd beaten us to the crossing.'

James was able to give accurate knowledge of the Darién to my father. He spoke Spanish, had met the chiefs of each village, had crossed via the same route as ourselves, knew every PNP (Panamanian police) station and its procedures and possessed an intimate understanding of the troubles the area was experiencing. I read through the various emails and suggestions that had bounced back and forth between James and my father. It was uncanny; it was almost as though he had been walking with us. He'd even predicted our place of ambush — Payita.

His guilt had been such that he'd offered to go back into the Darién to search for us, even going so far as to propose a detailed plan of action. My mother had told my father to put an end to such plans.

'I was horrified. I couldn't bear the thought of James risking his life in the Darién,' she said.

At the same time, James's friends and family discovered what his plan was and raised similarly vociferous objections. The idea was shelved.

'After this we had little choice but to use a detective agency,' my father said.

I read through the detective's reports. In October, one of them suggested that Tom and I were dead; the others made more accurate and intriguing reading, though few of them made any sense or gave a true indication of the areas we had travelled through. One even placed us in Puerto Obaldia, hundreds of miles up the Caribbean coast. During this time, James continued to pass comment on the reports my father forwarded to him. It seemed the detective was unable to get access to the PNP books that recorded movements within the outer Darién. With them, some sense could have been made of our route before Paya and Púcuro. Once again James offered to swoop in and out, to check the basic details, but only as far as Púcuro. Any further would have been too dangerous.

All was confusion, and there had been too many unconfirmed reports from mysterious sources. One thing for certain was that James Spring knew the Darién and had been the only person in the region for some time. He knew its day-to-day workings.

By November, hope was slowly fading.

'We were ninety-five per cent certain that you were dead,' Dad said.

They were even planning to hold a memorial mass for me.

Around late November, the guerrillas attacked a village on the Panamanian side of the Darién called Nazareth. This might have made the Panamanian government more aware of the situation in the area. The detective sent another

400

memo stating that a few of the guerrillas had been captured and the word was that we were alive. The report gave my parents renewed hope, but again, when I read it, there were too many inconsistencies and inaccuracies. For a start, it had us being captured in the wrong area and said we were being held with ten other prisoners, forced to do farm labour. It appeared that they were just rumours and the detective was raising false hopes, putting my parents through even more emotional turmoil.

Two days after our initial release, on 12 December, my parents received another memo. It mentioned a twenty-nine-year-old Panamanian who had just been released after fourteen months' captivity.

'This might have been our Bedfellow,' I told them.

It was the only report that made sense, though it still contained inaccuracies. It mentioned that the Panamanian had been able to speak to Tom and that we had been held in the Cristales area. Yes, we had passed close to Cristales on our walk into Colombia, but we never stayed there and Tom never spoke to him. The report suggested that contact with the guerrillas could be made through the Panamanian's father, who'd negotiated his son's release.

Buoyed by this news and another positive memo on 17 December, the idea of setting out to Panama and starting negotiations for our release was put in motion. It seemed that contact was only days away.

The next day, the British Embassy in

Colombia called to tell them that Tom and I had just walked out of the Darién.

★ ★ ★

On New Year's Eve I went out with my mate Chris, his girl-friend Mia, Chi, Steve, Neale and his girlfriend Mari. The alcohol flowed and I had a drunken mobile telephone conversation with my mate Mark, who lived miles away from London, about Lawrence of Arabia, for some reason. Nothing had changed. I still seemed to be the same person. That pleased me.

The culture shock of returning from my monastic nine months hit me quite hard. The delights of being drunk and surrounded by gaggles of semi-clad drunken women in a nightclub were a bit much. I could barely muster a word for a while, but I was content enough to be back and enjoying myself with my mates. The same mates I'd become convinced I'd never see again.

As the beers went down and the music blared, I became distracted by a tingling in my head and I scratched a slowly forming blister on the back of my skull. I went into the toilets for a closer look, but I could see nothing. The alcohol dulled the feeling, but the next morning it was there again, and this time the tingling felt like wiggling. Bleary-eyed, head screeching with pain, I trotted into the bathroom for a proper look. There on my scalp was what looked like a boil. From experience, I knew what it was: a worm. It had obviously taken its chance to escape the

Darién and see a bit of the world.

I went to see a doctor in casualty to see if he could remove it, but a lot of squeezing had little effect — he had neither the technique nor the know-how — and it remained wiggling around in my skull. I returned to my parents' house and asked my Darién *compadre*, James Spring, for help. He knew what to do. We heated my head with a hair dryer and then James squeezed hard. Out it popped, with the familiar spurt of blood and pus. It was big and fat. Tom had had more worms than me, yet it seemed I had suffered from the biggest, most obstinate ones.

He was due for a visit in a few days, so I put the worm in the freezer to show him when he arrived, a souvenir of our nine months in the jungle.

We do hope that you have enjoyed reading
this large print book.

Did you know that all of our titles
are available for purchase?

We publish a wide range of high quality
large print books including:
Romances, Mysteries, Classics
General Fiction
Non Fiction and Westerns

Special interest titles available in
large print are:
The Little Oxford Dictionary
Music Book
Song Book
Hymn Book
Service Book

Also available from us courtesy of Oxford
University Press:
Young Readers' Dictionary
(large print edition)
Young Readers' Thesaurus
(large print edition)

For further information or a free
brochure, please contact us at:
Ulverscroft Large Print Books Ltd.,
The Green, Bradgate Road, Anstey,
Leicester, LE7 7FU, England.
Tel: (00 44) 0116 236 4325
Fax: (00 44) 0116 234 0205

Other titles in the
Charnwood Library Series:

THE POPPY PATH

T. R. Wilson

It's 1920 and, the years of wartime rationing over, the inhabitants of the seaside resort of Shipden are turning again to the good things of life. The hottest news is that a new doctor has arrived in town: a handsome young man who would sweep any one of Shipden's many hopeful females off their feet. So when James Blanchard decides to marry pretty Rose Jordan the community is both shocked and outraged. Like many of the 'war widows' around her, Rose is an attractive, highly intelligent, single mother. But the scandalous difference is that Alec Taverner — the father of her four-year-old daughter — is still very much alive.

FALSE PRETENCES

Margaret Yorke

When her goddaughter is arrested during an anti-roads protest, Isabel Vernon is startled to discover that the fair-haired child of her memory has become a shaven-headed environmentalist and that Isabel herself is now regarded as Emily Frost's next of kin. Emily, released on bail to the Vernons, takes up a job as home help to a local family and forms an instant attachment to Rowena, the four-year-old girl in her charge. Emily's presence in the Vernons' house proves troubling, and is deepening the profound tensions within Isabel's marriage when the arrival of someone else threatens the safety of both Emily and the child, Rowena.

TREVOR McDONALD FAVOURITE POEMS

Trevor McDonald

Trevor McDonald, popular newscaster and also Chairman of the Campaign for Better Use of the English Language, has now compiled an anthology of his favourite poetry from across the ages. The collection is based on material published in his regular Anthology column in the *Daily Telegraph*. It is a comprehensive introduction to the poetry of the English language, from Milton to Ted Hughes, from Britain and abroad. He has included both perennial favourites and less familiar but accessible poetry. Each poet is introduced with a concise history of their work and there is something to suit all tastes and moods.

A PATCHWORK PLANET

Anne Tyler

Barnaby Gaitlin looks like a loser — just short of thirty he's the black sheep of a philanthropic Baltimore family. Once he had a home, a loving wife, a little family of his own. Now he has an ex-wife, a nine-year-old daughter with attitude, a Corvette Sting Ray that's a collector's item (but unreliable), and he works as hired muscle for Rent-a-Back, doing heavy chores for old folks. His almost pathological curiosity about other people's lives has got him into serious trouble in the past; but his feckless charm appeals to the kind of woman — like the angelic Sophia — who wants to save him from himself.